*The Poor and
the People Called
Methodists*

1729–1999

The Poor and the People Called Methodists

1729–1999

Edited by

Richard P. Heitzenrater

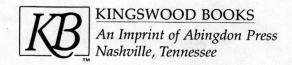

KINGSWOOD BOOKS
An Imprint of Abingdon Press
Nashville, Tennessee

THE POOR AND THE PEOPLE CALLED METHODISTS
1729–1999

Library of Congress Cataloging-in-Publication Data

The poor and the people called Methodists (1729–1999) / edited by Richard P. Heitzenrater.
   p. cm.
"Proceedings of an international conference held at Bridwell Library in October 1999."
Includes bibliographical references.
   ISBN 0-687-05155-X (pbk.: alk. paper)
   1. Church work with the poor—Methodist Church—History. 2. Methodist Church—Charities—History. 3. Poverty—Religious aspects—Methodist Church—History of doctrines—Congresses. 4. Methodist Church—Doctrines—History. I. Heitzenrater, Richard P., 1939–
   BX8347 .P66 2002
   261.8'325'08827—dc21

                                                                                2001008650

Unless otherwise indicated, all scripture quotations are from the King James or Authorized Version of the Bible.

All scripture quotations noted NRSV are taken from the *New Revised Standard Version of the Bible*, copyright 1989, Division of Christian Education of the National Council of the Churches of Christ in the United States of America. Used by permission. All rights reserved.

Material from Albert C. Outler, ed., vols. 2 and 3 of *The Works of John Wesley (Bicentennial Edition)* (Nashville: Abingdon Press, 1985–1986).

Material from Franz Hildebrandt and Oliver A. Beckerlegge, eds., vol. 7 of *The Works of John Wesley (Bicentennial Edition)* (Nashville: Abingdon Press, 1989).

Material from S T Kimbrough, Jr. and Oliver A. Beckerlegge, eds., vol. 2 of *The Unpublished Poetry of Charles Wesley* (Nashville: Abingdon Press, 1990).

Material from S T Kimbrough, Jr., ed., *Songs for the Poor: Hymns by Charles Wesley*, singer's ed., numbers 3, 7, 8, and 9. Copyright © 1997, General Board of Global Ministries of The United Methodist Church, New York, New York. Print license number 2197.

Excerpts from John Telford, ed., *The Letters of the Rev. John Wesley, A.M.* Copyright © 1931 by Epworth Press. Used by permission of Methodist Publishing House.

03 04 05 06 07 08 09 10 11 – 10 9 8 7 6 5 4 3

MANUFACTURED IN THE UNITED STATES OF AMERICA

Contents

Preface

This collection of essays provides a record of the proceedings of an international conference held at Bridwell Library in October 1999. It is part of the mission of Bridwell Library of the Perkins School of Theology at Southern Methodist University to foster scholarship. We do this not only by carrying out the traditional functions of a library—acquiring materials and making them accessible to students and scholars—but also by serving as a center for intellectual stimulation through conferences, concerts, workshops, publications, and our award-winning exhibition program. Through our programs we provide an outlet for sharing the results of scholarly research with a broader audience.

The idea for the conference came from discussions with Richard Heitzenrater of Duke University, whom we asked to curate an exhibition. Bridwell Library houses important collections of English and American Methodistica, and we invited Professor Heitzenrater, perhaps the foremost Methodist scholar in North America, to work with our collections. He suggested the theme of Methodist attitudes toward poverty, focusing on the denomination's response to the underrepresented and disenfranchised from its inception to the present day. As we thought about the topic and the many ways in which the issue has been addressed or neglected, we wondered how we might use the exhibition to explore the diversity of approaches over the centuries. What better way than to invite both historians and those currently working in this area to come together for conversation?

The topic allowed us to draw upon historians, theologians, pastors, and the Methodist lay community to tell the story of how Wesleyan theology influenced and continues to influence the way the church serves the world. Participants explored the ministries of John and Charles Wesley in response to the poor and underrepresented people of their day. In addition, the conference looked at the ways the Wesleys' theology and practices have influenced nineteenth- and twentieth-century Methodist attitudes toward the underprivileged. The event consisted of lectures, exhibitions, seminars, panel discussions, a concert, and a tour of the East Dallas Cooperative Parish. Our goal was to understand the history of Methodism's engagement with the disenfranchised in an effort to better serve the church, particularly in the area of urban ministry today.

The exhibition of rare books and manuscripts that formed the centerpiece of the Southern Methodist University conference, *The Poor and the People Called Methodists*, is re-created, in a way, in Appendix III, which reproduces the item label descriptions. A similar exhibit appeared online from the Methodist Archives and Research Centre of the John Rylands University Library of Manchester, curated by conference participant Gareth Lloyd. It can be accessed at *http://rylibweb.man.ac.uk/data1/dg/methodist/poor/*.

In the end, the conference resulted in an exchange of facts, anecdotes, and ideas. Most important, it brought together a diverse community of scholars, ministers, and laypeople who actively seek to live out Wesley's mandate to "gain all you can . . . save all you can . . . give all you can."

Valerie R. Hotchkiss
Bridwell Library
April 2001

Introduction

The reality of poverty as a human condition is evident from the beginning of history. The concept of poverty as a social problem is a relatively recent phenomenon. Christianity has always had a concern for the poor. The twenty-first century manifests the results of the politicization of the problem into a social obsession often largely out of touch with any religious or theological sensitivity.

The Wesleyan movement in the eighteenth century called attention to Christ's teachings and actions as a model for ministry to the deprived in contemporary society. The Methodist heritage, growing from those roots, has always been sensitive to the special issues related to the poor, as evident in the present United Methodist Bishops Initiative, "Children and Poverty."

The essays in this volume provide a selective survey of some of the significant issues, programs, and personalities that have emerged in Methodism's mission to the poor from its beginning to the present. The essays are arranged in chronological order of their topic, which approximates the order of their presentation at the conference. Read in this order, they provide a matrix for the evolution of questions and issues in the reader's mind that can mirror the emergence of issues in the movement itself.

The conference, however, grew out of vital concerns about poverty in the world today. This starting point of concern is the focal point of José Míguez Bonino's essay and of the panel on "Contemporary Issues and Models," which bring the whole work into contemporary focus. Looking at the problems evident especially in present-day Latin America, Professor Bonino claims that "Wesley's example should be for us an inspiration insofar as his theology rests on an organic unity between the personal encounter with Christ in the power of the Spirit and the commitment to a life of active love and service." In this light, Bonino claims that Wesley's willingness "to give Christian mercy and justice a specific and operative project" is an original and challenging approach that provides a model for Christian leaders today.

The panel presentations describe various ways by which Christians today can "love God" by "loving the poor [their neighbors] as part of ourselves" without romanticizing the issue in patronizing forms. Paul Escamilla, a pastor in urban Dallas, highlights the "converting and transforming" possibilities of working with the poor when people recognize that they need the poor more than the poor need them. Minerva Carcaño, also a pastor, now at Southern Methodist University, explains why effective ministry is about relationships, not programs, and provides several examples as models of mission. Stuart Jordan, a British pastor from London, suggests three models of engagement with the poor that he views as resonating with concerns expressed at the conference.

The first five chapters look at specific issues in John and Charles Wesley's work with the poor. Richard Heitzenrater's essay begins with a historical look at the definitions of *poverty* in Great Britain leading up to Wesley's day and attempts to answer the question, *Who were the poor?* After looking at the political, social, and economic background of the question, the author points to the fact that, given the quantitative guidelines of the government definitions of *relative deprivation*, most of the Methodists themselves could have been classified as poor. He then proceeds to outline Wesley's attitude toward and programs for the poor, which were grounded in part upon the distinctions between superfluities, conveniences, necessities, and extremities. He also illustrates how Wesley communalized programs of assistance, broadened the concept of community, reclassified the concept of poverty, universalized the concept of charity, and theologized the motivation for charitable activities.

Ted Campbell looks at the medieval roots of Wesley's ministry with the poor, especially showing the intertwined history of the notion of "apostolic poverty" with the image of Christ in the poor. He points out several parallels between Wesley's ministry with the poor and both the medieval piety of the *Devotio moderna* and mendicant itinerancy of the Franciscans and Dominicans, noting ironically that the medieval period was one that Wesley did not take very seriously. Campbell's point is not to prove that Wesley was in fact Catholic or Franciscan but rather to demonstrate that there was a long tradition in Christianity of "reverence for Christ's poverty and for the poor as they reflect the image of Christ," which became part of the Wesleyan movement.

The chapter by Randy Maddox examines the frequently over-looked connections between Wesley's concern for and engagement with the poor and his model for the sanctified life. After outlining the limitations of many traditional and contemporary stereotypes of Wesley and the poor, Maddox unpacks Wesley's principle that consistent and "faithful social action must be grounded in . . . communal spiritual formation." In the process, he illustrates how Wesley's writings consistently "connected engagement in ministry to and with the poor . . . to the existence or retention of the sanctified life," or, to put it another way, stressed the inherent interdependence of works of mercy and works of piety. The author sees the basic rationale for this connection in Wesley's conviction of "the holistic nature of salvation, as modeled by Christ," and in the nature of God's "responsible grace."

Joerg Rieger looks further at the relationship of works of piety and works of mercy, both of which are understood and emphasized as means of grace. After outlining the traditional tensions between those within the tradition who emphasize either the spiritual elements of right beliefs (orthodoxy) or the social aspects of right practice (orthopraxis), the author contends that a holistic Christian view of love of God and love of neighbor is strengthened by Wesley's view that both works of piety and works of mercy are means of grace. The author proceeds to give a theological rationale for understanding both orthodoxy and orthopraxis together as means of experiencing God's presence (grace), which he understands to be at the heart of Wesley's theology.

In a paper given at the Charles Wesley Society, meeting concurrently with the conference, S T Kimbrough looks at Charles Wesley's development of the ideas of "gospel poverty" and "perfect poverty" as part of Charles's understanding of Christian perfection. Through an examination of Wesley's poetry, Kimbrough illustrates the central place of the character and role of the poor in the Wesleyan understanding of the community of faith as the Body of Christ. Recognizing that the church has not often lived up to this expressed ideal, the author suggests that the theological imperative of "gospel poverty" is a realizable goal and that the community of faith is called to a social principle of befriending the poor, following Christ's example.

The next two chapters, while also grounded in the eighteenth century, move beyond the Wesleys to look more broadly at other centers of Methodist activity. Gareth Lloyd looks at the specific ways that the London Methodist Society assisted the poor in the eighteenth century. Relying upon documentary evidence of receipts and expenditures of the societies, he provides a glimpse into the inner workings of the local Methodist Society and describes the personnel, procedures, and programs that the Society instituted in relation to the poor. By looking at the data to the end of the century, the author is able to analyze shifts in priorities in the London Society toward a sort of maintenance budget that has become typical of many churches.

Tim Macquiban examines the work of the Strangers' Friend Society, an organization supported by Wesley and the Methodists but one that had a broader base. Looking at a fifty-year period that bridges the eighteenth and nineteenth centuries, the author uses this organization as a case study in the Methodist application of Wesley's "evangelical economics" to a particular cause. In the course of events, the development of the Society provides a mirror of the typical shift of interest away from urban poverty to foreign missions at the turn of the century (as Methodism became a church *for* the poor rather than *of* the poor) and illustrates the developing tensions between social concern and social control that are typical in many benevolent institutions.

William Abraham moves the discussion into the twentieth century with an examination of the life and ministry of Harry Ward, evangelist, professor, social theorist, and friend of the poor. After a quick glimpse at the major events in Ward's life and his production of Methodism's Social Creed in 1908, the author explores Ward's conception of "social evangelism" and places it within the larger conservative and liberal developments in the first half of the century, when revivals and trade unions seemed to be moving in different directions. While Ward's program of social idealism did not result in the transformation (regeneration) of society, Abraham suggests that it does provide some clues that might benefit the church's continuing attempts at evangelism, most especially the need for commitment to hard theological reflection within a deep doctrinal heritage that will sustain the task.

The appendices contain two other items that derive from the events at SMU. Especially for the occasion, Carlton Young composed a musical setting for a Charles Wesley poem, "Happy the multitude," which can be found in Appendix II. The poem was chosen for its particular pertinence to the theme of the conference on the poor. Appendix III contains the text from the panels and labels that were written by Richard Heitzenrater and used in "The Poor and the People Called Methodists," the exhibit that was featured in the Elizabeth Prothro Galleries of the Bridwell Library for several months during that period. Special appreciation is extended to Page Thomas, Wanda Smith, and Jon Speck for their extensive work in preparing the exhibit, and to Mr. Thomas in particular for his special role in organizing the conference.

The publication of this collection provides the opportunity to share on a wider scale the concerns and insights of those who gathered at Perkins School of Theology for the conference on the poor and the people called Methodists. Poverty is not a concern unique to Methodism by any means. But we trust that the Wesleyan and Methodist response over the years to the issues raised by poverty may provide some useful ideas as faithful Christians attempt to continue to imitate the life of Christ, "who went about doing good."

CHAPTER ONE

The Poor and the People Called Methodists[1]

Richard P. Heitzenrater

The general outlines of the early Methodists' work with the poor is well known and often repeated. Methodists gathered clothes and food to send to the poor; opened free medical clinics to draw in the sick from the streets; and stood on street corners and begged for the poor. Closer examination reveals that these descriptions are not fully accurate, and the particulars of the Methodists' efforts are even less familiar. The reasons for such a program of charitable activities are often ignored or misunderstood, and the context—the concept of poverty and the nature of the problem in eighteenth-century England—is largely unknown to most Methodists today. As a result, the picture of the poor and the people called Methodists, as typically portrayed, is largely incomplete, typically inaccurate, and therefore terribly inadequate.

Shortly after I had begun working on this topic, my wife, Karen, raised a simple but profound question. "Who were the poor?" she asked. "Well," I said, "the poor were . . . Well, the poor . . ." The terminology that had seemed so obvious when I accepted the assignment, now seemed hopelessly amorphous: "Well, the poor were just that—the poor." So, back to the drawing board we went to find out precisely who these people were.

---

1. This paper was given in conjunction with the opening of the exhibit, "The Poor and the People Called Methodists." While introducing and complementing the material in the exhibit,

As it turned out, that question is at the very heart of the whole issue. And to my knowledge, virtually all of the Wesleyan scholarship on the topic had successfully avoided asking it. I searched again through the typical bibliography on the topic—Manfred Marquardt, Theodore W. Jennings, M. Douglas Meeks, John Walsh, and so forth. Nothing appeared on the definition of poverty. One conversation with John Walsh led me to look at the French and English social and economic historians who have recently examined the history of the concept of poverty. Their writings, encompassing a wide range of economic, demographic, social, and philosophical studies on poverty, represent an emerging field that has only recently begun to take shape.

Defining Poverty

Who were the poor? Surprisingly, no definition of poverty prevails—there is no true, scientific, objective concept of it.[2] Poverty is a relative matter. Poverty is often considered deprivation, a condition marked by the lack of either the necessities of life or perhaps the comforts of life.[3] In either case, definitions are in order. Often, the portion of the population at the bottom of the economic ladder is considered to be poor. Then the question becomes, just how far up the ladder does the bottom go? Another complication is that many people are so-designated who do not consider themselves to be poor. At the same time, some who do consider themselves to be poor are not seen as such by others. To some degree, the whole question boils down to a matter of definitions.

Spurred by periods of poor harvest and consequent general hardship, the English started to develop a national policy to deal with the poor in the sixteenth century. There was some malnutrition among the population but no problem of mass starvation even in the worst years of crop failure, as was often the case on the continent (such as in France). Only in England, however, did officials come up with a public program of "poor relief" at this time, which was financed

---

this paper generally avoids duplication of the comments on the exhibit labels, which have been reproduced in Appendix III of this volume.

2. Wilfred Beckerman, "The Measurement of Poverty," in *Aspects of Poverty in Early Modern Europe I*, ed. Thomas Riis (Florence: Le Monnier, 1981), 48.

3. As Beckerman points out ("Measurement," 53), if poverty is defined in terms of necessities, then whatever constitutes poverty in any particular time and place depends on what is conventionally regarded as a necessity in that context.

by taxation. The system involved collective assistance for the infirm and impotent—the elderly, sick, widows, orphans, and disabled.[4] The question was never *whether* to provide help, but rather *who* would provide it. The shift from occasional and indiscriminant almsgiving toward a public program of relief entailed a closer look at the definition of poverty. The questions were: Who deserved what type of public support, and who was responsible for providing it?

The seventeenth century witnessed an increased public sensitivity to the concept of deprivation, which is, of course, a relative term. The English poor were never as bad off in absolute terms as those in some other countries. But the British developed a lively "intolerance of relative deprivation." The concept of the deserving poor was expanded beyond the infirm and impotent to include people who were able to work but were unemployed or underemployed and therefore not able to provide sufficient (again, a relative term) support for themselves and/or their families—that is, they could not provide the necessities of life (again, a relative concept). This sentiment of concern was then codified in the Poor Laws. This series of laws, in place by 1601,[5] defined a three-pronged national strategy to deal with the poor: The idle and able-bodied poor were put to work or punished, the infirm and impotent who could not work were given cash support, and begging and casual almsgiving were banned.[6] Putting the able-bodied to work meant providing not only materials and/or employment but also training for them, including children. This approach was generated by a national concern for the economy and a parliamentary effort to pass suitable laws, but the responsibility for implementation of the program was placed, not with national, county, or town officials, but in the hands of parish officers—churchwardens, overseers of the poor, and justices of the peace. They were charged with the tasks of surveying the poor, collecting the taxes, relieving the impotent, setting the able-bodied to work, and training the children. Local control was at the heart of the system and accounted for some small success to the extent that taxes were actually generated and used locally. The system generally failed, however, because there was no uniform enforcement or implementation. Many

4. The aged (people over sixty), never less than 7 percent of the population, required communal support, as did the sick and disabled, a similar proportion. Paul Slack, *The English Poor Laws, 1531–1782* (Cambridge: University Press, 1990), 5-6.

5. See 43 Eliz. c. 2, "An Act for the Relief of the Poor," in William Theobald, *A Practical Treatise on The Poor Laws . . . and an appendix, comprising a full collection of the statutes, with notes* (London: Sweet, 1836), 427-32.

6. Slack, *Poor Laws*, 9, 47.

areas followed the human inclination to do as little as possible that could still be considered acceptable.[7]

The Elizabethan set of laws had been established for a rural, agricultural society. *Poor* became quantitatively defined as having housing (a tenement) worth £10 or less per year. Since housing was about one-third of the annual expense, that definition points to people with less than £30 per year in earnings. People in that category would therefore have included most laborers of the day: husbandmen, manufacturers (spinners, weavers, dyers, shearers), small craftsmen (tinsmiths, blacksmiths, carpenters, tailors), and manual workers of all kinds.[8] One common understanding of poor in that context was "the laboring classes"—anyone who depended upon the wages of their labor for daily sustenance (i.e., those who had no investments, land, accumulated wealth, or independent income).[9] That group would have included more than half of the population of England, which was thus at the mercy of environmental extremes and market fluctuations.[10] One bad harvest could have been devastating. However, most people in this category apparently did not think of themselves as poor in the sixteenth and seventeenth centuries.[11]

Dealing with the Problem

The Poor Laws were passed by the rich to deal with the "problem" of the poor.[12] The motivation for such a program was threefold: (1) Christian charity, (2) moral reform (against idleness, dirt, disease, indiscipline), and (3) a rising concern for public policy on social and economic matters. There seems to have been some religious sense of

---

7. Ibid., 12.

8. Dorothy Marshall, *The English Poor in the Eighteenth Century* (London: Routledge, 1926), 1-2.

9. Bernard Mandeville, *Fable of the Bees* (1713), 294, cited by Gertrude Himmelfarb in *The Idea of Poverty: England in the Early Industrial Age* (New York: Alfred A. Knopf, 1984), 28. With no guarantee of subsistence, many of these people would be thrown into more desperate circumstances by any calamity.

10. Slack, *Poor Laws*, 4. Adam Smith saw the "laboring poor" as "the great body of the people." See Himmelfarb, *Idea of Poverty*, 56.

11. "On the eve of the industrial revolution poverty was essentially what it had always been: a natural, unfortunate, often tragic fact of life, but not necessarily a demeaning or degrading fact." Himmelfarb, *Idea of Poverty*, 41.

12. Thomas Riis makes the argument that the classification of the poor was created by the elite as part of their attempt to solve what they perceived as a social problem; the poor did not necessarily conceive of themselves as such. "Poverty and Urban Development in Early Modern Europe: A General View," in Riis, *Aspects of Poverty*, 16.

redemption for both the recipient and the donor.[13] By the time Adam Smith published his *Wealth of Nations* in 1776, he was able to give classic definition to the growing feeling that the health of the national economy depended on full employment of the population.[14] This developing sense that poverty was a social and economic problem (with emphasis on *problem*) began to supercede any earlier religious motivations. As the years wore on, more and more people called for more effectual methods of providing for the poor, both to sustain the aged and infirm and to make the idle and profligate more serviceable to the community. What started in Elizabethan England as an attempt to reform and remodel systems of charity was followed by a Jacobean tendency in the seventeenth century to see the problem in terms of the national economy—poor relief should be purposive and discriminatory.[15] By the eighteenth century, the whole system had become a social program of national welfare.

The extent of poverty, as defined by the government, can be seen in some national surveys of population and economic status in the seventeenth and eighteenth centuries. Gregory King, in 1688, and Joseph Massie, in 1760 (following King's scheme), provided estimates of the general population based on numbers of families, occupations, and incomes.[16] Since there was essentially no inflation between the surveys, they correlate well with each other. And with the present availability of subsequent inflation statistics, conversion formulas, and equivalency charts, one can correlate and compare those statistics with contemporary figures.[17]

Both charts contain six main groups: (1) nobility and gentry, (2) clergy and professionals, (3) freeholders and farmers, (4) merchants and tradesmen, (5) manufacturers and artisans, and (6) laborers and husbandmen. Among the latter two groups, which included cottagers,

---

13. Slack, *Poor Laws*, 7, 47. See John Wesley's letter to Miss March (26 Feb. 1776), *Letters* (Telford) 6:209: "The blessing which follows this labour of love [visiting the poor] will more than balance the cross."

14. See the label for exhibit 3 in Appendix 3 of this book. Unless otherwise noted, all references to exhibits are for Appendix 3.

15. Slack, *Poor Laws*, 41.

16. See the useful study by Peter Mathias, "The Social Structure in the Eighteenth Century: A Calculation by Joseph Massie," in *The Economic History Review* 10 (2nd ser., No. 1, 1957): 30-45, especially the chart on 42-43.

17. For this essay, the work of John McCusker was very useful. See Appendix B, "Consumer Price Indexes, Great Britain, 1600–1991," in *How Much is that in Real Money? A Historical Price Index for Use as a Deflator of Money Values in the Economy of the United States*" (Worcester, Mass.: American Antiquarian Society, 1992). Also see the "Conversion Table" in Frederic Morton Eden, *The State of the Poor: or, An History of the Labouring Classes in England from the Conquest to the Present Period*, 3 vols. (London: David, 1797), Vol. 3, Appendix I (p. viii).

fishermen, common soldiers, and so forth, most of the families in both surveys had an average income of not more than £30 per year, which would equate to approximately £2,800 ($4,480) today. In 1688, King estimated that 849,000 family units (more than half) decreased the wealth of the country by £622,000—that is, the cost of poor rates, which comprised half of the government budget of the day.[18] A century later in 1776, when Massie did his survey, the cost of the rates had more than doubled to £1,523,163.[19]

The Poor Laws increasingly tried to put everyone to work who could work, attempted to train the children, and endeavored to relieve the aged and infirm.[20] A correlative activity was to outlaw and punish the vagrants—whipping the beggars, sending home the transients. Parish officers carried out all of these activities.

Many of the able poor were simply underemployed.[21] They were first called the "laboring poor" by Daniel Defoe in 1701, although the reality is much older, of course. Hard times often did not allow them to earn enough money to support their family.[22] Many others were displaced, unemployed, sick, or otherwise unfortunately positioned because of times of dearth resulting from poor harvests, rising prices, death in the family, or other unpredictable causes. Rising unemployment resulted in lower wages, which increased the hardship of many families. Lack of work in the local situation represented a real problem, since the poor could not legally move out of the parish to seek employment elsewhere. Such a move made them illegal transients. Therefore, some localities established workhouses, cottage industries, and other means of supporting local employment of the poor through subsidies, which were paid for with the poor taxes. These provisions were intended to eliminate vagrancy and beggary. But many people asked whether the Poor Laws actually discouraged thrift and initiative among the able poor.[23]

---

18. Marshall, *English Poor*, 76. This figure did not include £100,000 in voluntary charitable contributions; Slack, *Poor Laws*, 44.

19. This figure did not include income of charitable trusts, which in 1788 amounted to £258,700. Slack, *Poor Laws*, 44. Inflation did not account for the difference.

20. Marshall, *English Poor*, 250.

21. Paul Slack points out that many of the poor were in fact employed but had insufficient earnings to support their families. "The Reactions of the Poor to Poverty in England, c. 1500–1750," in Thomas Riis, ed., *Aspects of Poverty in Early Modern Europe II* (Odense: University Press, 1986), 21.

22. Slack, *Poor Laws*, 4.

23. Donna T. Andrew, *Philanthropy and Police; London Charity in the Eighteenth Century* (Princeton: University Press, 1989), 29. See exhibit 1, 4a, and 4b.

Many times, those who were considered by others as "idle poor" were simply satisfied with their situation. Many of the so-called poor were not worried about their lack of contribution to the national economy. They would work just enough to have something to eat, drink, and a place to stay. There was little or no interest in savings or investments among most of the population.[24] This sentiment was often used against them by employers who were forced to hire the poor at stipulated rates. The complaint was that these folk worked only as long as they felt they needed to for mere subsistence and were therefore not reliable employees—after three days labor in a week, they would go home and drink. And, they wouldn't work for less than 2 shillings (s.) 6 pence (d.) a day since they could get 1s. per day on the dole.[25] Before 1760, the situation was further complicated by the fact that no clear-cut distinction existed between the agricultural and industrial sectors of the economy. Underemployed agricultural workers often did manufacturing work during slack times, but these workers commonly deserted the workshops for the fields during harvest season.[26]

Where poverty is the common condition of the population, as in large parts of England during that period, there is little realization or self-conception of being poor.[27] The situation depended largely on local definition and control at the turn of the eighteenth century and can be characterized as "parochial laissez-faire."[28] Generally, those over the £30 per year line paid the poor tax; those under the line benefitted from it. In many areas, there was a prevalent desire to keep the poor rates low. One of the continuing debates was whether the system should be based on a *flat* rate (equal pound rate) or a *relative* rate (based on ability to pay). In any case, the parish overseers of the poor generally earned about £20 to £30 per year, putting them just within the limits of the poverty level themselves.[29] The system inflicted especially undue hardships on single women, widows with dependent children, and married laborers in rural areas.

24. The Bank of England was not founded until 1702.
25. Many people felt that "they indeed who prefer an Idle and vagabond Life of Beggary before honest labour, ought not to be encouraged in it by Relief, but abandoned to the Wretchedness which they chuse." Andrew, *Philanthropy*, 19-20.
26. Mathias, "Social Structure," 37-38.
27. Wim Blockmans, "Circumscribing the Concept of Poverty," in Riis, *Aspects of Poverty I*, 43.
28. Marshall, *English Poor*, 9.
29. Ibid., 72-73.

Disparity Between Theory and Practice

Implementation of the Poor Laws was less than sufficient due to a number of causes ranging from incompetence to corruption.[30] There were some good models. Workhouses were the panacea after passage of the Poor Law of 1722, following the model established at Bristol.[31] However, most were a failure in the end.[32] A lack of clear purpose and careful administration resulted in many of the workhouses operating more like houses of correction.

There were some noble attempts at "associated philanthropy," which became more common further into the eighteenth century. Many hospitals, charity schools, and other organizations were set up on the basis of subscriptions from large numbers of donors, based on the example of joint-stock companies.[33] In 1720, Westminster Hospital was the first organization to be established in this manner. Shortly thereafter, Samuel Wesley, Jr. initiated the solicitation of contributions that eventuated in the establishment of Hyde Park Hospital (i.e., St. George's).[34] Also, Thomas Coram's Foundling Hospital was founded in 1739 as a haven for unwanted children; Magdalen Hospital was started in 1758 for "poor, young, thoughtless females"; and the list goes on. According to Joseph Massie, these projects appealed to charity, humanity, patriotism, and economy.[35]

In 1782, [Thomas] Gilbert's Act eliminated many of the problems of single parish administration and the domination of the parish officers, helped create a better attitude toward the poor, and brought some improvement in the operation of workhouses.[36] Generally, how-

---

30. Part one of the exhibit displays several aspects of the public policy and program toward the poor.

31. Marshall, *English Poor*, 128. Wesley says that in Ireland a workhouse was called the "House of Industry." *Journal* (17 May 1787), *Works*, 24:27. But in some cases, he observed English examples that seemed to function as a combination jail/workhouse; see *Journal* (24 June 1783), *Works*, 23:278. See also exhibits 6 and 7.

32. The 1798 figures for the workhouses in and around London reveal some pathetic facts. The total number of children born and/or received in the workhouses for the year is 8,185, of whom 906 were deemed "illegitimate" and 514 named as "casualties." The number of young children who died under the care of nurses in the workhouses or parish houses is very high—287 of the 389 who were being nursed in the environs of London. Of the 1,787 children under six years of age "sent to the country to be nursed," 110 died during that year, while 366 were "apprenticed out or put out to service." See exhibit 6.

33. Slack, *Poor Laws*, 42; see exhibits 8 and 9.

34. Richard P. Heitzenrater, *Mirror and Memory: Reflections on Early Methodism* (Nashville: Kingswood Books, 1989), 166; see also Adam Clarke, *Memoirs of the Wesley Family* (London: n.p., 1823), 386.

35. Slack, *Poor Laws*, 43.

36. See 22 Geo. III, c.83, in Theobald, *Practical Treatise*, appendix, "The Statutes Concerning

ever, the overall results were no better than any previous reforms of the Poor Laws. This particular attempt, combined with other laws of the day, increasingly classified and criminalized the poor. People were still whipped for begging (going door to door in the parish) and jailed for debt. Vagrants (also called rogues) could be "put to service" for seven years or put in houses of correction.

"Poverty" was *defined* by the elite, the wealthy, the officials, and the laws in terms of employment and wages as impacting the wealth and well-being of the nation. But poverty was *experienced* by the people in terms of hunger, exposure, and powerlessness, which impacted the health and well-being of the individual and family. Those who could be classified as poor in the eighteenth century still preferred self-help to the stigma of the dole, in spite of the increasingly prevalent notion of entitlements among some of them.

Attitudes

By the eighteenth century, the persistent attempts of the government to provide assistance to those in the lower economic levels of society had created an us-and-them mindset—those who paid the poor tax and those who benefited from it. The social managers of the scheme considered the poor a national economic and social problem to be solved by national legislation that would force increased productivity and thereby enhance national wealth. The poor participants in the scheme, however, began to think of the program of assistance in terms of entitlements, a level of relief that society owed them. The poor, therefore, came to consider public assistance a *right*, while the wealthy considered it a *burden*.[37]

The Poor Rates were high: at least 1 percent of the national income by 1750, which was relieving 8 percent of the population. After 1760, the payments began to shift from the impotent to the able, signaling a change in approach from "relief" or "subsidy" to "maintenance."[38] The jobs program never worked well since the poor were often reluctant to go off the dole for less than 2s. 6d. a day (about £30 per year), and the rich did not want to give jobs to "them"—they would rather have given to charity than employed the poor. Interestingly,

---

the Maintenance and Civil Regulation of the Poor," 497, which allowed parishes to combine efforts in maintaining workhouses.

37. Marshall, *English Poor*, 250.
38. Slack, *Poor Laws*, 46.

there were fewer poor in difficult economic times—general periods of hardship meant that it was harder to find food to eat, so there was more willingness to work.[39] The corn trade was no longer regulated, meaning, in part, that there were no more subsidized prices for the poor in years of scarcity (which more or less forced many of them to work). Increasingly, there was less regulation in employment, since most people felt it was easier to provide maintenance than to provide work or give encouragement and training to the poor.[40] By the mid-eighteenth century, humanitarian pressures had resulted in additional slackening of Poor Law enforcement, which had already lost any effective national oversight by the end of the seventeenth century anyway. To make the whole problem worse, the poor rates, as we have seen, had jumped from £660,000 to over £1.5 million in a mere seventy years.

Problems in the Public Scheme

The system described in the previous section contains several inherent problems. The first was the problem of definition: What is poverty? Who are the poor? Is poverty a condition that threatens survival? Or, is there some relative level of adequate maintenance that should be provided for everybody? Is there a minimal level of nutrition that everyone should rely on? If so, what is the standard by which it can be determined in qualitative as well as quantitative terms? Should poverty be defined in terms of minimum wage? If so, what is to say that such a wage would be used adequately or efficiently by all?

In addition, there were evident and persistent problems in the management of the system. First, there was the problem of finding suitable work for the unemployed or underemployed. Second, there was the expense of subsidizing it. Third, there was a fear of hurting the industrious by finding work for the idle. Fourth, there was the hardship that minimal wages would bring to unemployed laborers with large families. And fifth, there was the danger of developing a

---

39. Himmelfarb (*Idea of Poverty*, 51) points out that Adam Smith agreed with David Hume that "in years of scarcity when wages were low, 'the poor labour more, and really live better, than in years of great plenty, when they indulge themselves in idleness and riot.'" This could have led to the view that the poor must be kept poor or they will never be industrious.

40. Marshall, *English Poor*, 32, 250.

whole class of people who might lose a sense of self-sufficiency and begin to rely on others for subsistence.

The Poor Laws represent a legal system that was designed to solve a social and economic problem. In short, the program resulted in the conceptualization, classification, criminalization, and perpetuation of poverty.

Wesley and the Methodists

Into this setting came John Wesley and the Methodists. Several impressions about Methodism in eighteenth-century Britain are prevalent today:

- Early Methodists were primarily manual laborers and often destitute.
- Later Methodists became respectable and rich.
- Methodists had a mission to the poor of society.
- Methodists stood on the street corner and begged for the poor.

None of these statements is entirely accurate, as we shall see. Some other impressions can be gleaned from Methodist writings:

- Methodists were all poor (Wesley himself says that).
- Methodists distanced themselves from upper classes.
- Wesley himself lived on the edges of poverty.

Again, none of these statements is entirely accurate either. A short sketch of Wesley's involvement with the poor will help us introduce the Methodist attitudes and programs relative to the poor.

In his early years at Oxford, Wesley demonstrated a concern for the widows, orphans, and prisoners in the city. He contributed to the Grey-Coat School in town (a charity school). He helped provide a teacher for poor children in a school that William Morgan had started, by which the Methodists taught at least twenty poor children.[41] He gave money to debtors in the Castle prison and Bocardo jail. He gave of his resources to many in Oxford who lacked the necessities of life. Wesley often furnished more than just money. In some instances, he

---

41. See *Journal* (3 Oct. 1739), *Works*, 19:100. He visited the teacher, Mrs. Plat, and discovered that the school was "on the point of being broke up."

bought flax for children in the workhouses to use, and he gave food to families for their health and strength.[42] He was convinced that he should not enjoy the comforts of life if others did not have the necessities. In one instance, he tells the story of a poor girl (whom the Methodists kept in school) who, visiting him one winter day, looked cold and hungry. "You seem half starved," he said. "Have you nothing to cover you but that thin linen gown?" When she said that was all she had, Wesley put his hand in his pocket and found that he had scarcely any money left, having just purchased some framed pictures for his rooms. His later recollection of this scene drips with self-critical sarcasm:

> It immediately struck me, will not thy Master say, " 'Well done, good and faithful steward!' Thou hast adorned thy walls with the money which might have screened this poor creature from the cold!" O justice! O mercy! Are not these pictures the blood of this poor maid![43]

The Oxford Methodists regularly visited two workhouses—at Whitefriars in Gloucester Green and near Little High Bridge in the parish of St. Thomas—where they led services, assisted the elderly, taught the children, and provided supplies for their work. They visited inmates in the county prison (at the Castle) and the city jail at the north gate (Bocardo), leading services, giving counsel, furnishing relief, and in at least one case, drawing up a legal brief to assist in a prisoner's defense.[44] Benjamin Ingham visited Bartlemas House in St. Clement's several times looking to help the poor men who lived in that almshouse.[45] The Methodists also visited the poor in their homes, especially in The Hamel, a poor area in St. Thomas's parish west of the Castle.[46] And for all these causes, they raised money from friends and relatives to bolster their own funds in support of this important focus of their work.[47] These public activities helped earn them a suc-

---

42. See references to Wesley's philanthropy at Oxford, exhibits 16 and 17a.

43. Sermon 88, "On Dress," §16, *Works*, 3:255; see also exhibit 21; cf. MS Oxford Diary IV (1 Feb. 1734), Methodist Archives and Research Centre, John Rylands University Library of Manchester.

44. Wesley drew up papers for the trial of Thomas Blair, who the Methodists were convinced was falsely accused of sodomy. The trial at Thame proved their case. See Richard P. Heitzenrater, "John Wesley and the Oxford Methodists" (Ph.D. Diss., Duke University, 1972), 392-93.

45. Richard P. Heitzenrater, ed., *Diary of an Oxford Methodist* (Durham: Duke University Press, 1985), 27, 171-72.

46. For Wesley's later advice on visiting the poor, see exhibit 22.

47. Wesley's diary for the Oxford period is liberally sprinkled with entries that record funds raised and spent for these purposes.

cession of nicknames by which Oxford students derided them: Holy Club, Supererogation Men, Bible Moths, and finally, Methodists.

As the century wore on and the Methodist revival moved beyond Oxford, this combination of serious stewardship and personal concern for the plight of the poor became a hallmark of the Methodist movement. Not surprisingly, the Wesleyan revival attracted a large following from the ranks of those who might be considered poor. To say, as some do today, that Wesley had a "preferential option for the poor" is simply to say that he did not categorize more than half of the population as outsiders (as "them"), as the Church seemed to do.[48] In fact, if Massie's figures are right and more than half of the population in 1760 were in occupational categories that averaged under £30 per year in wages, the Methodists in the last half of the century seem themselves to have been even slightly poorer with 65 to 75 percent of the members falling into those same groups of the poor.[49] Based on a sampling of class lists from the period, 65 percent of Methodists belonged to occupational groups whose income averaged less than £20 per year, while 25 percent were in groups that averaged over £30.[50] In the former category, the poor, the largest number were in the manufacturing group—weavers, bakers, candle makers, and so forth.

Defining Poverty Within Methodism

We now must ask more particularly, *who* were these poor whom Wesley helped? Wesley had a fairly constant definition: The poor were those who lacked the necessities of life.[51] Many of them did not have enough good food to eat, decent clothes to wear, or a suitable place to live (although they never used the word "homeless"). Such

48. In fact, visiting the poor was not Wesley's preference, as he explained to Miss March (7 Feb. 1776), *Letters* (Telford), 6:207: "Creep in among these in spite of dirt and an hundred disgusting circumstances, and thus put off the gentlewoman. Do not confine your conversation to genteel and elegant people. I should like this as well as you do; but I cannot discover a precedent for it in the life of our Lord or any of His Apostles. My dear friend, let you and I walk as He walked."

49. See Clive D. Field, "The Social Structure of English Methodism: Eighteenth–Twentieth Centuries," *British Journal of Sociology* 28 (No. 2, June 1977): 202. It is difficult to derive specific percentages and annual wages from representative lists of occupations, not knowing where the particular individuals fell in the possible range of wages for that group.

50. Ibid. This information qualifies Wesley's own statement in *Advice to the People Called Methodists*, "You are poor, almost to a man, having no more than the plain necessaries of life" (*Works*, 9:126).

51. This definition is fairly common in the eighteenth century; see Eden, *State of the Poor*, 1:3.

conditions were the result of underemployment, unemployment, illness, age, or misfortune. These people were victims of a rapidly changing economy and of a failing parochial system of poor relief. And, most important to notice, many of them became members of the Methodist societies. Wesley did not have to search out the poor; they sat right there in front of him on the benches of his preaching houses. He did not have to go to another part of town to find some poor people to assist—he could have put signs on the Methodist preaching-houses that read, "The Poor R Us."[52]

Just how did Wesley deal with poverty and the poor? In short, Wesley declassified the concept of poverty, identified the breadth of the problem, and universalized the responsibility for dealing with it. Actually it might be more accurate to say that Wesley reclassified poverty, moving away from the absolute economic values established by the government and using instead a relative scale of human wealth and need. Instead of viewing the £30 per year benchmark as the poverty line, Wesley used the graduated terms of superfluities, conveniences, necessities, and extremities. His classic definition of the principle comes in a sermon on the Golden Rule (Matt. 7:12):

> We would that all men should love and esteem us, and behave towards us according to justice, mercy, and truth. And we may reasonably desire that they should do us all the good they can do without injuring themselves; yea, that in outward things (according to the known rule) their superfluities should give way to our conveniencies, their conveniencies to our necessities, and their necessities to our extremities. Now then, let us walk by the same rule: let us do unto all as we would they should do to us. Let us love and honour all men. Let justice, mercy, and truth govern all our minds and actions. Let our superfluities give way to our neighbour's conveniencies (and who then will have any superfluities left?); our conveniencies, to our neighbour's necessities; our necessities to his extremities.[53]

---

52. See Matt 26:11, "For ye have the poor always with you." Wesley's comment on this scripture is, "Such is the wise and gracious Providence of God, that we may have always opportunities of relieving their Wants, and so laying up for ourselves treasures in heaven." *John Wesley, Explanatory Notes upon the New Testament* (London: William Bowyer, 1755), 84.

53. Sermon 30, "Upon our Lord's Sermon on the Mount, X," §26, *Works*, 1:662. Wesley's terminology follows very closely that of Robert South: "The measures that God marks out to thy charity are these: thy superfluities must give place to thy neighbour's great convenience; thy convenience must vail to thy neighbour's necessity; and lastly, thy very necessities must yield to thy neighbour's extremity. . . . This is the gradual process that must be thy rule." South, *Sermons Preached upon Several Occasions*, 6 vols. (Oxford, 1823) 1:282-83, quoted by Outler in *Works*, 1:662.

The concept of "necessities" was not based on an absolute level of sustenance that would prevent destitution. His definition of "necessities" includes very significant descriptions: the necessities are seen in terms of *sufficient* food, *decent* apparel, and *proper* housing. Similar adjectival qualifications can be found in his sermons and letters. On housing, he says: "Who have not a dry, or warm, much less a clean abode for themselves and their little ones?"[54] In a letter to a friend in Ireland, he included (among some "small things" to inculcate among the people) the following suggestions regarding clothing:

Whatever clothes you have, let them be whole; no rents, no tatters, no rags. These are a scandal to either man or woman, being another fruit of vile laziness. Mend your clothes, or I shall never expect you to mend your lives. Let none ever see a ragged Methodist.[55]

Contentment seems to be a measure of necessities having been met. He frequently quotes 1 Timothy 6:8, "And having food and raiment ['includes lodging,' Wesley], let us be therewith content."

In using these qualified terms, Wesley was following the typical English view of "relative deprivation," soon to be enunciated (in 1776) by Adam Smith in *The Wealth of Nations:* "By necessaries, I understand not only the commodities which are indispensably necessary for the support of life but whatever the custom of the country renders it indecent for creditable people, even of the lowest order, to be without."[56] Wesley's level of relative necessities (sufficient, decent, adequate) may have been higher than what some of the rich felt was really necessary for the poor. Nevertheless, it was probably below what we would think of as necessary today.

Such expressions of relativity, however, do not necessarily indicate that Wesley was going noticeably beyond the government guidelines in his support of the needy. He did feel that the connection should provide support to maintain the preachers and their families, support that he defined as furnishing the necessities and conveniences of life to assure freedom from debt and sufficient provisions for the family, both before and after the preacher's death.[57] Just how much assistance did that entail in monetary terms? The connectional

---

54. Sermon 47, "Heaviness through Manifold Temptations," III.3, *Works*, 2:227. See his following passionate comments on the want of bread.
55. Letter to Richard Steel (24 April 1769), *Letters* (Telford), 5:133.
56. Quoted in Beckerman, "Measurement," 47.
57. See Wesley's "Address to the Clergy," *Works* (Jackson), 10:494-97.

level of support for retired preachers, their widows, and children was much lower than the £30 per year poverty line. The average pension from the Preachers' Fund for "tired and worn out preachers, their widows and children" in 1780 was £16 to four preachers and about £7 each to eight women. Presumably the local society helped supplement the connectional support since the Large Minutes of 1780 provided more generous guidelines for such support: preacher's wives were to be furnished with lodging, coals, and candles or £15 per year; widows and children were to receive £10 per year.[58] This level of support is, nevertheless, still well within the range of government-defined poverty at that time.

It is also important to notice that Wesley's scale was both relative and sliding. It was based not only on relative levels of need or comfort between the rich and the poor but also on a sliding scale that applied to everyone. Since his listeners ranged across the economic spectrum, he stressed that there were richer and poorer folks at every level. This approach differentiated Wesley's view from most of the social and legal programs of the day. From his point of view, everyone could find someone who was worse off than they were. And no one was so poor that they could not give something to their neighbor in need.[59] His biblical model for this last point was the widow with the two mites.[60]

Wesley not only relativized the concept of "necessity" on a sliding scale but also shifted the focus of his advice as more Methodists moved up the economic ladder and enjoyed the conveniences of life. By 1760, he felt it was permissible to have more than the bare necessities, so long as one did not actively pursue that goal.[61] Motivation—purity of intent—was thus a major consideration. Everyone should realize, he constantly pointed out, that having anything beyond the necessities makes one rich: "Whoever has sufficient food to eat and raiment to put on, with a place where to lay his head, and something over, is *rich*."[62] In some sense, then, Wesley thereby divided everyone

---

58. "Large Minutes," Q. 53, *Works* (Jackson), 8:326-27.

59. See Sermon 98, "On Visiting the Sick," III.4, *Works*, 3:393-94, where he quotes this "excellent rule" again.

60. Mark 12:42; Luke 21:2. For the former verse, Wesley exclaims, "How acceptable to [the judge of all] is the smallest [outward action], which springs from Self-denying Love!" Wesley, *Explanatory Notes*, 128.

61. Sermon 28, "Upon our Lord's Sermon on the Mount, VIII," §15 "Riches, dangerous as they are, do not always 'drown men in destruction and perdition'. But the *desire of riches* does." *Works*, 1:621. See also his comment on Thomas Jones: "Yet when riches increased on every side, he did not set his heart upon them." *Journal* (29 June 1762), *Works*, 21:371.

62. Sermon 87, "The Danger of Riches," I.1, *Works*, 3:230.

into two groups, the rich and the poor. But he never stated a quantifiable standard or dividing line—one's conscience must be the guide. And in the end, all, even the poor, are compelled to help those who are worse off than oneself. No one is exempt from the law of love for neighbor.[63]

Giving to the Poor

Wesley used both a personal and an institutional approach to charity. He gave liberally from his own pocket, and he raised money through the Methodist connection. Wesley's rule with regard to money, applicable (as we have seen) to persons at all levels of society, was his well-known advice to gain all you can, save all you can, and give all you can—with an emphasis on the third point.[64] In this matter, he seems to have consistently followed his own dictum. In 1790, he decided to stop keeping his financial accounts (which he had kept since 1725), "being satisfied," as he noted after the last entry, "with the continual conviction that I save all I can, and give all I can, this is, all I have." Among other channels of charity, John occasionally gave coins to beggars on the street even though such begging was illegal. His brother Charles was often annoyed by such public actions, which he considered to be self-righteous displays of charity.[65]

John also raised money and collected resources of all kinds from those who could help. He privately "begged" from the rich, many times soliciting known benefactors door to door. One particular week, he noted his disappointment that he could find only six or seven people that would give £10 apiece (now worth £900 or $1,400). On another occasion, he spent the week slogging through the slush of the wintry London streets to "beg" £200 from such friends. This was no tin cup on the street corner method—he had raised today's equivalent of $30,000 for his programs of charity for the poor.[66]

A more efficient way for Wesley to raise money within Methodism was to establish connectional collections in the societies.[67]

---

63. One of his stories tells of one of the Oxford Methodists (himself?) who, though his annual income ranged from £30 to £120, lived on £28 and gave away the remainder; Sermon 89, "The More Excellent Way," VI.4, Ibid., 275-76.

64. Sermon 50, "The Use of Money," in *Works*, 2:266-79. See exhibits 11 and 23.

65. Rupert Davies, A. Raymond George, and Gordon Rupp, eds., *A History of the Methodist Church in Great Britain* (London: Epworth Press, 1965–), 4:222.

66. See exhibit 18.

67. See exhibits 17b and 20.

It might seem ironic to be collecting money from the poor for the poor. But as early as 1742, Methodist people were expected to give a penny a week to their class leader in support of the beneficent programs of the connection. Captain Foy, a lay leader in Bristol, suggested that if a poor person could not meet that expectation, the class leader should make up the difference. He backed up his suggestion by volunteering to assume responsibility for twelve of the poorest people in the society.[68]

The Methodist program of assistance to the poor was, first and foremost, a way to help those in their own societies who had special needs. Wesley pointed out that, like the Quakers, the "poor despised" Methodists felt that their primary responsibility was to provide for their "own" poor.[69] He hoped that the Methodists would differ from the Quakers, however, by helping those of other societies when they themselves were able to relieve more than their own poor.[70]

Wesley appointed stewards in each society to manage the incoming funds and administer the various distributions of money.[71] In this sense, the Methodist system within each society was not unlike the parish administration of the poor tax—some money was used locally, some was sent to a regional or national fund. Although many of Wesley's friends gave money to the Methodists, Wesley was always careful to let the stewards manage the funds, though he provided direction for them and was very particular about their exactness in the matter.[72]

The Wesleyan Program

Wesley's program of assistance to the poor followed the general outline of national policy categories but with a different attitude and

---

68. For Wesley's work with the poor in Bristol, see exhibit 14.

69. This practice also follows the priorities enunciated in Galatians 6:10, "let us do good unto all men, especially unto them who are of the household of faith."

70. *Farther Appeal to Men of Reason and Religion, Part II*, III.7 (in 1746 Bristol edition and following), *Works*, 11:257. Wesley did support the work of the Strangers' Friend Society, which was organized in London to assist people in society at large; see chapter 6.

71. See exhibits 19a and 19b.

72. Wesley never took any money for himself directly. He was supported by a quarterly allowance from the London steward, just like the other preachers. This protected him from the charge of becoming rich from the collections, the gifts, and the profits from the publishing enterprise. One of his letters (exhibit 24) explains to his friend Ebenezer Blackwell the exact distribution of the banker's most recent benefaction.

a different approach.[73] To begin with, Wesley did not consider the poor to be lazy and indolent, as did many of the upper class and some of the lawmakers. He worked very hard to counteract that view, which was contained in much of the literature of his day, especially as voiced by critics of the Poor Laws. From his extensive traveling about the country, Wesley concluded that the problems of hunger and unemployment were caused by poor government policy, economic management, and societal choices, seen especially in three areas: distilling, taxes, and luxury.[74] For instance, he pointed out that too much grain had been used for distilling liquor, leaving a shortage of grain to make bread, which drove the price up and especially hurt the poor. From his point of view, most everyone who was able to work was, in fact, working, and yet many were still hungry. In one sermon, Wesley lambasts those who quote the classical poet who said that "poverty brings no unhappiness worse than this: it exposes men to ridicule."[75] His response exudes his passion for the poor:

> Has poverty nothing worse in it than this, that it "makes men liable to be laughed at"? . . . Is it not worse for one after an hard day's labour to come back to a poor, cold, dirty, uncomfortable lodging, and to find there not even the food which is needful to repair his wasted strength? . . . is it not worse to seek bread day by day, and find none? Perhaps to find the comfort also of five or six children, crying for what he has not to give. Were it not that he is restrained by an unseen hand, would he not soon "curse God and die"? O want of bread! Want of bread! Who can tell what this means unless he hath felt it himself?[76]

---

73. Some of the particulars of the Wesleyan program of ministry to the poor are outlined in exhibits 25–36.

74. See his "Thoughts on the Present Scarcity of Provisions" (exhibit 12), which contains a political tirade against views held by people such as Joseph Townsend (*Dissertation on the Poor Laws, by a well-wisher to mankind*, see exhibit 4a) and John M'Farlan, D.D. (*Inquiries Concerning the Poor*, see exhibit 1). Townsend, a former Calvinist Methodist preacher, viewed the Poor Laws as, in effect, providing a guaranteed wage for the indigent and lazy and promoting "drunkenness and idleness cloathed in rags," while being paid for by the industrious farmers who were thus oppressed themselves by poverty. M'Farlan, a minister of Canongate, Edinburgh, began his work by pointing out that poverty has a number of unavoidable and adventitious causes, but the most frequent causes are sloth, intemperance, and other vices. He proceeds with the assumption that charities are designed "to relieve absolute want." He then criticizes those programs that seem to promote a social and political agenda beyond that basic goal. See exhibits 1 and 2.

75. *Nil habet infelix paupertas durius in se,*
    Quam quod ridiculos homines facit! (Juvenal, *Satires*, iii.152-53 [Loeb, 91:42]).

76. Sermon 47, "Heaviness through Manifold Temptations," III.3, *Works*, 2:227-28.

Wesley continually developed programs to deal with a variety of problems faced by his people. First, To relieve the *helpless* (the impotent poor), he took nourishing food to the hungry, collected decent clothes for the threadbare, and furnished adequate housing for widows and orphans.[77] Second, To assist those who were *unfortunate* (the able poor), he boosted their employment by sending the weavers yarn for their looms and establishing a loan program to distribute seed money to struggling merchants or manufacturers.[78] Third, For the *children*, Wesley established schools to train the minds, bodies, and spirits of young boys and girls.[79] Fourth, For the literate but *uneducated* adults, Wesley established a prolific publishing program that provided important literature for his people—much of which was produced inexpensively—to be given away to those who could not afford to purchase it.[80] Fifth, To assist the *sick* and infirm, Wesley hired apothecaries and doctors to staff free medical clinics in his preaching houses in London, Bristol, and Newcastle.[81] Behind these programs lay a desire to encourage industry, thrift, learning, health, and godliness.

Wesley was in some ways ahead of his time, though in many ways his programs and attitudes would not measure up to twentieth-century standards. On the one hand, although "perfect poverty" was an ideal that Charles Wesley had enunciated for the Methodists in his hymns,[82] John's quarterly allowance was twice the poverty level and five times that of many Methodist preachers. Wesley's views of providence also led him occasionally to see poverty as God's punishment to bring people to an awareness of their sin.[83] On the other hand, it is interesting to note that Wesley did pinpoint some of the systemic causes of the problem in the structures and attitudes evident in gov-

---

77. See exhibits 17b, 18, and 20.

78. See exhibit 35. One beneficiary, James Lackington, was an especially remarkable success story financially, but he left the Methodist society and became a critic of the Wesleyans; see exhibit 36.

79. See exhibits 30–32.

80. The establishment of the Tract Society by Wesley in 1782 is the best example of the institutionalization of this ministry, which is evident from nearly the beginning of Wesley's publishing interest: an advertisement in the front of his first edition of *Christian Pattern* (London: Rivington, 1735) announces a forthcoming smaller-sized edition for which there will be given "a handsome allowance . . . to all such who shall take a number to be disposed of charitably." See exhibits 33 and 34, and Richard Heitzenrater, *Faithful Unto Death* (Dallas: Bridwell Library, 1989), 46-47.

81. See exhibits 27–29.

82. See his hymn on Matt. 5:48 in *Short Hymns on Select Passages of The Holy Scriptures* (Bristol: 1762) 2:139; reprinted by S T Kimbrough in *Songs for the Poor* (New York: General Board of Global Ministries, 1993), no. 7. See also exhibit 15.

83. Sermon 113, "The Late Work of God in North America," II.14, *Works*, 3:607.

ernment and society. He did occasionally connect poverty with human oppression.[84] On occasion, he also used the language of justice in relation to the need to free the poor from their plight.[85] And he did think that poverty could actually be eliminated from the Methodist societies. In answer to the question, *Is it possible to supply all the poor in our Society with the necessaries of life?* Wesley answered that it certainly was possible in larger societies than theirs, such as the early church in Jerusalem as well as the Quakers and Moravians in their own day. His estimate was that with two thousand pounds, the Methodists "could supply the present wants of all our poor, and put them in a way of supplying their own wants for the time to come." And he was quick to point out that there were Methodists who could provide those funds if they were so inclined and if they simply practiced his rule of "giving all you can."[86]

Summary

In his attitudes toward and programs for those in need, John Wesley was a man of his time. He followed models that were available to him from Scripture, government, Church, and society. But there were important differences in his approach from the societal models that defined, criminalized, and perpetuated poverty in his day.

(1) Wesley *communalized* the program of assistance. His people were expected to help each other in the community of faith. This was not just a local program for individual societies. They were expected to contribute to connectional funds that cut across the boundaries of societies, parishes, towns, and cities.

(2) Wesley *broadened* the concept of community to include everyone, from the top to the bottom of the economic scale. No longer was there an us-and-them dichotomy. In a sense, this view reverts to a pre-seventeenth-century perspective in which the poor are not made to

---

84. See his *Doctrine of Original Sin* (Part I, ¶11) in which he poses several questions to test whether or not "the generality of Attorneys and Solicitors in Chancery" follow the Great Commandment or the Golden Rule, such as "Do they never deliver the poor into the hand of his oppressor, and see that such as are in necessity have not right? Are they not often the means of withholding bread from the hungry, and raiment from the naked, even when it is their own, when they have a clear right thereto, by the law both of God and man?" *Works* (Jackson), 9:229.

85. See, for instance, his desire for "truth, justice, mercy, and common sense" in his impassioned plea against the Declaration Bill and its victims; *Journal* (3 July 1761), *Works*, 21:332-33.

86. Sermon 122, "Causes of the Inefficacy of Christianity," §§10 and 11, *Works*, 4:92-93.

think of themselves as distinguished by their poverty or as a disadvantaged class. In fact, in this period of English history, most of the people were in that condition at some point in their lives.

(3) Wesley *relativized* (reclassified) the concept of poverty, ignoring the idea of an absolute or quantifiable poverty line. He viewed deprivation in terms of relative needs based on a sliding scale (superfluities, conveniences, necessities, extremities) with each level defined in terms of specific contexts. There could almost always be someone found with fewer conveniences or less adequate necessities, if not destitute of extremities.

(4) Wesley *universalized* the concept of charity so that no one was exempt from responsibility for assisting the needy. Everyone could be a Christian neighbor, even the widow with her two mites.

(5) Wesley *theologized* the motivation for charitable activities. His basic goal in this regard was for Methodists to imitate the life of Christ not improve the national economy. He conceived of the problem theologically in terms of love of God and love of neighbor rather than in terms of defining minimum wage, improving the country's wealth, or solving a social problem. Everyone in every level of society was a child of God and deserved to be treated as such. He tried to remove the stigma of poverty—we are all poor in some way or another. Wesley's goal appears to have been a harmonious society not unlike the Christian community idealized in the Acts of the Apostles.[87] His method was not to pacify the poor or manipulate their submissiveness and industry but rather to prick the conscience of everyone by breaking down the barriers that helped cause and perpetuate poverty.[88]

Conclusion

The Methodist program to help alleviate poverty was not as successful in eliminating it as Wesley had hoped. However, his method did not exacerbate or perpetuate the problem of poverty either, as was often the case with the Poor Laws. But Wesley's approach, which included encouragement for all people to practice industry, thrift, and

87. For a time, he promoted economic communism on the model of the early church, as in Acts 2:44-45. See John Walsh, "John Wesley and the Community of Goods," in Keith Robbins, ed., *Protestant Evangelicalism: Britain, Ireland, Germany, and America, c. 1750–c.1950: Essays in Honor of W. Reginald Ward*, Studies in Church History 7 (Oxford: Basil Blackwell, 1990), 25-50.

88. E. P. Thompson, *The Making of the English Working Class* (London: Gollancz, 1963), 351.

charity, did cause another unforeseen problem by virtue of its success: Methodists moved up the economic scale. They did well at making and saving money. But some forgot their roots and neglected the third element of the Wesleyan scheme: charity—giving all you can. This situation left them in danger of falling back into an "us-and-them" mindset with the same economic and social class barriers that Wesley had tried so hard to tear down. There is nothing more proud than a self-made person. It is very easy to forget one's roots in such circumstances. And few are more oppressive than the oppressed who are liberated and then become oppressors.

Methodism, however, did well serve both the rich and the poor as long as the group syndrome did not become part of the defining structure or self-conscious identity.[89] Any degree of success was proportional to the degree in which they recognized and dealt with any and all degrees of poverty in their midst. This approach entailed tearing down the barriers that separated the children of God and the community of faith, as well as turning with compassion to all neighbors and responding to their needs as Christ would have, "who went about doing good."

Can the problem of poverty be solved? Wesley thought so. At the very least, he thought the Methodists could do away with destitution in their midst—and not simply by eliminating the poor from their membership roles or by narrowing the definitions of poverty. He saw the model solution in the New Testament—in the sharing community in Acts, which was bound not by secular laws but by the law of love.[90] To love God and neighbor will always result in acts of assistance for those with needs greater than one's own.

Love and empathy are at the heart of the Wesleyan theology and the "method" of the Methodist mission. As he told the stewards in his societies, "Put yourself in the place of every poor [person] and deal with *him* as you would God should deal with *you*."[91] Dealing with the poor was simply a consistent part of his overall scheme that looked toward the building of a community of faith in which everyone's needs would be sufficiently met. Wesley launched toward that goal, held to that hope, and acted consistently with that purpose, supported by a host of followers who were themselves mostly "the poor."

---

89. Ibid., 356.
90. Walsh, "John Wesley," 50.
91. *Journal* (4 June 1747), *Works*, 20:177.

The question that faces us today is whether we, like the rich of the eighteenth century, will follow the natural tendency to impose our ideologies upon the human condition of poverty in order to define "the problem," or whether we, like Wesley, can imitate the life of Christ and conscientiously become one with the reality of poverty in order to let the deprivations of all our neighbors help shape our moral imagination, our ethical consciousness, our theological categories, and our social programs.[92]

92. See Himmelfarb, *Idea of Poverty*, 19.

CHAPTER TWO

The Image of Christ in the Poor: On the Medieval Roots of the Wesleys' Ministry with the Poor

Ted A. Campbell

"If we want the poor people to see Christ in us," Mother Teresa wrote to a group of her supporters, "we have to see the image of Christ in the poor."[1] In this challenge to see "the image of Christ in the poor," Mother Teresa was enunciating a long-standing theme in Christian devotion and activism. This theme appeared most clearly in the mendicant movements of the Middle Ages, but it has persisted at least in Catholic culture. The Second Vatican Council's Dogmatic Constitution on the Church (*Lumen Gentium*) declared that the Church "recognizes in the poor and suffering the likeness of her poor and suffering Founder."[2] John and Charles Wesley also reflected this particular theme from medieval spirituality and social engagement in their lives and writings.

My 1984 dissertation at Southern Methodist University dealt with John Wesley's ancient, or patristic, roots, and it made the point that Wesley generally shared the Reformation's distaste for the Middle Ages.[3] But in considering at least one of the Wesleys' medieval

---

1. Mother Teresa of Calcutta, "Mother's message to the co-workers," cited from the website http://www.tisv.be/mt/cw.htm#message. The Co-workers are a group of supporters of the mission of Mother Teresa.
2. Vatican Council II, Dogmatic Constitution on the Church (1964), 1:8, in John H. Leith, ed., *Creeds of the Churches: A Reader in Christian Doctrine from the Bible to the Present*, 3d. ed. (Atlanta: John Knox Press, 1982), 461.
3. Ted A. Campbell, *John Wesley and Christian Antiquity* (Nashville: Kingswood Books, 1991), see 49-51.

roots, I'm offering something of a correction to my earlier thesis. My mentors at S.M.U. taught me to be suspicious of generalizations. They tried their best to hold me to the concreteness of historical moments, events, people, and (above all) texts. In the words of Arthur Darby Nock, "A fact is a holy thing, and its life should never be laid down on the altar of a generalization."[4] But themes and ideas do persist throughout history. They change; they take new guises; and they flourish in new contexts (these are all facts). So I hope that, rather than a generalization (in the pejorative sense of the term), I can offer an accurate study of an evolving theme, notion, or idea, that may go toward explaining, or at least understanding, the radical commitment to the poor expressed consistently by John and Charles Wesley.

Consider the following lines from Charles Wesley:

> Saviour, how few there are
> Who thy condition share,
> Few who cordially embrace,
> Love, and prize thy poverty,
> Want on earth a resting-place,
> Needy and resign'd like Thee![5]

In this poem, Charles Wesley sounds a theme that goes toward explaining his and his brother's concern for the poor. The point is not simply that we ought to love and help the poor , nor is it only that the poor have something to offer us. The point is the central role of Christ, "who, though he was in the form of God, did not regard equality with God as something to be exploited, but emptied himself, taking the form of a slave" (Phil. 2:6-7, NRSV). Christians are called to be conformed to the image of the Savior by living out the ideal to which Charles Wesley refers as "gospel poverty."[6] These notions of "gospel poverty" and the image of Christ in the poor have a long and intertwined history.

---

4. Zeph Stewart, ed., *Arthur Darby Nock: Essays on Religion and the Ancient World*, 2 vols. (Oxford: Oxford University Press and Cambridge, Mass.: Harvard University Press, 1972), 1:333.

5. *Unpublished Poetry*, 2:115; also in S T Kimbrough, Jr., ed., *Songs for the Poor: Hymns by Charles Wesley*, singer's ed. (New York: General Board of Global Ministries of The United Methodist Church, 1997), no. 8.

6. *Unpublished Poetry*, 2:298-99; also in Kimbrough, *Songs for the Poor*, no. 9.

Apostolic Poverty and the Image of Christ in the Poor

"Gospel poverty," otherwise known as "apostolic poverty," is a medieval notion that expressed the belief that Christ and the first apostles were themselves *deliberately* poor. A corollary of this belief is that the poor uniquely bear the image of Christ. However, we should be very clear about two matters: (1) The issue is not whether Wesley was basically Franciscan or Catholic. The simple case is that there was a long-standing tradition of reverence for Christ's poverty and for the poor as they reflected the image of Christ and that this distinctive tradition was incorporated into the Wesleyan movement in eighteenth-century Britain. (2) Such notions as "apostolic poverty" and "the image of Christ in the poor" may well suggest a romanticized or even paternalistic notion of the poor, although there may be some question whether these notions are simply romanticized or whether they do serve to recognize the dignity of those who suffer. But poverty is not pretty: St. Francis and St. Clare knew that; John and Charles Wesley knew it; William and Catherine Booth knew it. None of them took Jesus' poverty—"Gospel poverty"—to mean that the poor somehow ought to remain poor.

The Mendicant Understanding of the Poor

The roots of medieval understandings of the poor lie in the Christian scriptures and in the writings of Christian antiquity. Ambrose of Milan, for example, referred to the poor as "Christ's poor," and his contemporary John Chrysostom pressed the point that we store up treasures in heaven by giving our earthly treasures to the poor.[7] But under the influence of the mendicant movement (and its predecessors in such groups as the Waldensians), at least three distinctive and specific attitudes developed regarding "Christ's poor."

The first distinct notion characteristic of the mendicant movement is the *salvific significance of the poverty of Christ*. In its broader context, the mendicant stress on the poverty of Christ must be seen as

---

7. Ambrose of Milan, "Sermon against Auxentius on the Giving Up of the Basilicas," in vol. 10 of *A Select Library of the Nicene and Post-Nicene Fathers of the Christian Church*, Philip Schaff and Henry Wace, eds., 2d. ser. (Grand Rapids, Mich: Wm. B. Eerdmans Publishing Company, 1955), 435, ¶33. John Chrysostom, "Concerning the Statues, homily 2," in vol. 9 of *A Select Library of the Nicene and Post-Nicene Fathers of the Christian Church*, Philip Schaff, ed., 1st ser. (Grand Rapids, Mich.: Wm. B. Eerdmans Publishing Company, 1956), 353, ¶24.

part of a renewed stress on devotion to the humanity of Christ in the Middle Ages. This devotion was expressed in the Crusades to Palestine to recover sacred shrines and relics that reflected Christ's human life. It was also to be seen in St. Francis's use of the manger to honor the infant Jesus and in his reception of the stigmata.[8] But Franciscans and Dominicans went on to insist that Christ himself owned no possessions. Christ's absolute poverty became a central object of devotion to the humanity of the Savior, and this belief was formalized as doctrine in the mendicant orders.[9]

A second note of mendicant attitudes toward the poor follows from the first: not only was the Savior poor but also *the poor are distinctly the beloved of Christ*. This notion was Francis's great discovery when he left his home and served the *minores*—the lepers and the poor—of his native Umbria. Not surprisingly, his order is the *Ordo Fratrum Minorum*, the Order of Minor, Lesser, or Poor Brothers. This attitude is expressed in Thomas of Celano's *St. Francis of Assisi*: "Not even lowness of birth or any condition of poverty stood in the way of building up the work of God in those in whom God wished to build it up, God who delights to be with the outcasts of the world and with the simple."[10]

Thomas quotes Francis as saying, repeatedly, "Who curses a poor man does an injury to Christ, whose noble image he wears, the image of him who made himself poor for us in this world."[11]

Given this commitment to the poor as those who bear Christ's image, it followed that the mendicant orders became the cornerstone of medieval Christian efforts for the relief of the poor. The commitments of the mendicant Third Orders (and later the Beguines, following the model of the Third Orders) gave them an especially clear mandate for service to the poor.[12]

---

8. The narrative of Francis's use of the manger is given in Thomas of Celano's *St. Francis of Assisi: First and Second Life of St. Francis*, tr. Placid Hermann (Chicago: Franciscan Herald Press, 1963), book 1, chap. 30. The narrative of the stigmata is given in the same source, book 2, chap. 3, ¶¶94-96. On the broader context of devotion to Christ's humanity, see J. Mead, "Passion of Christ III (Devotion to)" in the *New Catholic Encyclopedia*, 15 vols. (New York: McGraw-Hill, 1967), 10:1059-61.

9. In Umberto Eco's novel *The Name of the Rose* (San Diego: Harcourt, Brace, Jovanovich, 1983), this issue was the subject of formal debate in the monastery. See C. H. Lawrence, *The Friars: The Impact of the Early Mendicant Movement on Western Society* (London and New York: Longman, 1994), 15-19, 31-37; cf. M. D. Lambert, *Franciscan Poverty: The Doctrine of the Absolute Poverty of Christ and the Apostles in the Franciscan Order, 1210–1323* (London: SPCK, 1961), chaps. 1 and 2.

10. Thomas of Celano, *St. Francis of Assisi*, book 1, chap. 12, ¶31.

11. Ibid., book 1, chap. 28, ¶76.

12. On the origins of the Franciscan Third Order, see Raffaele Pazzelli, St. Francis and the *Third Order: The Franciscan and Pre-Franciscan Penitential Movement* (Chicago: Franciscan Herald

A third distinctive note of mendicant attitudes toward the poor is *the call to a life of voluntary poverty* both in imitation of Christ and in service to Christ's beloved poor. Where earlier monastic communities had rejected individual property (but allowed monastic communities to amass considerable wealth), the mendicants insisted on the rejection of all moveable or stored property including property held in common. The Franciscans and Dominicans believed that in this approach they were quite literally following Christ. A particular praise was given by Walter Map, archdeacon of Oxford, who recorded his impression of seeing the Waldensians at the Third Lateran Council in 1179. They were, in his words, *nudi nudum Christum sequentes*, "Naked, following a naked Christ."[13] These words came to be applied broadly to the mendicants and expressed their belief that the renunciation of property is a mark of the perfect following of the Savior. Moreover, the life of Christ-like poverty enables the mendicant to fulfill literally Jesus' evangelistic instructions to the apostles. So Thomas of Celano describes Francis's conversion:

> The holy Francis, hearing that the disciples of Christ should not possess gold or silver or money; nor carry along the way scrip, or wallet, or bread, or a staff; that they should not have shoes, or two tunics; but that they should preach the kingdom of God and penance, immediately cried out exultingly: "This is what I wish, this is what I seek, this is what I long to do with all my heart."[14]

The embrace of absolute poverty and the proscription against moveable or stored property, however, led to the long-disputed issue of whether a "spiritual friend" of a mendicant community could grant the use of property to a community. The *usus pauper* controversy extended for a hundred years after the founding of the mendicant orders and shows both the seriousness and the distinctiveness of the ideal of voluntary poverty embraced by the mendicants.[15]

Press, 1982). On the charitable institutions of the Third Orders (Lawrence uses the more inclusive term "lay confraternities"), see Lawrence, *Friars*, 112-16.

13. Walter Map, *De Nugis Curialium*, cited in G. Gonnet, *Enchiridion Fontium Valdensium* (Torre Pellice, 1958), 122-23; cited (in turn) in Giorgio Tourn, *You Are My Witnesses: The Waldensians across 800 Years* (Turin: Claudiana, 1989), 20. Map's quotation in Latin is given in an article by Walter Mohr, "Waldes and die Frühe Waldensertum," *Zeitschrift für Religionsgeistesgeschichte* 9 (1957): 352.

14. Thomas of Celano, *St. Francis of Assisi*, book 1, chap. 9, ¶22.

15. See Lambert, *Franciscan Poverty*, chaps. 3-10; Lawrence, Friars, 60-64.

Piety Toward the Poor in the *Devotio Moderna*

Near the end of the Middle Ages, these three mendicant attitudes toward the poor were transformed in a prominent movement called the *Devotio Moderna* or "Modern Devotion." With its social location in the growing mercantile cities of northern Europe, especially the Low Countries and Germany, the *Devotio Moderna* offered a spirituality well adapted to its "modern" (urban) social context. Its spirituality lay in the immediate background of the Protestant Reformation.[16]

One of the central features of the *Devotio Moderna* was its stress on the humanity of Christ, evident in its abundant use of crucifixes and such literature as Thomas à Kempis's classic work, *The Imitation of Christ* (1418). In this vision, Christ's material poverty (but not absolute poverty) was emphasized as a feature of the Savior's humility, and believers were encouraged to identify affectively with this aspect of Christ's life. But the overwhelming emphasis in the *Devotio Moderna* was not on this material poverty but on the passion and sufferings of Christ (for example, devotion to the wounds of Christ), and Christ's material poverty no longer held the position of centrality in devotion that it held for the mendicants.[17]

The advocates of the *Devotio Moderna* did retain a sense of the poor as Christ's beloved. Thomas à Kempis expresses the idea that the poor are favored by God: Whereas *nature* causes us to revel in the things of this world, grace, according to à Kempis, "favors the poor to the rich."[18] He explains further,

> Woe to those who think themselves too good to humble themselves willingly with the children, for the lowly gate of the heavenly kingdom will not allow them to enter. Woe also to the rich who have their comforts here, for while the poor enter into the kingdom of God, they will stand outside lamenting. Rejoice, you humble! Exult, you poor! The kingdom of God is yours if you walk in the way of the truth![19]

Despite this sense of the spiritual superiority of the poor, though, the stress on "interiority" in the *Devotio Moderna* made the service to

---

16. See David Steinmetz, "Luther against Luther" in his *Luther in Context* (Bloomington: Indiana University Press, 1986), 1-11.

17. On devotion to the humanity of Christ in the *Devotio Moderna*, see the introduction to *Devotio Moderna: Basic Writings*, tr. John van Engen, Classics of Western Spirituality series (New York: Paulist Press, 1988), 25.

18. Thomas à Kempis, *The Imitation of Christ*, book 3, chap. 54, tr. William C. Creasy (Macon, Ga.: Mercer University Press, 1989), 118.

19. Ibid., chap. 58, 125-26.

the poor an obligation to be fulfilled in the Christian's quest to do all that we can for the good. Service to the poor, we might say, becomes an ordinance (borrowing Baptist language) rather than a sacrament of encounter with Christ.

The *Devotio Moderna* also transformed the mendicants' call to a life of radical poverty. The focus was no longer on the finer distinctions of the *usus pauper* controversy but on the need for a simple life, free from the affective restraints of possessions. Geert Grote, considered by many to be the founder of the *Devotio Moderna*, advised his directees as follows:

> Allot yourself therefore a frugal portion of clothing and food, more to the poor and the deserving, and more still for the salvation of souls. Never give anything to someone not in need, because you can find many poverty-striken people. And if you give to someone with more than enough, you have not dispensed faithfully nor prudently as regards your salvation.[20]

This approach is consistent with the "Customary" (or customs) of the Brethren of the Common Life, which rules private possessions among the Brethren and encourages frugality and simplicity of life. The literature of the movement on the eve of the Reformation abounds in stories of the extreme frugality of sisters and brothers.[21]

The Legacy of Mendicant Attitudes in the Age of Reformation

The Renaissance invented the notion of the "Middle Ages" as its *literati* looked back over centuries of "superstition" to the purer cultural models of classical and Christian antiquity. The Reformation followed, and in their rejection of all things hinting of medieval and "popish" superstition, the Reformers rejected the institutions of monasticism, including the mendicant orders.[22] Church institutions for

---

20. Geert Grote, "Resolutions and Intentions, But Not Vows," in van Engen, *Devotio Moderna*, 75.

21. See the stories given in van Engen, *Devotio Moderna*, 127-31. See the discussion "Common Life and Poverty," in the "Customary for Brothers," ibid., 170-71.

22. Francis of Assisi would later become a favored medieval saint among Protestants but not until after the Gothic revival of the nineteenth century with its more positive approbation of the Middle Ages in general. Respect for Francis among Protestants rose markedly after the publication of Huguenot Paul Sabatier's *Life of Saint Francis of Assisi* (1894). On this point, see

the relief of the poor, largely led by the mendicants and their Third Orders, were secularized in Protestant countries—hence the Elizabethan Poor Law of 1601, to which Wesley repeatedly appealed.

Given the Renaissance and Reformation's distaste for the Dark Ages, how could the inheritance of medieval spirituality and activism have influenced the Wesleys? One answer, I believe, lies in the flourishing of Anglican spiritual writers of the seventeenth century who came to value the medieval inheritance of the *Devotio Moderna*. A second answer lies in the popularity of a few Catholic spiritual writers (themselves made popular by Caroline Anglicans) whose works John Wesley had read.

Seventeenth-century Anglicanism had positioned itself against Catholicism on the one hand and Puritanism on the other. As the conflict with Puritanism escalated during the seventeenth century, Anglican theologians and spiritual writers began to appropriate more and more of the Catholic inheritance of faith, including such works of late medieval piety as à Kempis's *Imitation of Christ*.[23] In Anglican works of the late seventeenth and early eighteenth centuries, and especially those of nonjuring authors, medieval notions about the poor had been diffused within the Anglican tradition. So William Law's *A Serious Call to a Devout and Holy Life* (1728) urges readers to acknowledge the sanctity of the poor: "Love poverty and reverence poor people as for many reasons, so particularly for this, because our blessed Savior was one of the number and because you may make them all so many friends and advocates with God for you."[24]

Similarly, nonjuror Robert Nelson, a friend of the Wesley family, challenged the readers of his *Address to Persons of Quality* (1715) with a call to renunciation of surplus wealth, "All the ancient Fathers who are wise instructors in matters of piety, as well as the best witnesses to necessary truth, agree in this notion; that after we have satisfy'd

---

John R. H. Moorman, *The Sources for the Life of S. Francis of Assisi* (Manchester: Manchester University Press, 1940), 9-10.

23. That Caroline Anglicans should have been more open to the contributions of the mendicants appears from that fact, and although Franciscans and other mendicants were regarded with contempt in continental Protestant countries, there was at least a scintilla of interest in them in England. Thus, an English Franciscan (Anthony Parkinson) wrote a history of his Order in 1726, addressed to Protestants, with these words in the preface: "They were a Society of well-meaning Christians, and our Country-Men; and on these considerations, I presume, they cannot be disagreeable to all. . . . It's true they were *Friers* [sic]; but they are dead and gone many a fair Year ago, and it is Pity, methinks, that all the Memory of their Merits shou'd die too." Anthony Parkinson, *Collectanea Anglo-Minoritica* (1726), cited in Moorman, *Sources*, 7.

24. William Law, *A Serious Call to a Devout and Holy Life*, Paul G. Stanwood, ed., Classics of Western Spirituality series (New York: Paulist Press, 1978), 275.

our necessities, and supply'd our reasonable occasions, we should employ the rest for the relief of our poor neighbours."[25]

So John Walsh comments (and his comment was, at least in part, what inspired this research) that, "In their attitude to poverty and riches, however, [the] inbred authoritarianism [of the Anglican High-Church party] was often softened by an ethic of charity inherited from the Middle Ages and reinforced by patristic learning. Reverential views of the poor as 'Christ's poor' were still current."[26] This brings us directly to the time of the Wesleys.

The Wesleys and the Medieval Understanding of the Poor

Finding the traces of this notion of the poor in the Wesleys' thinking is not as straightforward as one might hope. We have noted John Wesley's general disdain for the medieval, a disdain he largely shared with his fellow eighteenth-century Anglicans. A search of Wesley's works shows no references to Francis of Assisi (beyond one quoted from another source) and little awareness of the positive contributions of mendicants beyond John Wesley's approval of a certain provision in the Dominican Rule that allowed for lay preachers.[27] Although Albert C. Outler used the medieval catch phrase "Christ's poor" in describing John Wesley's attitudes,[28] a computer search of the *Works*, again, shows no instances of this particular term.

Clearly, Wesley inherited from his parents a strong respect for high-Church Caroline Anglicanism, including familiarity with the works of nonjurors and that strain of Caroline spirituality (including à Kempis) that Susanna Wesley identified as "practical divinity."[29] John Wesley's study in Oxford led him to deeper reading in the nonjurors, in the writings of Christian antiquity, and in the study of some contemporary Catholic writers. Richard Heitzenrater has emphasized the importance of the motif of following Christ (again,

---

25. Robert Nelson, *An Address to Persons of Quality and Estate* (London, 1715), 229-30; cited in John Walsh, "John Wesley and the Community of Goods," in Keith Robbins, ed., *Protestant Evangelicalism: Britain, Ireland, Germany, and America, c. 1750–c. 1950, Essays in Honour of W. R. Ward*, Studies in Church History Series, no. 7 (Oxford: Basil Blackwell, 1990), 32.

26. Ibid.

27. Wesley's positive comments on the Dominican Rule appear in his *Farther Appeal to Men of Reason and Religion*, Part III, III.12, *Works*, 10:298.

28. Introduction to Sermon 50, "The Use of Money," *Works*, 2:263.

29. Susanna Wesley, letter to John Wesley (23 February 1725), *Works*, 25:160.

à Kempis is emphasized) in John Wesley's experience with the Oxford Methodists.[30]

John and Charles Wesley undertook the Georgia mission with the intent of living out the vision of pure Christianity they had inherited from these varied sources. On his first day to preach in Savannah, John Wesley recorded in his *Journal* that he had preached on Luke 18, and that it foreshadowed the persecution that would come to those who were resolved, *nudi nudum Christum sequi*, "naked to follow a naked Christ."[31] It may well be that the phrase came to him by way of his study of the Latin text of à Kempis's *Imitation of Christ*.[32]

One might say that although these Catholic sources affected the Wesleys early in their careers (before their evangelical experiences of 1738), they did not affect them beyond the beginnings of the Methodist Revival. But in fact the Wesleys continued to rely on many of these sources, especially for their understanding of sanctification. What is more important, perhaps, is that Wesley continued to believe in the sanctity of the Catholic authors he knew. In 1765 John Wesley wrote:

> "Oh, but Mr. Hervey says *you* are *half* a Papist." What if he had *proved* it too? What if he had proved I was a *whole* Papist? (though he might as easily have proved me a Mahometan). Is not a Papist a child of God? Is Thomas à Kempis, Mr. De Renty, Gregory Lopez gone to hell? Believe it who can. Yet still of such (though Papists) the same is my brother and sister and mother.[33]

---

30. Richard P. Heitzenrater, "*The Imitatio Christi* and the Great Commandment: Virtue and Obligation in Wesley's Ministry with the Poor," in M. Douglas Meeks, ed., *The Portion of the Poor: Good News to the Poor in the Wesleyan Tradition* (Nashville: Kingswood Books, 1995), esp. 57-59. The theology of the *Devotio Moderna* (as exemplified by Gabriel Biel) and of many Caroline Anglicans (such as Jeremy Taylor) did in fact claim a kind of "justification by faith" but with the critical proviso that the Christian would not be given faith (and justification) until he or she had done all within his or her power (*fac quod in te est*). My own surmise is that the theology and ethics of the Oxford Methodists were grounded in just this understanding of faith and works, and it was this understanding that most of the Reformers had rejected as requiring *prior* human effort. This would explain why John Wesley's study of the Anglican Articles and Homilies (beginning in November 1738) came as such a surprise to him.

31. *Journal* (7 March 1736), *Works*, 18:153.

32. Ibid., see note 64 by Ward and Heitzenrater on this passage. John Wesley's own edition of à Kempis's work, under the title *The Christian's Pattern*, had the following: "Let this be thy prayer, let this be thy desire: that being stripped of all selfishness, thou mayst follow naked the naked Jesus, and dying to thyself, mayst live eternally with me" (New York: The Methodist Book Concern, n.d.), 122. See Frank Baker, ed., *John Wesley's Own Choice: The Heart of True Spirituality*, 2 vols. (Grand Rapids, Mich.: Francis Asbury Press, 1985), 2:37; and see the table given by Baker, 2:86.

33. Letter to John Newton (9 April 1765), *Letters* (Telford), 4:293.

Such quotations as this make it clear that however Wesley may have differed with the theology of Catholic (or Caroline Anglican) writers, he was willing to see evidence of their sanctity.[34] He was also willing to incorporate some of their understandings of the poor in the apostolate of the Methodist movement. We may turn, then, to the three distinctive characteristics of mendicant attitudes toward the poor and see how John and Charles Wesley reflect their inheritance.

The Poor Christ

The first point has to do with the material poverty of Christ—in the distinctive formulation of the mendicants, the *"absolute* poverty" of Christ and the disciples. The Wesleys did not defend the notion of "absolute poverty," and indeed, John Deschner's study of *Wesley's Christology* finds no significant emphasis on the material poverty of the Savior in discussing Christ's humiliation.[35] The places where John Wesley does approach language suggesting the significance of Christ's poverty could be seen as echoes of à Kempis or other authors. Consider, for instance, the following passage from John Wesley's "Plain Account of Christian Perfection" (as revised in 1777):

> To abandon all, to strip one's self of all, in order to seek and to follow Jesus Christ naked to Bethlehem, where he was born; naked to the hall where he was scourged; and naked to Calvary, where he died on the cross, is so great a mercy, that neither the thing, nor the knowledge of it, is given to any, but through faith in the Son of God.[36]

These words sound as if they have come directly from à Kempis. And even here, the "nakedness" of Christ is associated with his birth, his passion, and his crucifixion, not with material poverty per se.

In the Wesleys' poetry—and primarily in Charles Wesley's work—we can apprehend an even greater significance attached to Christ's poverty. In the drama of the Wesleys' verse, the incarnation

---

34. See Wesley's comment in Sermon 107, "On God's Vineyard" (1787), I.5, that Catholic authors had written "strongly and scripturally on sanctification" (*Works*, 3:505-6).

35. John Deschner, *Wesley's Christology: An Interpretation*, rev. ed. (Dallas: Southern Methodist University Press, 1985), 48-52. Deschner does not state this conclusion positively, but in dealing with several aspects of Christ's humiliation, it is significant that Deschner makes no mention of material poverty, even in his section on Christ's ministry (p. 49, the shortest by far of all the sections).

36. John Wesley, "A Plain Account of Christian Perfection," *Works* (Jackson), 11:437. Although the text at this point is in quotation marks, it is quoted from an earlier version of the same tract.

consistently appears as the staggering paradox of the incomprehensible and omnipotent deity who nevertheless takes his place among the poorest of human sisters and brothers:

> Thou, who didst so greatly stoop
> To a poor virgin's womb.[37]

The paradox can be put in a simple juxtaposition: "Praise we all our lowly King."[38] And the believer's challenge is to follow Christ in humiliation: "My lowly Master's steps pursue!"[39]

Consider again the following lines from Charles Wesley. Reflecting on Luke 9:57-58 ("Foxes have holes, and birds of the air have nests; but the Son of man hath not where to lay his head"), Charles Wesley writes:

> Savior, how few there are
> who thy condition share,
> few who cordially embrace,
> love, and prize thy poverty,
> want on earth a resting place,
> needy and resigned like thee![40]

This perspective will be relevant to our third point as well, but Charles Wesley's point is that our own call to poverty is a call to follow Christ. So, in another poem, he writes that to attain poverty is to attain Christ:

> Thus, thus may I the prize pursue,
> and all the appointed paths pass through
>   to perfect poverty:
> thus let me, Lord, thyself attain,
> and give thee up thine own again,
>   forever lost in thee.[41]

On this point, then, Charles Wesley's verse seems to express more of the distinct medieval understanding of the poor than anything in John Wesley's writings.

---

37. *A Collection of Hymns*, no. 401, *Works*, 7:577.
38. Ibid, 562, no. 388.
39. Ibid, 502, no. 341.
40. In Kimbrough, *Songs for the Poor*, no. 8.
41. Ibid., no. 7. A hymn from Charles Wesley, *Short Hymns on Selected Passages of the Holy Scriptures* (Bristol: Felix Farley, 1762).

The Poor as Christ's Beloved

The second distinctive note of mendicant attitudes toward the poor was the idea that they are uniquely loved by Christ. The notion of the human dignity of the poor as God's creation appears robustly in John Wesley's prose. Consider, for example, the following passage from John Wesley's sermon "On Pleasing All Men" (1787):

A poor wretch cries to me for an alms: I look and see him covered with dirt and rags. But through these I see one that has an immortal spirit, made to know and love and dwell with God to eternity: I honour him for his Creator's sake. I see through all these rags that he is purpled over with the blood of Christ. I love him for the sake of his Redeemer.[42]

In a sense, this simply marks John Wesley's attempt at an egalitarian response to the poor, and his conclusion on this point is that we owe courtesy to the poor as well as the rich.[43]

But the more distinctive nuance of this theme, the poor as uniquely beloved of Christ, appears especially prominent in Charles Wesley's long-unpublished verse:

> The poor, as Jesus' bosom-friends,
>   The poor he makes his latest care,
> To all his successors commends,
>   And wills us on our hands to bear:
> The poor our dearest care we make,
>   Aspiring to superior bliss,
> And cherish for their Saviour's sake,
>   And love them with a love like his.[44]

So also:

> The poor in every age and place
>   Thou dost, O God, approve
> To mark with thy distinguish'd grace,
>   T'inrich with faith and love.[45]

---

42. Sermon 100, "On Pleasing All Men," II.5, *Works*, 3:425.
43. Ibid. See the concluding sentences of the preceding quotation.
44. *Unpublished Poetry*, 2:404; see also Kimbrough, *Songs for the Poor*, no. 3.
45. *Unpublished Poetry*, 2:90; see also Kimbrough, *Songs for the Poor*, no. 6.

In another poem, Charles Wesley makes the point—so character-istic of mendicant spirituality—that the poor are appointed to Christ's place on earth:

> Yes; the poor supply thy place,
> Still deputed, Lord, by Thee,
> Daily exercise our grace,
> Prove our growing charity;
> What to them with right intent
> Truly, faithfully is given,
> We have to our Saviour lent,
> Laid up for ourselves in heaven.[46]

Given this notion of the poor as the beloved of Christ, even as those who occupy Christ's place in our world, we can understand both John and Charles Wesley's frequent indications of their own love for the poor and their frequent disdain for the rich. John Wesley wrote to Dorothy Furly in 1757, "I love the poor; in many of them I find pure, genuine grace, unmixed with paint, folly, and affectation."[47] "O what an advantage have the poor over the rich! These are not wise in their own eyes, but all receive with meekness the engrafted word which is able to save their souls."[48] For this reason, John Wesley con-sistently represented the Methodist movement as having a distinct apostolate among the poor. He wrote, "The rich, the honourable, the great, we are thoroughly willing (if it be the will of the Lord) to leave to you. Only let us alone with the poor, the vulgar, the base, the out-casts of men."[49] The poor were Christ's beloved and the distinct con-stituency of the Methodist movement.

The Call to Voluntary Poverty

The third aspect of mendicant attitudes toward the poor was the call to a life of voluntary poverty following Christ's example.[50]

---

46. *Unpublished Poetry*, 2:46; see also S T Kimbrough, Jr., "Charles Wesley and the Poor," in Meeks, *Portion of the Poor*, 156 and 190 n. 29.

47. Letter to Dorothy Furly (25 September 1757), *Letters* (Telford), 3:229.

48. John Wesley, *Journal* (19 September 1788), *Works*, 24:110. For a variety of such quotations indicating affection for the poor, see Theodore W. Jennings, Jr., *Good News to the Poor: John Wesley's Evangelical Economics* (Nashville: Abingdon Press, 1990), 48-53.

49. *Farther Appeal to Men of Reason and Religion, Part III*, III.35, *Works*, 8:316.

50. John Wesley did express an objection to the interpretation of the beatitude "Blessed are the poor in spirit" as a direct call for vows of poverty, as Catholic interpreters had argued; see

Charles Wesley's poem that begins "Savior, how few there are/who thy condition share" (cited previously) continues:

> I dare not ask thy pain
> and sorrow to sustain:
> but if thou vouchsafe me power
> thee by want to glorify,
> blessed with love I ask no more,
> poor I live, and patient die.[51]

Similarly, Charles Wesley commends those who offer an example of Christ-like poverty:

> See here an Apostolic priest,
>   Commission'd from the sky,
> Who dares of all himself divest,
>   The needy to supply!
> A primitive example rare
>   Of gospel-poverty,
> To feed the flock his only care,
>   And like his Lord to be.[52]

In the light of this call to voluntary poverty we can understand John Wesley's consistent warnings against surplus accumulation. He was aware of medieval precedents for the church's use of money in the help of the poor. According to his own edition of Anthony Horneck's "Letter to a Person of Quality," even the Christians of the Middle Ages regarded "ecclesiastical revenues" as being "sacred to God and the poor."[53] What he meant by the third rule for "The Use of Money," namely, "give all you can," was "If there be an overplus still," after supplying the needs of one's family and dependents, then " 'as you have opportunity, do good unto all men.' "[54] Consistent with this ethic, Wesley claimed that to keep possessions beyond the necessities of life amounted to robbery of the poor:

---

his Sermon 21, "Upon our Lord's Sermon on the Mount, I," I.3, *Works*, 1:476-77. But Wesley's point here was that the Sermon on the Mount laid a universal foundation for Christian faith, so no part of it should be taken as referring to the particular vocation of those called to vows of poverty, chastity, and obedience.

51. In Kimbrough, *Songs for the Poor*, no. 8.

52. *Unpublished Poetry*, 2:298-99; in Kimbrough, *Songs for the Poor*, no. 9.

53. Anthony Horneck, "Letter to a Person of Quality, concerning the Heavenly Lives of the Ancient Christians," ed. John Wesley, in the *Christian Library* (Bristol, 1753), 29:115, 126-27; cf. Claude Fleury, *Manners of the Ancient Christians*, 2:4, ed. John Wesley, 6th ed. (London, 1798), 8.

54. Sermon 50, "The Use of Money," *Works*, 2:277; see Outler's introductory comments at the beginning of this sermon, 2:263-65.

Do you not know that God *entrusted* you with that money (all above what buys necessaries for your families) to feed the hungry, to clothe the naked, to help the stranger, the widow, the fatherless; and indeed, as far as it will go, to relieve the wants of all mankind. How can you, how dare you, defraud your Lord by applying it to any other purpose![55]

Consistent with this ethic was Wesley's personal involvement with the poor, for instance, the often-cited example of his collection of significant funds for the poor when he was eighty-two.[56]

Did not Wesley live as a *de facto* mendicant? Consider that the immovable property of Methodism (including the preaching houses, the New Chapel [City Road] in London, and the residences in Bristol, London, and Newcastle) was owned communally and managed by the Methodist trustees. With respect to moveable or stored property, Wesley himself consistently claimed that he owned very little in this world. Except for the months in the 1750s when he lived with his wife, it seems that his life was actually lived on the model of the mendicant. His time was taken with itinerant preaching, and he constantly warned his flock about the dangers of stored or surplus accumulation. Moreover, he believed in the restoration of the primitive Christian ideal of a "community of goods," as John Walsh has pointed out, and he suggested that members of the Select Societies should contribute to a common store of goods, "till we can have all things common."[57]

Conclusions

First, the literature concerning the Wesleys and the roots of their various doctrines and practices typically conclude that the Wesleys were very complicated people, and that amongst the various influences that have been considered, the details of the present study must have a prominent place. The Wesleys were indeed complicated folk who lived at the very intersection of overlapping historic epochs. But it is not necessary to say that medieval piety had a prominent place in

---

55. Sermon 131, "The Danger of Increasing Riches," §12, *Works*, 4:184.

56. *Journal* (4 January 1785), *Works*, 23:340. For further examples of this type of benevolent work, see Jennings, *Good News for the Poor*, 53-62.

57. Walsh, "Wesley and Community of Goods," 32. The quotation is from John Bennett's copy of the Minutes of the 1744 Conference for June 28, Publications of the Wesley Historical Society 1 (London, 1896), 14; see Campbell, *John Wesley and Christian Antiquity*, 87-88.

the Wesley's thought and practice. If we want to understand their passion for ministry with the poor, perhaps it is only important to say that we must understand the medieval traditions they had imbibed, especially the intimate connection between Christ and the poor in those traditions.

Second, I want to acknowledge Henry Rack's concern with putting too much emphasis on the books Wesley read along with their religious pedigree and meaning. Too many analyses of Wesley's experience and theology have proceeded in this way. It is true that the books mentioned did influence him, some of them (even the mystics) long after his conversion, but he read and abridged them very selectively and built them into patterns of his own.[58]

I have always suspected that Professor Rack was referring to those American interpreters of Wesley, such as myself, who often read John Wesley's works and the books he read with poor sensitivity to the historical context and to the ways in which Wesley used and transformed them. Perhaps we should make the point that the Middle Ages did not come to John and Charles Wesley only in the books they read. The Middle Ages came to the Wesleys in the very world in which they lived from day to day.

As a student at Lincoln College, Oxford, I had the opportunity to see the Latin letter that John Wesley wrote to the College resigning his fellowship on the occasion of his marriage in 1751. The College liked to claim that they funded the first decade of the Evangelical Revival because John Wesley received an annual stipend from the College throughout that period. During the Reformation, the universities had been spared from the dissolution of the monasteries, and the colleges retained some of the character of their origins as monastic houses including the stipulation that college fellows had to be single and were expected to live in the college. John Wesley was aware that Lincoln College had been founded for the extirpation of Lollardy, and he knew that fellows of Lincoln were given, by charter, a distinct license, or permission, to preach throughout England for the eradication of heresy.

We have seen that Wesley's later life took the form of a mendicant itinerant. But it might also be worth remembering that he had lived in community during his days at Charterhouse (a former

---

58. Henry Rack, *Reasonable Enthusiast: John Wesley and the Rise of Methodism* (Philadelphia: Trinity Press International, 1989), 97.

Carthusian establishment) as well as at Oxford. That is to say, there were only a few points in his life beyond Epworth when he did not live in some kind of community.

Moreover, one cannot walk the streets of Oxford or visit the colleges and their chapels without seeing the visible signs of medieval piety. So, perhaps we should recall that medieval notions came to John and Charles Wesley not only in the contents of books but also in their daily lives. For all the developments of the Enlightenment, modernity, and the nascent Industrial Revolution, they lived in a world that remained in many ways quite medieval. Given this context, as well as the various literature the Wesleys read, it should come as little surprise that medieval conceptions of the sanctity of the poor should have influenced them deeply.

Third, it would be fair to conclude that, at many points, Charles Wesley's verse comes much closer to the distinctiveness of mendicant understandings of the poor than John Wesley's prose. Perhaps this has something to do with the particular personality of Charles in contrast to John, but it may have something to do with the nature of poetry as contrasted with prose, for poetry sometimes carries echoes of notions that have long since perished in prose. For example, although the church lost sight of the doctrine of the poverty of Christ, devotion to Christ's material poverty persisted in the dramatic paradoxes of religious verse. But it appears that, very consistently, Charles Wesley's verse embodies much more of the medieval sense of the saving significance of Christ's poverty, of the distinct love that Christ has for the poor, and even of the distinct call to a life of renunciation and voluntary poverty.

The fourth point has to do with my surprise, on looking back, at what a small role Christ's material poverty plays in Protestant understanding. Even the Lutheran tradition's emphasis on the *theologia crucis* as contrasted with the *theologia gloriae* gives relatively little place to Christ's poverty as a significant element of his humiliation. Why is this? I suspect it has something to do with the Protestant rejection of monasticism, although as we have seen, even in the *Devotio Moderna* the theme had been downplayed. It may have something to do with Protestantism's connection with nascent mercantilism and capitalism. I do not know the literature of contemporary systematics to know if this is an issue that has been sufficiently addressed, but I am struck with the fact that the notion of Christ's identification with the poor is hardly a novel theme. It was at the center of medieval Christian devotion.

Finally, I think we have to raise the question about Protestantism's lack of options for those who are distinctly called to a life of poverty and celibacy. Lacking options for monastic vocations, Protestants are left with the impossible task of framing a one-size-fits-all spirituality. This dilemma was, as you know, a very personal problem for John and Charles Wesley. It is a problem for that small but significant train of students who have come to me in the decade and a half I have taught in seminaries and who feel that there are almost no options for their own sense of calling except to become Orthodox or Catholic. I suppose one could argue that a theology of vocations, especially applied to issues of wealth and poverty, could become a crutch for middle-class complacency. But on the other hand, some of Protestantism's most significant work with the poor has been undertaken by those who were *de facto* committed to a single life, at least for a particular span of their lives (here I am thinking of the work of Methodist deaconesses).

I concluded my study of *Christian Confessions*, comparing the historic doctrines taught by the various confessional families of Christianity, with the claim that "the Christian faith is historically constituted by the teaching that Jesus Christ is God . . . [and] by the worship of Jesus Christ as God."[59] In my most recent study of *Methodist Doctrine*, I have made the claim that historic Methodist doctrine, as communal consensus on what to teach, has also affirmed the centrality of this most distinctively Christian claim.[60] The most important thing about the medieval understanding of the poor reflected by the Wesleys is that in *this* vision the poor become central to the very meaning of Christian faith itself. That is to say, the poor are connected intimately with Christ. If unconnected to the central *religious* meaning of Christian faith—unconnected to Christ—the poor become a problem, an obligation, an exception, and in any case, they become peripheral.

You may, as I suggested at the beginning, reject medieval talk of the "sanctity of the poor" as pious, paternalistic, or romanticizing. But how else can we hand down a Christian culture that takes the plight of "Christ's poor" as being, not at the periphery, but at the very heart of our religious commitment?

---

59. Ted A. Campbell, *Christian Confessions: A Historical Introduction* (Louisville: Westminster John Knox Press, 1996), 282.

60. Ted A. Campbell, *Methodist Doctrine: The Essentials* (Nashville: Abingdon Press, 1999), 41-47.

CHAPTER THREE

"Visit the Poor": John Wesley, the Poor, and the Sanctification of Believers

Randy L. Maddox

Few will question the warrant for holding a conference such as this one, a conference focused on the concern for and engagement with the poor that was clearly demonstrated by the Wesleys and many of their spiritual descendants. Nor will there be much surprise about discussion of differing models for the sanctified life within the Wesleyan tradition. By contrast, the connection between these two topics may provoke some puzzlement. There is little emphasis on such a connection in standard studies of either John Wesley's economic ethics and social ministries or his model of spiritual formation. I could ignore this reality and plunge ahead with my argument. But it might be more helpful to set these standard studies in contextual perspective as a way of "clearing the ground" to consider Wesley afresh.

A Frequently Overlooked Connection

The topic of Wesley and the poor has been a popular one in the twentieth century. It drew particular attention as North Atlantic Methodists engaged the Social Gospel movement in the first half of this century,[1] and it has become prominent again in the last quarter of

---

1. Note how this issue predominates in Francis J. McConnell's survey, "New Interest in John Wesley," *Journal of Religion* 20 (1940): 340-58.

the century as Wesley's various descendants have struggled to come to terms with the challenge of (particularly Latin American) Liberation Theology.[2]

The strength of these twentieth-century analyses of Wesley and the poor has been the passion that drives their reconsideration of traditional images and materials and the forthrightness with which they have championed alternative readings of Wesley. But this strength has its correlated dangers: Historical appeal can turn into hagiography, and present ideologies and concerns can obscure relevant evidence that challenges one's reading—and proposed appropriation—of the past. Liability to such dangers is also evident in twentieth-century analyses of Wesley and the poor.

For example, the desire to emphasize Wesley's concern for and ministry among the poor has tempted some authors toward hagiographical exaggeration, in part by taking Wesley's own rhetorical exaggerations at face value. Such interpretations do not do justice to the socioeconomic complexity of either eighteenth-century Britain or early British Methodism. There is a tendency to paint a picture that places the large masses of Britain in abject poverty, abandoned and ignored by their government, the church, and the upper class until noble Wesley comes along. Wesley is then portrayed as spending his ministry almost entirely among the poor, voluntarily embracing poverty himself to stand in their midst. Early Methodism, resulting from this focus of his ministry, is assumed to be comprised primarily of manual laborers and the destitute. Then the drama ends on a tragic note as the second generation is presented as being ushered *en masse* (by their parsimonious Methodist lifestyle) into the ranks of the respectable middle class, at which point they summarily abandon their ministry to and with the poor.

This version of the Wesley story must be judged as a caricature and my summary perhaps as a caricature of a caricature—it emphasizes existing characteristics by overdrawing them and flattening out their contextual background.[3] While caricature is a legitimate and often highly appropriate form, it tends to provoke responses that are

2. See especially *Sanctification and Liberation*, ed. Theodore Runyon (Nashville: Abingdon Press, 1981); *La Tradición Protestante en la Teología Latinoamericana*, ed. José Duque (San Jose, Costa Rica: DEI, 1983); *Faith Born in the Struggle for Life*, ed. Dow Kirkpatrick (Grand Rapids, Mich.: Wm. B. Eerdmans Publishing Company, 1988); Theodore W. Jennings, Jr., *Good News to the Poor: John Wesley's Evangelical Economics* (Nashville: Abingdon Press, 1990); and *The Portion of the Poor*, ed. M. Douglas Meeks (Nashville: Kingswood Books, 1994).

3. A good moderate example to consult in testing my summary would be Oscar Sherwin, *John Wesley: Friend of the People* (New York: Twayne Publishers, 1961).

little more than inverse caricatures.[4] What is needed, instead, is to balance the aspects highlighted in the caricature by fleshing out the less dramatic characteristics of the subject and filling in the contrasting backdrop. In the case of Wesley and the poor, this means seeking greater historical clarity about the contributing causes, self-understanding, and numbers of the poor in eighteenth-century Britain; the types of government and ecclesiastical efforts already being made to address the situation of the poor; and the actual socioeconomic constitution of Methodist societies. The fruit of such work (which is underway) is a growing agreement about what was truly characteristic, and possibly unique, about Wesley's ministry to and with the poor.[5] We will examine some of these agreed-upon characteristics later in this essay.

The passionate nature of twentieth-century considerations of Wesley and the poor has also produced a number of directly contrasting readings, which sometimes appear to lose touch with their historical base in the argument. There is no better example of this than the range of evaluations of Wesley's economic ethic—an ethic that Wesley once paraphrased (in specific relation to money) in three rules: Gain all you can, save all you can, and give all you can.[6] Some have quoted this maxim (in either praise or condemnation) as evidence that Wesley epitomized Max Weber's "Protestant Ethic," embracing laissez-faire capitalism.[7] Others have vigorously protested this characterization[8] with a few arguing instead that Wesley was a prototype of Christian socialism.[9] The reality is that while each of

4. A relevant example would be Henry Diamond Abelove, *The Evangelist of Desire: John Wesley and the Methodists* (Stanford: Stanford University Press, 1990), which portrays Wesley's focus on and success among the poor in neo-Freudian categories as his "seduction" of the poor. Cf. the incisive critique by Richard Heitzenrater in *Methodist History* 30 (1992): 118-20.

5. Many historians of early Methodism are working on aspects of this larger task. For an overview of the findings, see chapter one of this book, "The Poor and the People Called Methodists," by Richard P. Heitzenrater.

6. Sermon 50, "The Use of Money," *Works*, 2:266-80.

7. See Ernst Cahn, "John Wesley als Vorkämpfer einer christlichen Sozialethik," *Die Christliche Welt* 46 (1932): 208-12; Robert Kingdon, "Laissez-Faire or Government Control: A Problem for John Wesley," *Church History* 26 (1957): 342-54; Bernard Semmel, *The Methodist Revolution* (New York: Basic Books, 1972), 75ff; and Roy Sturm, *Sociological Reflections on John Wesley and Methodism* (Indianapolis: Central Publishing, 1982), 137.

8. For specific critique of the Weber comparison see Charles Elliott, "The Ideology of Economic Growth: A Case Study," in *Land, Labour and Population in the Industrial Revolution*, eds. E. L. Jones & G. E. Mingay (New York: Barnes & Noble, 1967), 75-99; Yuki Kishida, "John Wesley's Ethics and Max Weber," *Wesleyan Quarterly Review* 4 (1967): 43-58; Manfred Marquardt, *John Wesley's Social Ethics: Praxis and Principles* (Nashville: Abingdon Press, 1992), 41-42; and Thomas Madron, "John Wesley on Economics," in Runyon, *Sanctification and Liberation*, 102-15 (p. 109).

9. See W. H. Meredith, "John Wesley, Christian Socialist," Methodist Review 83 (1901): 426-39; Kathleen Walker MacArthur, *The Economic Ethics of John Wesley* (New York: Abingdon-

these later models find points of similarity in Wesley, none capture his overall position.

Wesley's actual economic ethic can be summarized in four points: (1) ultimately everything belongs to God; (2) resources are placed in our care to use as God sees fit; (3) God desires that we use these resources to meet our necessities (i.e., providing shelter and food for ourselves and dependents), and then to help others in need; thus, (4) spending resources on luxuries for ourselves while others remain in need is robbing God![10] On the one hand, we sense that Wesley did assume the (socialist) ideal of community of goods as he saw it described in Acts, but he supported only voluntary means for effecting this ideal, not sociopolitical coercion.[11] On the other hand, his encouragement of his Methodists to earn and save money is suggestive of—but hardly an endorsement of—laissez-faire capitalism. In the sermon where Wesley introduced this threefold rule, his discussion of the first rule (earn) focused on enjoining social responsibility in the manner in which one acquires property, capital, or the means of production. Concerning the second rule (save), he placed primary emphasis on self-denial in the use of one's resources, not wasting them on idle expenses or luxuries. Then, in the third rule (give), he renounced accumulation of anything above what meets one's basic needs, directing it instead to meet the needs of one's neighbors.[12]

In other words, while Adam Smith held that surplus accumulation was the foundation of economic well-being, Wesley viewed it (at least in the present situation of being surrounded by those whose basic needs are not yet met) as mortal sin! However, he found it hard to convince his people of this. They were prone to retain any hard-won surplus for themselves. Wesley considered this more than a minor deviation. Through the final decade of his ministry, he issued a series of warnings that the increasing tendency of Methodists

---

Cokesbury Press, 1936); and Robert Hughes, "Wesleyan Roots of Christian Socialism," *The Ecumenist* 13 (1975): 49-53.

10. This stance is first articulated in Sermon 28, "Sermon on the Mount, VIII," §§11, 25-26, *Works*, 1:618-19, 628-29. A good overview is Gary Ball-Kilbourne, "The Christian as Steward in John Wesley's Theological Ethics," *Quarterly Review* 4.1 (1984): 43-54. See also Clarence Haywood's helpful comparison of Wesley to the traditional Aquinian ethic of a just price in "Was John Wesley a Political Economist?" *Church History* 33 (1964): 314-21.

11. See the study by John Walsh, "John Wesley and The Community of Goods," in *Protestant Evangelicalism*, ed. Keith Robbins (Oxford: Blackwell Publishers, 1990), 25-50.

12. This distillation of "The Use of Money" is taken from Albert Outler, "How to Run a Conservative Revolution . . . ," in *Albert Outler the Preacher*, ed. Bob Parrott (Anderson, Ind.: Bristol House, 1995), 411.

to retain wealth instead of sharing it with those in need correlated directly with a decline in their spiritual growth and in the progress of the revival.[13]

This suggested correlation between engagement with the poor and spiritual growth sets the background for noting one other impact of their partisan contexts on twentieth-century studies of Wesley and the poor. Most of the studies appropriate, in varying degrees, the tendency to cast concern for personal spirituality in antithetical relationships to concern for social ministry and activism.[14] This tendency was becoming prominent in North American Protestantism by the turn of the century. At its most extreme this appropriation could lead Wesley's heirs to misapprehend and disavow his precedent in defense of either a "pure" spirituality or a "social" Christianity. Thus we find the ground-breaking Black Liberation theologian and African Methodist Episcopal elder James Cone initially dismissing Wesley's relevance on the assumption that his concern for "the warm heart and all that stuff" necessarily distracted Wesley from attention to social, political, and economic needs.[15] The appropriation shines through more discretely in studies where discovery of Wesley's concern for the poor has served to rehabilitate the author's interest in a founder whose broadly touted emphasis on religious experience and disciplined spiritual life had not been attractive, in part because of caricatured presentations of the latter emphasis.[16] In its most subtle expression the appropriation has become an interpretive filter that translates potentially contrasting aspects of Wesley into supporting evidence for one-sided emphases on social concern or spiritual formation. A particularly relevant example of this is how arguments in Methodist circles for embracing both the Social Gospel and Liberation Theology have often appealed, for warrant, to Wesley's claim that there

---

13. See Sermon 87 (1781), "The Danger of Riches," *Works*, 3:228-46; Sermon 61 (1783), "The Mystery of Iniquity," §34, *Works*, 2:468; Sermon 68 (1784), "The Wisdom of God's Counsels," §§16–18, *Works*, 2:560-63; "Thoughts upon Methodism" (1788), *Works*, 9:527-30; Sermon 108 (1788), "On Riches," *Works*, 3:519-28; Sermon 122 (1789), "Causes of the Inefficacy of Christianity," §§9, 17–18, *Works*, 4:91, 95-96; Sermon 125 (1789), "On a Single Eye," *Works*, 4:120-30; Sermon 126 (1790), "On Worldly Folly," *Works*, 4:132-38; and Sermon 131 (1790), "The Danger of Increasing Riches," *Works*, 4:178–86. Cf. the discussion in Jennings, *Good News to the Poor*, 118ff.

14. For more on this, see Jean Miller Schmidt, *Souls or the Social Order: The Two-Party System in American Protestantism* (Brooklyn, N.Y.: Carlson Publishing, 1991); and David Moberg, *The Great Reversal: Evangelicalism versus Social Concern* (Philadelphia: J. B. Lippincott, 1970).

15. James Cone, *Black Theology of Liberation* (Philadelphia: J. B. Lippincott, 1970), 72.

16. Note the disarming admission of this in Jennings, *Good News to the Poor*, 9-11.

is "no holiness but social holiness."[17] One could hardly guess from these appeals that the primary stress of Wesley's original claim was on the vital contribution of "society" with other Christians to our pursuit of holiness of heart and life.[18]

Wesley assumed that consistent and faithful social action must be grounded in such communal spiritual formation. The tendency to counterpoise concern for spiritual formation against concern for social service and activism, which his twentieth-century heirs appropriated from their culture, has inclined them to overlook this connection. Thus recent works calling for a recovery of Wesley's ministry to and with the poor devote little attention to the spiritual formation that Wesley believed empowers and inclines one to be involved in this ministry. The authors appear to assume that it is sufficient simply to make clear the "duty" of such involvement.[19] Meanwhile books calling for a recovery of Wesley's spirituality devote little attention to the formative role he assigned to works of mercy. These authors appear to view such works mainly as ways in which we express our spirituality not ways in which we develop it.[20] My goal in this essay is to clarify the more integral connection that Wesley was convinced existed between one's sanctification (as the recovery of holiness of heart and life) and one's involvement with the poor.

The Consistency of the Connection

When one surveys Wesley's writings with this specific issue in mind, it is striking how consistently he connected engagement in ministry to and with the poor, often under the heading of "works of

---

17. See, for example, the programmatic article by Herbert Welch, "The Church and Social Service," *Methodist Review* 90 (1908): 707-15 (quotes Wesley on p. 710); Mortimer Arias, "Distortions in the Transmission of the Original Legacy of Wesley," in *Faith Born in the Struggle for Life*, 229-43 (p. 230); and Aldo Etchegoyen, "Theology of Sin and Structures of Oppression," in ibid., 156-66 (p. 164).

18. The two relevant passages are: *Hymns and Sacred Poems* (1739), preface, §§4–5, *Works* (Jackson), 14:321; and Sermon 24, "Sermon on the Mount, IV," I.1, *Works*, 1:533-34. In the latter passage Wesley explains: "I mean not only that [holiness] cannot subsist so well, but that it cannot subsist at all without society, without living and conversing with [others]."

19. Note how little discussion there is of any positive contribution of spiritual disciplines in either Marquardt's *John Wesley's Social Ethics* or Jennings's *Good News to the Poor*. Cf. the critique of one-sided emphasis on "duty" in Richard P. Heitzenrater, "The *Imitatio Christi* and the Great Commandment: Virtue and Obligation in Wesley's Ministry with the Poor," in *The Portion of the Poor*, ed. M. Douglas Meeks (Nashville: Kingswood Books, 1995), 49-63.

20. See, for example, Steve Harper, *Devotional Life in the Wesleyan Tradition* (Nashville: Upper Room Books, 1983), 64; and Gregory S. Clapper, *As if the Heart Mattered* (Nashville: Upper Room Books, 1997), 95.

mercy," to the existence or retention of the sanctified life. The connection is evident already in *The Character of a Methodist* (1742), which Wesley considered his first tract on the subject of Christian perfection. There he offers the following emphases as most characteristic of his movement:

4. By *salvation* [the Methodist] means holiness of heart and life. . . . We do not place the whole of religion (as too many do, God knoweth) either in doing no harm, or in doing good, or in using the ordinances of God. . . .

5. "What then is the mark?" . . . a Methodist is one who has "the love of God shed abroad in his heart by the Holy Ghost given unto him"; one who "loves the Lord his God with all his heart, and with all his soul, and with all his mind, and with all his strength". . . .

9. And while he thus always exercises his love to God . . . this commandment is written in his heart, that "he who loveth God, loves his brother also." . . .

13. . . . His obedience is in proportion to his love, the source from whence it flows. And therefore, loving God with all his heart, he serves him with all his strength. . . .

16. Lastly, as he has time, he "does good unto all men"—unto neighbours, and strangers, friends, and enemies. And that in every possible kind; not only to their bodies, by "feeding the hungry, clothing the naked, visiting those that are sick or in prison", but much more does he labour to do good to their souls, as of the ability which God giveth.[21]

The connection recurs in the sermon "The Scripture Way of Salvation" (1765), which marks Wesley's mature integration of the twin emphases that (1) salvation is by grace, yet (2) God upholds a place for our responsive appropriation of this grace. In this sermon Wesley insists that both works of piety and works of mercy are "necessary to sanctification," being the way that God has appointed us to "wait for complete salvation."[22] And the connection remains prominent in his classic sermon "On Working Out Our Own Salvation" (1785), where the major mean that Wesley recommends for working out full salvation is faithful engagement in both works of piety and works of mercy.[23]

The integral connection for Wesley between sanctification and concern for the poor is even more evident when one considers the

---

21. *Works*, 9:35-41.
22. See Sermon 43, "The Scripture Way of Salvation," III.5–10, *Works*, 2:164-66.
23. See Sermon 85, "On Working Out Our Own Salvation," II.4, *Works*, 3:205-6.

structures he created for his movement. These would include the various structures he created specifically to offer help to the poor: clinics, boarding schools, loan programs, and the like.[24] But even more relevant to our topic is the "select society," a substructure that he created specifically for those in the Methodist movement who had claimed the experience of entire sanctification—to help them *press after perfection.*" Wesley decided that not many rules were needed for folk in select societies since "the best rule of all [was] in their hearts." Therefore he stipulated only three matters: that they maintain confidence about their discussions, submit to their minister as spiritual director, and bring all the money they could spare once a week "toward a common stock."[25]

The third stipulation is striking as the only programmatic suggestion specific to these Methodist subgroups, and it is important to see that it was not tangential nor only a passing fancy for Wesley. It reflected one of the most consistent assumptions he held throughout his life about the nature and evidence of a community of fully sanctified believers. This assumption was grounded in his characteristically Anglican commitment to the pristine nature of the New Testament church and his specific definition of that church by the Pentecostal passages in Acts. Wesley came early to understand these passages to be affirming that the community present at the first Christian Pentecost was so open and responsive to the Spirit that they were *unanimously* and *immediately* transformed into *full* holiness of heart and life and that a primary expression of this transformation was the members' love for one another, which constrained them to hold all things in common.[26] In good Anglican fashion he lamented the way that the later Christian church had fallen from this pristine model, and he longed for his Methodist movement to become the pioneering community that led to the church's recovery.[27]

---

24. The best survey of these is in Marquardt, *John Wesley's Social Ethics.*

25. See Minutes, 28 June 1744, Q. 5, *Minutes* (Mason), 1:23; and *A Plain Account of the People Called Methodists,* VIII.2–3, *Works,* 9:269-70.

26. This romantic view of "Pentecostal communalism" and its assumed precedence for the current church are evident in his Letter to John Burton (10 October 1735), *Works,* 25:441. Likewise, his famous 1744 sermonic indictment of contemporary Anglicanism was framed by specific reference to the model of the Pentecost church; cf. Sermon 4, "Scriptural Christianity," I.10, *Works,* 1:165.

27. Wesley's (weakening) hope in this regard is most evident in late sermons such as Sermon 61, "The Mystery of Iniquity," *Works,* 2:452-70 (note the appeal to Pentecost in §8); Sermon 63, "The General Spread of the Gospel," *Works,* 2:485-99 (note hope for a New Pentecost evidenced by sharing all things in common in §20); and "Thoughts upon a Late Phenomenon," *Works,* 9:534-37.

But Wesley also wanted to keep participation in the Methodist movement open to all who sensed a spiritual need. He did so by not requiring assurance of saving faith for initial membership, let alone a claim of entire sanctification. This put the select societies in the default role of mentors, modeling the sanctified life for the larger movement. For Wesley this modeling necessarily included a voluntary sharing of one's resources with the poor in order to return to the biblical ideal of holding all things in common. The programmatic guideline of contributing toward a common stock was his prod toward this goal, issued as the spiritual director of the movement. His profound disappointment over how few (even in the select societies) actually embraced the voluntary program becomes increasingly apparent.[28]

The Rationale for the Connection

Once it is recognized that Wesley so consistently connected affirmation of the sanctified life with encouragement to engage in works of mercy, the obvious issue becomes the nature of this connection. What rationale does he offer for why these two go together?

We have already seen one way that Wesley could answer this question, namely, that the connection reflects faithfulness to the model of the early church. But this simply pushes the question back a level: Why did the early church connect these two together? Wesley's likely response would be that they were simply seeking to "imitate Christ." As he put it in one sermon, all those who claim to be Christ's disciples will (or should) embrace lives of self-denial, because self-denial for the sake of the other was a defining characteristic of Christ's life.[29] By probing this response we can discern the foundational level of Wesley's rationale for connecting the reality of sanctification in our lives to our active ministry to and with the poor.

One way to probe this response is to ask why Christ himself was so concerned with works of mercy or ministering to the physical needs of people. While some might wonder whether the question is sacrilegious, it has been debated often in the history of the church. This debate was set up by a tendency that made its way into the tradition

---

28. See in particular Sermon 68, "The Wisdom of God's Counsels," *Works*, 2:552-66 (appeal to Pentecost in §7).
29. Note the prominence of this theme at the beginning of Sermon 48, "Self-denial," *Works*, 2:238-50.

to understand "salvation" primarily, if not entirely, in terms of the spiritual dimension of life. On such terms, Jesus' mission was to offer people the chance for their souls to attain eternal life, and it becomes puzzling what ministry to their physical or temporal needs would contribute to this goal. One common answer to this puzzle was to assume that Jesus engaged in works of mercy for strictly instrumental reasons, that is, he ministered to people's bodies only because this helped him gain the access needed to offer real "saving" ministry to their souls.

The integral connection that Wesley makes between works of mercy and the sanctified life reflects his deep disagreement with any such merely instrumental valuation of the works of mercy and with the spiritualized view of salvation that underlies it. When viewed both in his specific context and against the broader Christian tradition, Wesley's concern to retain (or recover) the holistic understanding of salvation in scripture is unmistakable. This concern is evident in the way he weaves together the juridical emphasis of salvation as forgiveness (justification) with the therapeutic emphasis of salvation as healing the various faculties or dimensions of the human soul (sanctification). It shines through in his insistence that God is the physician of not only the soul but also the physical body, demonstrating that God longs to aid us, as well, in recovering and maintaining physical well-being in this life. And it is particularly striking in his growing retrieval of the biblical theme that ultimate salvation includes the whole creation, not just humanity.[30]

When salvation is understood in such holistic terms, Christ's ministry to the temporal and physical needs of people is not viewed as merely instrumental to offering them salvation; it is an integral part of his saving work. Likewise, Wesley considered providing such things as subsidized boarding schools for children of the poor, free health clinics, and a carefully collected set of inexpensive medical remedies (his *Primitive Physick*) to be an integral part of the salvific mission of Methodism. That is why the select societies, which were committed to promoting the "full salvation" of their members, were specifically instructed to focus attention on addressing the needs of those who lacked basic temporal well-being.

Because he understood salvation in truly holistic terms, Wesley was quick to insist that it was both unfaithful and unloving to minis-

---

30. For more details on these points, see Randy L. Maddox, *Responsible Grace: John Wesley's Practical Theology* (Nashville: Kingswood Books, 1994), 141-47, 252-53.

ter only to people's physical needs, neglecting to convey to them God's offer of gracious transformation of the spiritual dimensions of their lives as well. Indeed, if (in theory) we had to choose between these two, Wesley would prioritize the need to address their spiritual healing because of its eternal dimensions.[31] But in practice Wesley resisted acquiescing to such a forced priority, and he specifically rejected valuing works of mercy in mere instrumental connection to evangelization. Throughout his ministry he admonished his people that they should not limit their works of mercy to only those who respond (or are likely to do so), but rather they should offer this ministry as Christ did—to all who are in need and simply because of their need.[32]

Wesley did not overlook the possible positive evangelistic impact resulting from Christian engagement in such open-ended works of mercy. But the specific potential effect that he highlighted was not the enticement of uncommitted people to embrace the Christian faith by addressing their physical needs. Rather, he hoped to overcome the widespread crisis of credibility of Christian witness through the increased number of Christians who would model authentic loving care for others. Wesley considered the failure of most Christians to imitate Christ-like sharing with those in need to be the grand stumbling block that prevented other groups from taking Christian evangelistic efforts seriously. He could even suggest ironically that the so-called Christian British were the ones standing in need of conversion into "honest heathens" like the native Americans, whom he praised for more typically sharing with those in need than hoarding their resources.[33]

In all of this we see that one central aspect of Wesley's rationale for connecting the reality of sanctification in our lives to our active ministry to and with the poor was his conviction of the holistic nature of salvation as modeled by Christ. Another aspect of this underlying principle emerges when we probe specifically into why he believed that Christians (particularly those seeking or claiming "full salvation")

---

31. Recall the language in *Character of a Methodist*, §16, that love moves Methodists to minister "not only to [other people's] bodies . . . but much more . . . to do good to their souls" (*Works*, 9:41). See also Sermon 98, "On Visiting the Sick," I.5 and II.4, *Works*, 3:389, 391. For emphasis on this priority see Kenneth Collins, "The Soteriological Orientation of John Wesley's Ministry to the Poor," *Asbury Theological Journal* 50 (1995): 75-92.

32. On this point see Sermon 98, "On Visiting the Sick," I.1, *Works*, 3:387; and Sermon 24, "Sermon on the Mount, IV," III.7, *Works*, 1:546.

33. Cf. *Journal* (8 February 1753), *Works*, 20:445; Sermon 28, "Sermon on the Mount, VIII," §9, *Works*, 1:617; and Sermon 63, "The General Spread of the Gospel," §21, *Works*, 2:495.

will—or *should*—imitate Christ's model. (I have italicized the alternative helping verbs to reflect polar directions in the classic Christian debate over the relation of "good works" to Christian status and character.) At one end of the spectrum in this debate are those who view (or are accused of viewing) good works as duties that we must fulfill to qualify for Christian status or to maintain pure Christian character. At the other end of the spectrum are those who decry such apparent "works-righteousness" and argue that good works are simply the *expression* of the faith or holy dispositions that are graciously infused in Christians by the Spirit at their conversion. For this group, good works are impossible prior to attaining Christian status and character but become natural (at the most extreme, inevitable) after regeneration.

When Wesley's comments connecting works of mercy with the sanctified life are read in light of this debate it is striking how he strives to weave together these supposed polar emphases, reflecting his conviction of God's responsible grace.[34] For example, the rhetoric of some of his exhortations to engage in works of mercy casts them as duties that serve as the crucial test for determining our holy standing and, hence, our eternal salvation.[35] He can even encourage their practice by promising supplementary heavenly reward.[36] If such language is isolated, Wesley appears in danger of straying into works-righteousness, where works of mercy earn one's sanctification. But when confronted with such accusations, Wesley insists that our works of mercy are always dependent on God's gracious transforming work in our lives.[37]

Coming at this integration from the other direction, we noted that, in *The Principles of a Methodist*, Wesley described the charitable work of Methodists as flowing from the love of God and neighbor in their heart (§13). This language could suggest that works of mercy should be expected only after one attains holiness of heart, as a natural expression of this holiness. Such suggestion comes through even stronger in places where ministry to the poor is highlighted as

---

34. For how central this "orienting concern" is to all of Wesley's theology see Maddox, *Responsible Grace*.

35. See, in particular, Sermon 98, "On Visiting the Sick," III.2, *Works*, 3:392-93.

36. See particularly *Journal* (15 January 1777), *Works*, 23:40; and his comment on Matthew 26:11 (The poor you have always with you) in the *Explanatory Notes on the New Testament*: "Such is the wise and gracious Providence of God, that we may have always opportunities of relieving their Wants, and so laying up for ourselves treasures in heaven."

37. See particularly Sermon 99, "The Reward of Righteousness," *Works*, 3:400-414 (pp. 403-5).

the decisive evidence that God has poured the sanctifying Spirit into one's heart. Consider a hymn from *A Collection of Hymns* (1780), that Wesley wove from two separate hymns in Charles Wesley's *Scripture Hymns* (1762):

1. Jesus, the gift divine I know,
   The gift divine I ask of thee;
That living water now bestow,
   Thy Spirit and thyself on me.
Thou, Lord, of life the fountain art:
Now let me find thee in my heart!

2. Thee let me drink, and thirst no more
   For drops of finite happiness;
Spring up, O well, in heavenly power,
   In streams of pure, perennial peace,
In peace, that none can take away,
In joy, which shall forever stay.

3. Father, on me the grace bestow,
   Unblameable before thy sight,
Whence all the streams of mercy flow;
   Mercy, thy own supreme delight,
To me, for Jesu's sake impart,
And plant thy nature in my heart.

4. Thy mind throughout my life be shown,
   While listening to the wretch's cry
The widow's and the orphan's groan,
   On mercy's wings I swiftly fly
The poor and helpless to relieve,
My life, my all for them to give.

5. Thus may I show thy Spirit within,
   Which purges me from every stain;
Unspotted from the world and sin
   My faith's integrity maintain,
The truth of my religion prove
By perfect purity and love.[38]

In isolation, such texts value acts of relief for the poor and help-less primarily as manifestations of the sanctifying work that God has already completed in our lives. But Wesley balances affirmation that

---

38. *A Collection of Hymns*, no. 354, *Works*, 7:521-22.

works of mercy flow from the love of God and neighbor existing in our hearts with reminders that this responsive expression of love is not inevitable. While God's gracious, sanctifying work enables us to love God and others, it does not coerce this response. As Wesley saw clearly among his Methodist people, humans can resist even the strongest loving inclination to reach out to the poor and helpless. His rhetorical appeals to the "duty" of works of mercy were actually aimed at breaking through such resistance to God's gracious leading.

In short, the second central aspect of Wesley's rationale for connecting the reality of sanctification in our lives to our active ministry to and with the poor was his rejection of the false dichotomy of (1) works of mercy, or any other "good works," as mere human efforts to earn holiness, and (2) works of mercy as epiphenomena of unilaterally infused holiness. But how do we move beyond this dichotomous understanding in a way that preserves both the reality of God's gracious prevenience to all human response and the integrity of that response? The most distinctive avenue that Wesley chose centralized a dimension of the connection between sanctification and works of mercy that he believed was often overlooked.

The Empowering/Formative Dimension of the Connection

This distinctive way of transcending dichotomous understandings of the works of mercy was to defend their role as "means of grace." Wesley recognized that many Christians equate the means of grace solely with activities such as Bible study, prayer, and worship, practices that he grouped together as "works of piety." As such, in discussions of the works of mercy he frequently emphasized that these, too, can be means of grace.[39] One of his most enlightening comments comes in a proposed sketch of the relative comparative value of the different aspects of the Christian religion:

In a Christian believer *love* sits upon the throne, . . . namely, love of God and man. . . . In a circle near the throne are all *holy tempers*: long-suffering, gentleness, meekness. . . . In an exterior circle are all the *works of mercy*, whether to the souls or bodies of men. By these we exercise all holy tempers; by these we continually improve them, so that all these are real *means of grace*, although this is not commonly adverted to. Next

---

39. See esp. Sermon 98, "On Visiting the Sick," §1, *Works*, 3:385.

to these are those that are usually termed *works of piety*: reading and hearing the Word; public, family, private prayer, receiving the Lord's Supper; fasting or abstinence. Lastly, that his followers may the more effectually provoke one another to love, holy tempers, and good works, our blessed Lord has united them together in one—*the church*.[40]

Embedded in this quote are the assumptions that undergirded Wesley's conviction that engaging in works of mercy has an empowering and formative impact on those *offering* help, beyond whatever positive impact there is upon the recipients of the works.

The foundational level of these assumptions is reflected in the immediate connection that Wesley makes between our love for God and others and having specific holy tempers. Many people find this connection puzzling because "temper" is usually associated with connotations that have little to do with either love or holiness. Wesley's use of the term reflects both a meaning that was more typical in the eighteenth century and his distinctive convictions about the dynamics that account for human moral choice and action, that is, his moral psychology.

Moral psychology deals with the range of possible responses to such questions as: Are our options truly open in any sense at the juncture of a moral choice or act? If so, what hinders us from choosing as we should? And, what would most effectively free us to choose differently? Christian debates over these issues have often divided into two groups: those who insist that humans are graciously created with a resident ability to initiate moral choice and those who deny all human initiative in truly moral actions, at times reducing these to passive experiences of God-choosing-through-us. There has also been great divergence over the specific contribution of reason to enabling authentic human moral choice.[41]

Wesley struggled within the various reigning stances of these issues to articulate his fundamental conviction that all human choice and action is rooted in God's redemptive (not just creational) initiative but that God exerts this initiative in a way that honors the integrity of our human response. He progressed by transferring his empiricist commitments in epistemology to the arena of moral psychology. Central to empiricist philosophy is the rejection of any innate ideas or

40. Sermon 92, "On Zeal," II.5, *Works*, 3:313.
41. For more reflection on alternative moral psychologies and details of Wesley's stance, see Randy L. Maddox, "Reconnecting the Means to the End: A Wesleyan Prescription for the Holiness Movement," *Wesleyan Theological Journal* 33.2 (1998): 29-66.

truths in the human mind. This philosophy emphasized that people only begin to form ideas after they have been exposed to sufficient experiences. Analogously, Wesley argued that there is no innate reservoir of love (or any other power from which moral acts might flow) in the human soul. We are only enabled to act in response to experiencing the actions of others. In what Wesley held as the crucial instance, our love for God and others can awaken and grow only in response to experiencing God's gracious love for us, shed abroad in our hearts by the Holy Spirit.[42]

The technical way that Wesley expressed this general conviction was by equating the human faculty of the "will" with our "affections." Since the will is usually understood to be the springboard of human acts, Wesley's equation allowed him to stress that we must be affected before we can act; in other words, the will is more like a mirror than a pre-charged battery. He also valued the connotations of desire in "affections," which allowed him to stress that reason alone is never a sufficient motivation for action—intellectual conviction without desire remained merely theoretical. Ultimately, we are able to act only when there is a holistic inclination, which was initially awakened responsively.

While the affections are responsive, they are not simply transitory, but rather, through engagement, they are progressively strengthened and shaped into enduring dispositions. Wesley's term for such dispositions was "tempers." Enduring sinful dispositions are "unholy tempers," while "holy tempers" encompass the range of virtues that are awakened by our experience of love and dispose us to responsive acts of love to God and others. On these terms, the essential goal of all true religion becomes the recovery of holy tempers.[43]

But how does this recovery take place? How did Wesley assume that our sin-debilitated affections are re-empowered and the distortions of their patterning influence reshaped? He was quite clear that we cannot accomplish this through our human efforts alone. The possibility of change lies instead in God's gracious regenerating work in the lives of believers. But God does not infuse holy tempers instantaneously complete. Rather, God awakens in believers the seed of every

---

42. This point permeates Wesley's works. For a few examples see *The Character of a Methodist*, §13, *Works*, 9:39; *An Earnest Appeal to Men of Reason and Religion*, §61, *Works*, 11:70; *A Farther Appeal to Men of Reason and Religion, Part 1*, I.3, *Works*, 11:106; Sermon 10, "The Witness of the Spirit I," I.8, *Works*, 1:274; and Sermon 120, "The Unity of the Divine Being," §17, *Works*, 4:67.

43. Sermon 91, "On Charity," III.12, *Works*, 3:306.

virtue. These seeds then strengthen and take shape as we responsively "grow in grace."[44]

The specific context that God has graciously provided for such growth, Wesley insisted, was the means of grace. This insistence reflects his hard-won conviction, against various other one-sided perspectives in the Christian tradition, that the means of grace serve as both avenues by which God conveys empowering gracious encounter and formative disciplines by which we strengthen and shape our character into Christ-likeness.[45] He charged those desiring holiness of heart and life to seek it in the means of grace because within these various means they will be opened to the ever deeper empowering affect of God's presence thus motivating them to exercise their affections, shaping them into holy tempers.

The importance of the works of mercy for those pursuing full salvation takes on an added dimension when they are considered as means of grace in Wesley's sense. We do not engage in works of mercy just because we "feel like it" or only when we feel like it, nor do we engage in them only because it is what God commands or because it helps others. We are encouraged to engage in works of mercy because God has graciously designed this engagement to have an empowering and formative impact on us.[46] To pursue the sanctified life while leaving out this or any other means of grace would be foolhardy. It would be falling into the mistake of the "enthusiasts," who fail to reach their desired end because they ignore the graciously provided means.[47]

When one looks at Wesley's specific instructions for promoting works of mercy it becomes clear that he was also sensitive—arguably to a unique degree for his time—to the potential empowering (or disempowering) and formative (or deformative) impact of works of mercy upon those receiving help. One way this comes through is his repeated critique of stereotypes of the poor as "lazy," testifying to the legitimacy of their need and the integrity of their efforts to help themselves.[48] This critique served not only to counteract a rationalization

---

44. See Minutes, 2 August 1745, Q. 1, *Minutes* (Mason), 1:10. See Maddox, *Responsible Grace*, 178-79, for discussion of two passages where Wesley argues that holy tempers can be implanted in a fully mature state.

45. Cf. Maddox, *Responsible Grace*, 192-201.

46. See in this regard Joerg Rieger, "The Means of Grace, John Wesley, and the Theological Dilemma of the Church Today," *Quarterly Review* 17 (1997): 377-93. While our foci are different, there is significant overlap between Rieger's major point and my own—we both insist that the works of mercy convey transforming encounter with and knowledge of God.

47. See Sermon 16, "The Means of Grace," I, *Works*, 1:378-80.

48. Cf. *Journal* (9-10 February 1753), *Works*, 20:445.

of withholding aid by the well-to-do but also to help the needy resist the subtle pressures to think of themselves as distinguished by their poverty or as a disadvantaged class. Taking it a step further, Wesley rejected static classifications into the "rich" and the "needy." He relativized poverty by suggesting that those who barely have their necessities met should still ask whether there was someone in more dire need with whom they might share. And he gave specific instructions that poor Methodists should be allowed, and expected, to contribute to the aid of the poor as they were able.[49] Behind these instructions is his concern that poor Methodists should experience themselves not only as *recipients* of grace but also as *responsible participants* in sharing that grace. Given his conviction of the empowering and formative impact of such balanced experience, he could not withhold it from the poor.

The Indispensable Contribution of Works of Mercy

In the quotation that began the previous section of this paper, one final assumption of Wesley stands out. Not only does he insist that works of mercy belong among the means of grace along with works of piety, but also he seems to place works of mercy in more immediate relation to forming holy tempers than he does works of piety. Once again, any relative comparison here does not mean that Wesley would easily acquiesce to forced choices between engaging in works of mercy or works of piety. He considered the empowering and formative impact of both to be essential to nurturing holiness of heart and life. However, it appears that he believed works of mercy made a unique contribution among the other means of grace to well-rounded Christian formation and worried that his followers were neglecting its benefit. What might this contribution be?

One way to understand this uniqueness is to suggest that certain virtues constitutive of the holy life are best awakened and strengthened into enduring patterns by the works of mercy. As Theodore W. Jennings shows, Wesley repeatedly warned that hoarding one's resources in the face of the needy others directly endangers such virtues as humility and patience while fostering such vices as resentment and contempt.[50] These warnings echo the insights emerging from

---

49. See particularly Sermon 98, "On Visiting the Sick," III.4, *Works*, 3:393-94.
50. Jennings, *Good News to the Poor*, 33-38.

recently renewed interest in the moral psychology of the virtues that neither development of virtues nor counteraction of vices is a generic process.[51]

A particularly relevant example is compassion. The fact that we argue over whether compassion is more an emotion (something we suffer) or more a disposition (something over which we have control) reflects an awareness that one is not likely to develop compassion without undergoing specific experiences. We must usually experience some type of hardship ourselves to be able to identify with the hardships of others. But we must also experience true suffering or neediness on the part of another.[52] This means that it is not enough to "send in our money" dutifully in response to reports of need. Authentic compassion can only take form through sincere encounters with those in need. This is why Wesley emphasized the need to *visit* the poor and sick even more than he did the need to offer them aid. He recognized that failure to visit was the major contributing cause of the lack of compassion that lay behind withholding aid.[53]

Wesley's extended correspondence with Miss J. C. March is revealing on this point. Miss March was a woman of wealth and education who became active in the Methodist revival around 1760. Wesley's initial correspondence with her reflects that she was very serious about pursuing full salvation and his worry that she was setting the goal for this experience too high.[54] His respect for the seriousness of her commitment remains clear throughout their correspondence, but his concern shifted. Miss March eventually admitted that she struggled with the fact that affiliating with the Methodists put her in connection with so many who were of "lower character" or unrefined. Wesley gently reminded her that she was no longer just a gentlewoman, but now had a "higher character" as one whose life was a temple of the Holy Spirit.[55] He returned to this point a year later and advised her that the best way to "improve her life and use her health" was to visit the poor:

51. See in particular, Robert Kruschwitz and Robert Roberts, *The Virtues: Contemporary Essays on Moral Character* (Belmont, Calif.: Wadsworth Publishing, 1987); and G. Simon Harak, *Virtuous Passions: The Formation of Christian Character* (Mahwah, N.Y.: Paulist Press, 1993).

52. For a particularly insightful analysis of this dynamic (in a more specific context), see Richard B. Steele, "Unremitting Compassion: The Moral Psychology of Parenting Children with Genetic Disorders," *Theology Today* 57.2 (2000): 161-74.

53. See esp. Sermon 98, "On Visiting the Sick," I.3, *Works*, 3:387.

54. See the letters of 17 June 1761 (*Letters* [Telford], 4:157), 30 January 1762 (4:170), and 24 June 1764 (4:251).

55. Letter to Miss March (3 June 1774), *Letters* (Telford), 6:88.

> Go and see the poor and sick in their own poor little hovels. Take up your cross, woman! Remember the faith! Jesus went before you, and will go with you. Put off the gentlewoman; you bear an higher character. You are an heir of God and joint-heir with Christ! Are you not going to meet Him in the air with ten thousand of His saints? O be ready![56]

When Miss March objected that a Christian should associate with people of taste and good character, Wesley responded:

> I have found some of the uneducated poor who have exquisite taste and sentiment; and many, very many, of the rich who have scarcely any at all. But I do not speak of this: I want you to converse more, abundantly more, with the poorest of the people, who, if they have not taste, have souls, which you may forward in their way to heaven. And they have (many of them) faith and the love of God in a larger measure than any persons I know. Creep in among these in spite of dirt and an hundred disgusting circumstances, and thus put off the gentlewoman. Do not confine your conversation to genteel and elegant people. I should like this as well as you do; but I cannot discover a precedent for it in the life of our Lord or any of His Apostles.[57]

Miss March continued to protest that she could not form real friendships with the poor. With some resignation, Wesley replied:

> What I advise you to is, not to contract a friendship or even acquaintance with poor, inelegant, uneducated persons, but frequently, nay constantly, to visit the poor, the widow, the sick, the fatherless in their affliction; and this, although they should have nothing to recommend them but that they are bought with the blood of Christ. It is true this is not pleasing to flesh and blood. There are a thousand circumstances usually attending it which shock the delicacy of our nature, or rather of our education. But yet the blessing which follows this labour of love will more than balance the cross.[58]

Within a couple of months Wesley reveals his concerns about the potential (de)formative impact of this concession when he tells Miss March, "Sometimes I have been afraid lest you should sustain loss for want of some reproach or disgrace. . . . The knowledge of ourselves is true humility; and without this we cannot be freed from vanity, a desire of praise being inseparably connected with every degree of pride."[59]

---

56. Letter to Miss March (9 June 1775), *Letters* (Telford), 6:153-54.
57. Letter to Miss March (7 February 1776), *Letters* (Telford), 6:206-7.
58. Letter to Miss March (26 February 1776), *Letters* (Telford), 6:208-9.
59. Letter to Miss March (30 May 1776), *Letters* (Telford), 6:220.

Her apparent response to Wesley's renewed prodding was to protest that she needed times of seclusion for her spiritual life and could not add visiting the sick and poor to her schedule without being overly busy, such as he was. In his final extant response Wesley first insisted that, while he was indeed always active, he did not lack calmness of spirit nor times of seclusion. Then he added:

> Yet I find time to visit the sick and the poor; and I must do it, if I believe the Bible, if I believe these are the marks whereby the Shepherd of Israel will know and judge His sheep at the great day. . . .
> . . . . I am concerned for you; I am sorry you should be content with lower degrees of usefulness and holiness than you are called to.[60]

Note how his final concern is that her lack of willingness to visit the poor will leave her with "lower degrees of holiness" than God desires of her. Wesley clearly saw some virtues in the life of holiness as only available through engaging in works of mercy.

Beyond this role of helping to form certain virtues, two broader conceptions of the indispensable contribution of works of mercy among the means of grace are hinted at in Wesley's dialogue with Miss March and developed elsewhere. One of these conceptions considers the contribution of works of mercy to the formative effectiveness of the various other means. Wesley develops this conception most directly in his sermon on "Self-Denial." He argues therein that self-denial is central to the Christian life because it most directly counters the corruption of our nature by sin. Developing this point, he notes that while *neglect* of such means of grace as sermon, sacrament, and fellowship will surely weaken our growth in grace, *use* of these means might still be accompanied by hindered growth. In these cases, he suggests, the lack of self-denial is what limits the full effectiveness of the other means.[61] Since Wesley equated engaging in works of mercy with self-denial, this would tie the effectiveness of the other means of grace to some engagement in the works of mercy as well.[62]

The other way Wesley developed the interdependence of works of piety and works of mercy in the Christian life was in his insistence on the interdependence of love of God and love of neighbor. We

---

60. Letter to Miss March (10 December 1777), *Letters* (Telford), 6:292-93.
61. See Sermon 48, "Self-denial," *Works*, 2:238-50, esp. I.10 (244) and II.1 (245-46).
62. On the equation of works of mercy with self-denial, see Sermon 85, "On Working Out Our Own Salvation," II.4, *Works*, 3:205-6.

previously noted Wesley's conviction that we cannot return our love for God until we first experience God's love for us and that as we return this love our ability to experience God's love is deepened. But where do we experience God's love for us, and how do we return it? Wesley recognized that God's love is conveyed to us in a variety of mediated forms, and he gave particular prominence to corporate forms of mediation such as the class meeting and the love feast, occasions where we experience the love of God through the love others show for us.[63] Similarly, he connected our love for God integrally to our love for our neighbors, which he defined to include specifically those around us in need. This connection means that we cannot really love our neighbor without loving God.[64] But it also means that we cannot truly love God without loving our neighbor.[65] Therefore, Wesley refused to let Miss March play off times of seclusion experiencing God's presence against times of ministry to and with the poor. To limit ourselves to either of these options would drastically impair our transformative engagement with God's love.

Conclusion

While Wesley wove engagement with the poor integrally into his model of holiness of heart and life, the movements descended from his ministry have repeatedly severed this connection. The reasons behind this are complex. Among those frequently identified are the dynamics of rising class status and the cultural trend to divide the public from the private. Another significant contributing factor, however, is that Wesley's later descendants lost touch with his assumptions about the responsive and formative nature of the will. Instead, they adopted the "decisionistic" assumptions of modern culture—where humans are considered most free when we throw off external expectations and break out of past habits, liberating our innate power of choice. This switch has rendered Wesley's affectional model of sanctification puzzling and reduced his appreciation for the various

---

63. Note the hymn for the love feast, which talks about how God nourishes us with "social grace," *Collection of Hymns*, no. 507, st. 1, *Works*, 7:698.

64. See his comment on Galatians 5:14 in *Explanatory Notes on the New Testament* and his attack on Francis Hutcheson's claim that gratitude or love of God is NOT the foundation of love of our fellow creatures, in Sermon 90, "An Israelite Indeed," *Works*, 3:279.

65. See Letter to John Glass (1 November 1757), *Letters* (Telford), 3:237.

dimensions of the means of grace into an exclusive emphasis on the "duty" of observing them.[66]

Our churches have thereby largely inherited an approach to the means of grace that focuses on reminding our people, at each new point of decision, of their duty to fulfill these acts. Their natural response has been to question who has the right to impose duties upon them and why they have a duty to do something they do not "feel" like doing. In all of this, what is lost is the sense that activities like ministry to and with the poor are not simply duties, they are also gracious means that God has provided to "free" us to become progressively the kind of people that we really long to be. I suspect that ministry to and with the poor will become central to contemporary Methodist/Wesleyan practice of Christian life only as we recover this richer sense, and experience, of the means of grace.

---

66. For more on this change and its impact on both the understanding of holiness and the role of means of grace in forming holiness, see Randy L. Maddox, "Holiness of Heart and Life: Lessons from North American Methodism," *Asbury Theological Journal* 51.1 (1996): 151-72; and Maddox, "Reconnecting the Means to the End."

CHAPTER FOUR

Between God and the Poor: Rethinking the Means of Grace in the Wesleyan Tradition

Joerg Rieger

A number of years ago a study on John Wesley and the sacraments concluded that modern Methodism has "little spiritual power and very limited intercourse with God."[1] Some people would still agree. Others, however, would contend that our main problem might not be a lack of spiritual power as such but rather what use we make of it.

At first sight, these may seem to be the only two options available in this debate that reflects one of the overarching tensions in the contemporary church. On one side of the gulf are those who focus on the socioethical implications of Christian existence and emphasize orthopraxis, literally "right praxis," including a strong focus on what Christians can do for others. On the other side are those who focus on things they consider more spiritual, such as issues of Christian identity and the divine mystery. Here the emphasis is on orthodoxy, "right belief." The history of conflict between these two perspectives goes back at least as far as the nineteenth century.

My intent is to explore ways of moving beyond these two options that in many ways have steered us to a dead end. My design

An earlier version of this essay appeared in *Quarterly Review* 17 (Winter 1997–98): 377-93, under the title, "The Means of Grace, John Wesley, and the Theological Dilemma of the Church Today."

1. Ole E. Borgen, *John Wesley on the Sacraments: A Theological Study* (Nashville and New York: Abingdon Press, 1972), 281.

is to investigate new ways of connecting the spiritual and practical quests in light of alternative ways of relating to God and neighbor. At the basis of my argument is the Wesleyan understanding of the means of grace, which has often become one of the pawns in the struggle between the two dominant camps.

No doubt, each of the two camps—often classified in the terminology of the culture wars as "liberal" and "conservative"—raises important questions of the other. The conservative, or *orthodox*, camp, in keeping with some of the more trendy postmodern critics, points out the limits of the aspirations of the liberal position. Modern liberal Christianity, they argue, relies too much on its own political correctness and moral powers and, thus, takes for granted the workings of grace and the power of God. What if the current mentality of corporate America—best characterized perhaps by the slogan of the Nike Corporation: "Just do it"—were to take over the modern church, thus causing it to lose both spiritual power and intercourse with God? From the conservative perspective, the solution of the dilemma looks rather simple: Just put more emphasis on God's power and God's free gift of grace.[2]

The *orthopraxis* camp on the other hand, often labeled as liberal, is worried that such critiques might lead to the abandonment of Christian social action. They may ask, how can one make sure that faith in God really does make a difference in this world? The church must not abandon uncompromising Christian praxis, the call to make a difference in this world where people are hurting. In this view, the solution to the problem lies in a conscious effort to improve Christian praxis.[3]

However, both solutions are in danger of becoming self-referential. In liberal theology, God is at times assimilated to the benevolent activism of people, usually white and "first world," who tend to take things into their own hands and, in the process, turn the things they touch into their own image. Here, neither God nor neighbor can be seen fully for what they are. The orthodox camp, on the other hand, often forgets that even their most sincere efforts of building deeper relationships to God easily become distorted if they are not related to building deeper relationships with their neighbor.

---

2. Borgen, for example, thought this concern would bring together the "sacramentalists" and the evangelicals.

3. In the process, Wesley's own praxis often serves as a model that Christians need to imitate in the present. See, for example, Theodore W. Jennings, Jr., *Good News to the Poor: John Wesley's Evangelical Economics* (Nashville: Abingdon Press, 1990).

Ironically, both approaches end up losing their primary concern; the relation to both God and neighbor suffer. In this context, Wesley's understanding of the means of grace can provide not only a better grasp of the problem but also a first step beyond the impasse.

The Means of Grace

Generally speaking, the means of grace remind us that God and humanity must not be played off against each other. Keeping with his Anglican tradition, Wesley defines means of grace as "outward signs, words, or actions ordained of God, and appointed for this end—to be the *ordinary* channels whereby he might convey to men preventing, justifying, or sanctifying grace."[4] His initial list of the means of grace includes three elements: "prayer, whether in secret or with the great congregation; searching the Scriptures (which implies reading, hearing, and meditating thereon), and receiving the Lord's Supper."[5] Later he adds fasting and Christian conference.[6]

This list brings to mind again images of the two dominant camps. On the one hand are those who see the whole purpose of the Christian life in terms of the means of grace, not always in terms of the whole list of course, but at least of some of its elements. Scripture is still the primary focus, especially in the "Bible Belt," although others may focus more on the sacraments or on personal relationship to God expressed in prayer. On the other hand are some who feel that we should look elsewhere for what really matters in today's church.

This dichotomy reflects a basic problem in Wesley's own time also, and he was not happy with either side.[7] Although at this point the issue has been clarified, Methodist theologians have usually not considered it further.[8] Thus, we are left with the challenge to find a more constructive way of dealing with the means of grace.

---

4. Sermon 16, "The Means of Grace," II.1, *Works*, 1:381.

5. Ibid. The three notions of Scripture, prayer, and Holy Communion " 'have a sound basis in the official Anglican formularies: Prayer Book, Ordinal, Homilies, Catechism,' " ibid., 377.

6. *Minutes* (Mason), 1:548-53 (the so-called "Large Minutes").

7. See Sermon 16, "The Means of Grace," I.1-2, *Works*, 1:378-80.

8. The latest book written on the means of grace still addresses precisely this dilemma. See Henry H. Knight III, *The Presence of God in the Christian Life: John Wesley and the Means of Grace* (Metuchen, N.J.: The Scarecrow Press, 1992).

Expanding the Means of Grace Tradition

How can we make sure that we are not perpetuating the conundrums of that old impasse whose entrenchments are no longer helpful? At a time when even mainstream sociological studies confirm that the opposition between conservatives and liberals is still in full swing, a mere affirmation of the importance of the previous list of the means of grace hardly seems to be sufficient.[9]

Trying to expand our vision, we might find a clue in Wesley's theological focus on Christian love of God and love of neighbor, sparked by God's own love in Christ. This theme is a central element of many of his writings from the beginning,[10] and it leads him to a radical expansion of his definition of the means of grace later on. In his sermon "On Zeal" (1781), Wesley locates the means of grace in a larger framework, unfolding the double focus of his theology in terms of the means of grace.

One can see how seriously the mature Wesley takes the love of neighbor by the fact that he now includes "works of mercy"—good deeds for the benefit of the neighbor—into the list of the means of grace. Although this idea is one of the distinctive marks of his theology, Wesley is fully aware that "this is a point exceeding little considered."[11] Developing a vision of what really matters in the Christian life, Wesley worked out a framework of four concentric circles. At the center is love, more precisely the double focus of love of God and love of neighbor. In the circle closest to the center Wesley locates what he calls "holy tempers."[12] The next circle contains works of mercy and in the third circle are works of piety (the traditional means of grace). In the outermost circle Wesley locates the church.

The most remarkable thing about this framework is the place of works of mercy in relation to works of piety, which some of Wesley's interpreters have noted correctly but not developed further. In agree-

---

9. See, for example, Robert Wuthnow, *The Restructuring of American Religion: Society and Faith since World War II* (Princeton: Princeton University Press, 1988). Wuthnow argues that we now have two civil religions—one liberal and the other conservative.

10. On Wesley's emphasis on the primacy of God's love, see Sermon 10, "The Witness of the Spirit, I," I.8, *Works*, 1:274; and Sermon 36, "The Law Established through Faith, II," III.3, *Works*, 2:42. This observation is also affirmed by historians such as Richard P. Heitzenrater; see "God With Us: Grace and the Spiritual Senses in John Wesley's Theology," in *Grace upon Grace: Essays in Honor of Thomas A. Langford*, ed. Robert K. Johnston, et al. (Nashville: Abingdon Press, 1999), 87-109.

11. Sermon 92, "On Zeal," II.5, *Works*, 3:313.

12. Ibid. Wesley lists some of those fruits of the Spirit that Paul mentions in Galatians 5:22-23: "long-suffering, gentleness, meekness, goodness, fidelity, temperance."

ment with both the prophet Hosea and the evangelist Matthew, Wesley notes that " 'God will have mercy and not sacrifice.' "[13] Whenever works of mercy and works of piety interfere with each other, the former "are to be preferred." Wesley explains to the surprised reader that "even reading, hearing [the Word], prayer, are to be omitted, or to be postponed, 'at charity's almighty call'—when we are called to relieve the distress of our neighbour, whether in body or soul."[14]

This same pattern can also be found in the present *Book of Discipline of The United Methodist Church* in the General Rules. The three General Rules start with the concern for doing no harm and doing good—thereby integrating the works of mercy—and then conclude with the attendance "upon all the ordinances of God"—thereby reminding us of the importance of the works of piety.[15]

Works of mercy are commonly acknowledged to be of fundamental importance to Wesley. However, one must try to understand the purpose of his including them in the means of grace tradition. In this new model, works of mercy are more than just correct actions, or orthopraxis. As real means of grace, they are channels that convey God's grace to the one who acts mercifully. A work of mercy is, therefore, no longer a one-way street leading from the well-meaning Christian to the other in need. Something comes back in return, which transforms the doer of mercy as well. In doing works of mercy—and this is absolutely crucial—a real encounter with God takes place that cannot be separated from the encounter with the other.[16]

A fresh reflection on works of mercy as means of grace might help us overcome the old impasse to which the opposition of orthodoxy (right belief) and orthopraxis ("politically correct" praxis) has led us. By bringing together both works of piety and works of mercy as means of grace, Wesley keeps together the love of the divine Other and the human other in a special way. This union is the fundamental challenge. Can the fact that the relation to the divine Other cannot be

---

13. Ibid., II.9, *Works*, 3:314 (the footnote cites Hos. 6:6; Matt. 9:13, 12:7).

14. Ibid. On this background, Borgen (*Wesley on Sacraments*, 105) lays too much emphasis on the works of piety, which he says are "of the greatest importance for Wesley."

15. Cf. *The Book of Discipline of The United Methodist Church, 1992* (Nashville: The United Methodist Publishing House, 1992), 71-73. In the first two parts of the General Rules, there is an extended list of works of mercy.

16. For Wesley, the works of mercy are not just "prudential" in the sense that they would be optional means of grace that may or may not be used according to changing circumstances. Many authors, such as Knight (*Presence of God*, 5) have overlooked that Wesley's distinction between "instituted" and "prudential" means of grace does not apply here, for works of mercy are not listed in either category. See *Minutes* (Mason), 1:548-57.

separated from the relation to the human other help to overcome the current impasse in the church?

We must consider the full range of this challenge, following the lines of this argument. It has been argued, for instance, that works of mercy are means of grace that point to God's presence but not to God's identity. In that model, God's identity would be defined solely by works of piety.[17] But is not God's identity also at stake in works of mercy, for instance when we encounter Christ's presence in the face of the neighbor? Can someone have an encounter with God's presence without receiving even a glimpse of God's identity? We need to see the relationship between works of piety and works of mercy in more constructive ways.

Between the Other and the other

Those who say, "I love God," and hate their brothers or sisters, are liars; for those who do not love a brother or sister whom they have seen, cannot love God whom they have not seen. (1 John 4:20 NRSV)

The platitude that both works of piety and works of mercy are important is obvious. No one would disagree with that. My basic point is more specific: We need to give a theological account of the fact that works of mercy are to be understood as means of grace. Whether we realize it or not, works of mercy are actually means of grace. All that the church can do is acknowledge this reality. The problem is that people in both the orthodoxy and the orthopraxis camps have blind spots at this point.

The problem has two distinct aspects. First, a one-sided concern for works of piety and orthodoxy denies to works of mercy their status as means of grace. Second, a one-sided concern for the works of mercy and orthopraxy often forgets the same thing, namely, that works of mercy are not only good deeds but also real means of grace.

Works of Mercy

Let us examine the latter problem first. If works of mercy are not seen as real means of grace, we are stuck on a one-way street. In that

---

17. Knight defines works of mercy as means of grace that "encourage openness to the presence of God" as opposed to means that "describe the character and activity of God." According

case, works of mercy might promote good deeds, or "outreach" projects, whereby Christians are doing good things for others. But even if those works are done out of love for the neighbor, a certain condescending and controlling attitude is hard to avoid. In that case, the fate of the other in need is placed in the hands of the one who is acting in a merciful way. What is less clear to them, and usually overlooked, is that the encounter with people in need might also have a powerful impact on the doer of mercy—an impact that goes far beyond "feeling good about oneself" for charitable activities.

This lack of clarity is still one of the major blind spots of some Christians who honestly seek to help others in need. Many social action programs have had to deal with this misunderstanding. In the Civil Rights movement, for instance, some well-meaning white Americans ended up turning their backs on the African American struggle when they did not recognize that their own liberation was at stake too. The exclusive concern for what one can do for the other is not only incomplete, it is also problematic. The contribution that the other might make in return is overlooked. Worse yet, the inability to take others seriously in their difference from us leads to the temptation to mold them into our own image.

This attitude has had detrimental consequences for those who were supposed to be the recipients of works of mercy. George Tinker, a Native American scholar, tells the "history of good intentions" of the missions to Native Americans.[18] The missionaries facilitated exploitation despite their moral integrity and the fact that they did not benefit from exploitation themselves.[19] Tinker traces this phenomenon back to an unconscious attitude of condescension tied to the idealization of the missionaries' own white culture. At the root of the problem is the inability to enter into relationship with and learn from the Native American other.[20]

In regard to the more recent context, Robert Allen Warrior, another Native American scholar, sees a problem with "liberals and conservatives alike" who have decided to come to the rescue of Native Americans: They are "always using their [own] methods, their

---

to Knight, God's character is described by "Scripture, preaching, the Eucharist, and the prayers of the tradition" (*Presence of God*, 13).

18. George E. Tinker, *Missionary Conquest: The Gospel and Native American Cultural Genocide* (Minneapolis: Fortress Press, 1993), 112.

19. Ibid., 17.

20. Ibid., 3.

ideas, and their programs."[21] Warrior sees hope only where Christians finally start to listen more carefully to the other in need.

Among those who promote orthopraxis apart from the means of grace, a similar pattern of condescending control also seems to be present in the relation to God, a problem that the orthodox critics have sensed very well. The patronizing tendency for the charitable self to usurp the other in need is also implicit in its relation to God. The focus on orthopraxis, centered in the power of the modern human self, tends to concentrate on the self's reach for God. There is a very real danger that God becomes a function of the well-meaning individual.

If, however, works of mercy are understood as means of grace, they can be seen as what they are: channels of grace not only to the recipients of mercy but also to the acting self. The one-way street of liberal charity, leading from the self to the other and from the self to God, opens up into a two-way street. The self becomes a recipient of grace by acting on behalf of the other. In working for others, Christians become recipients of the grace of God. Those who do works of mercy are themselves transformed in their encounters with the other. In this connection, their relationship to the other person contributes to their relationship to the divine Other as well. Liberated from turning around ourselves, we gradually open up to the transforming power of God's grace. Only as orthopraxis becomes a two-way street can we realize what many of the oppressed have known all along: The liberation of the oppressed and the transformation of those who volunteer to help are inextricably connected.

This account helps explain the experience of many present-day Christians of all walks of life who have, on occasion, been forced out of their personal safety zones. Some people in the church have been transformed when they encountered their neighbors, whether on mission trips to other countries or in places of need close to home. Once again, praxis precedes theology. Unfortunately—and this is the problem much of my work seeks to redress—we do not have the theological tools yet to interpret these experiences.[22] At this point, the

---

21. Robert Allen Warrior, "A Native American Perspective: Canaanites, Cowboys, and Indians," in *Voices from the Margin: Interpreting the Bible in the Third World*, ed. R. S. Sugirtharajah (Maryknoll, N.Y.: Orbis Press, 1991), 288.

22. See also my book, *Remember the Poor: The Challenge to Theology in the Twenty-First Century* (Harrisburg, Pa.: Trinity Press International, 1998) and my essays, "Whaling Our Way into the Twenty-First Century," in *Theology from the Belly of the Whale: A Frederick Herzog Reader*, ed. Joerg Rieger (Harrisburg, Pa.: Trinity Press International, 1999), 1-19; and "Developing a Common

contemporary church faces the problem of being unable to lead people to the next steps, not so much due to a complete lack of praxis but rather due to a lack of adequate theological reflection.

Works of Piety

The one-sided concern for the works of piety, which also forgets that works of mercy are means of grace, is perhaps more difficult to analyze. Wesley was quite concerned about this because he knew that people fall from grace simply because they do not pay attention to works of mercy.[23]

No doubt, an exclusive focus on works of piety, including prayer, Scripture reading, and Holy Communion, would appear to be inadequate. But what, beyond that, is precisely the problem? One might assume that those concerned with works of piety might know what those concerned with works of mercy did not know: that Christianity is not a set of one-way streets moving from ourselves to the other and from ourselves to God. For those who correctly understand the significance of works of piety, the focus is reversed. The divine-human relationship is no longer initiated by humanity leading to God but rather is begun by God reaching out to humanity. Means of grace are channels of God's grace and must be used accordingly.

While it may appear that the only necessity, then, is to add works of mercy on top of works of piety, the real problem cuts deeper. A singular focus on works of piety may cover up yet another blind spot. The most drastic problem occurs when the means of grace are mistaken for the thing itself, the grace of God. One example in many Protestant circles is the confusion between the Bible as *containing* the Word of God and as *being* the Word of God itself. If reading the Bible is a means of grace and a channel of God's speech, that does not necessarily make the Bible itself identical to the Word of God. This problem is addressed by Wesley in his sermon "The Means of Grace" and picked up faithfully by his interpreters.[24]

But even when this confusion is cleared, an exclusive focus on the works of piety tends to neglect a concern for the other person in need, which is God's own concern. The problem is that, with a singular

---

Interest Theology from the Underside," in *Liberating the Future: God, Mammon, and Theology*, ed. Joerg Rieger (Minneapolis: Fortress Press, 1998), 124-41.

23. See Sermon 98, "On Visiting the Sick," §1, *Works*, 3:385.

24. For example, Knight, *Presence of God*, and Borgen, *Wesley on Sacraments*.

focus on God's relation to humanity in the works of piety, the grace-filled character of one's involvement with the neighbor cannot be fully appreciated. Simply adding works of mercy on top of works of piety without accounting for their interrelation does not make much of a difference. Such works of mercy become mechanical actions, mere applications of a more important set of truths.[25]

Another problem, perhaps even more troublesome, is often overlooked. When the relation to the neighbor is not taken into account as a means of grace, even the traditional means of grace—reading the Bible, participating in Holy Communion, and praying—are easily distorted. The singular concern for the move from God to humanity might lead to an implicit scheme in which God's grace becomes self-serving to the person. What if the faithful are not interested in anything but themselves and their own salvation? In this case, the Christian self is not transformed, and the works of piety lose their challenge. The simple addition of works of mercy on top of works of piety does not lead automatically to the quantum leap that we seek.

In this way, both the liberal and the orthodox modes ultimately miss the love of not only the human other but also the divine Other. The orthodox concern for God's relation to us in works of piety is in constant danger of covering up Christian self-interest in the name of God. If the relation to the other person is lost, there is no double-check of our relation to the divine Other, as the writer of 1 John knew. A heightened concern for God does not automatically overcome the self-centeredness of theology. Theologians must constantly be aware of the various ways that the concern for God's sovereignty can be misused to disguise the self-centeredness and parochial character that is so typical of contemporary "first world" theology.

On the other hand, the simple concern of orthopraxis, even if pursued with the purest of intentions, is in danger of leading to a form of self-centeredness that is unable to find anything in the other but a mirror image. It is no wonder that one is not able to find God present there either! The people who focus on right praxis need to clarify how a concern for others properly functions. How can the

---

25. There seems to be a connection between this theological analysis and the findings of a recent study by the Pew Research Center that "religious teachings have remarkably little influence in shaping people's attitudes on broad social issues like welfare and the role of women in the workplace." Quoted in the *New York Times*, 25 June 1996. At the same time, the survey found that religious teaching had its greatest effect on moral and sexual issues, especially abortion and homosexuality.

other become a channel of God's grace that helps us better understand who God is and who we are? Those who take this approach must be able to face the self-critical question, *Who put the other in this place?* and thus become aware of their own need for God's liberating and transforming power.

Beyond Orthodoxy and Orthopraxis

The challenge of taking a clue from Wesley's position is that often the results cannot easily be appropriated either by the orthodoxy or the orthopraxis camp. Preaching on the Sermon on the Mount, Wesley made it clear that orthodoxy is not sufficient: "Whatever creeds we may rehearse; whatever professions of faith we make; whatever number of prayers we may repeat, whatever thanksgivings we read or say to God," we may still miss the mark.[26] The same is true for those in the orthopraxis camp who follow the first two General Rules of doing no harm and doing good.

Nevertheless, simply seeking a middle road, one of the biggest temptations of the Methodist mainline, is not enough either. Wesley's concern for the means of grace and the power of the Spirit was not simply " 'high-church' evangelicalism," as Albert Outler assumed, in the sense of having it both ways.[27] While Outler noted correctly that Wesley was not interested in playing off works of piety and works of mercy against each other,[28] this assertion does not mean that Wesley was leaving both virtually unchanged in a harmless division. Wesleyan spirituality transformed both elements—orthodoxy and orthopraxis.

First of all, love of God and love of neighbor, seen in proper relation, can transform one's understanding of the orthodox and High Church traditions. Mainstream Anglican theology did not include works of mercy in the means of grace tradition in the same way that Wesley did. Following in the tradition of Wesley, we need to explore how faithful Christian praxis (which does not forget about people in need) helps reshape matters of doctrine. Outler's helpful point that Wesley was a "folk-theologian"[29] must be understood in a more fundamental and dialogical sense. Most people assume that, as a folk-

---

26. Sermon 33, "Upon Our Lord's Sermon on the Mount, XIII," I.1-3, *Works*, 1:688.
27. Introduction to Sermon 16, "The Means of Grace," *Works*, 1:377.
28. Sermon 14, "The Repentance of Believers," *Works*, 1:343 n. 65.
29. Introduction, *Works*, 1:67.

theologian, Wesley was mainly concerned about transmitting the Christian faith to common people. But in taking works of mercy seriously, he also developed theological tools that (even though perhaps only in preliminary form) allowed him to listen to and learn from the people. And, more importantly, we must expand the commonly accepted insight that Wesley always related doctrine to issues of Christian praxis. Wesley's emphasis on the relation of works of piety and works of mercy was aimed at reconstructing both elements.

Second, Wesley's spirituality also transforms the concern for right action. The inclusion of works of mercy into the means of grace—and thus relating love of God and love of neighbor—is a radical challenge, both for those who are *not* concerned about right action and especially for those who *are*. Works of mercy can no longer be understood as one-way streets. Combined with works of piety, they invite an encounter with God that offers a substantial reconstruction of the modern liberal self and its tendency to assimilate everything to its own interests. This reality is what many of the so-called contextual theologies still need to realize. The theological task is not simply to adapt Christianity to one's own context. The works of piety (reading the Bible, celebrating Holy Communion, praying) help guide works of mercy in the search for those contexts where God's saving presence is most needed today.[30] The basic challenge for the church, then, is to look for God's own actions among those in need and to join God there.

Holy Communion is an example of how both works of mercy and works of piety come together. The Christ whom we meet at the Communion table and in the liturgy of the church cannot be another Christ than the one we meet in the other person, the marginalized. Holy Communion is communion with Christ who is both "sitting at the right hand of God" (as we confess in the Apostolic Creed) and walking the dusty roads of this world. Communion is, therefore, no longer merely a mystical and private transaction between God and the church. Communion includes God's concern for all of creation (especially those who are most needy), eating and drinking together with them at the table.[31]

---

30. For a discussion of the difference between what is now called "contextual theology" and liberation theology, see my essay, "Developing a Common Interest Theology from the Underside."

31. See the work of Frederick Herzog and my "Whaling Our Way into the Twenty-First Century," 14-15.

Any attempt to combine the concern for orthodoxy and ortho-praxis into a middle road between both would, therefore, be fatal. To leave it there would mean to perpetuate the bifurcation commonly found in the contemporary church. If the orthodox and liberal camps do not communicate, both will ultimately leave the modern self untouched and in charge: the liberals glorifying in the power of the self and the conservatives sheltering the self in a religious escape. The challenge for theologians is to give an account of how both ele-ments—works of mercy and works of piety—reconstruct themselves whenever they are brought into a dialogue. More specifically, both types of works need to be reconstructed in light of God's own praxis. Both the concern for right doctrine and the concern for right praxis are far too important to be left to each camp alone. Contrary to what much of contemporary theology still seems to tell us, the Christian faith is not primarily about orthopraxis or orthodoxy, taking one or the other (either doctrine and piety or the acting self) as a starting point.

Theology needs to discern God's presence in relation to the church's self-presence. Wesley seems to have sensed this in his call for a "religion that is spirit and life; the dwelling in God and God in thee."[32] This mutual presence is the true importance of the means of grace. The key to understanding these means is not primarily the concern for right doctrine or right action. The means of grace are essential for the experience of God's gracious presence in specific locations with those who need help the most.

God's gracious presence, experienced through the various means of grace, is the context in which both orthodoxy and orthopraxis come together. In the experience of God's presence, Christian doctrine and Christian praxis are interrelated. This truth is at the very heart of Wesleyan theology and doctrine.[33] If theology is no longer viewed as either a catalog of doctrines subsequently applied to ethics or an undertaking preoccupied with questions of praxis or personal piety, the theological task can then be properly understood as reflection on praxis, especially God's praxis in relation to our own. In this way, the-ology and the church can be renewed and transformed creatively.

---

32. Sermon 33, "Upon Our Lord's Sermon on the Mount, XIII," III.9, *Works*, 1:697. See also the conclusion of Sermon 92, "On Zeal," III.12, *Works*, 3:321, "For 'God is love; and he that dwelleth in love, dwelleth in God and God in him'" (1 John 4:16).

33. It has been argued that the notions of orthodoxy and orthopraxis are tied together by a third term, *orthopathy*. Cf. Theodore H. Runyon, "A New Look at 'Experience,'" *Drew Gateway* (Fall 1987): 44-55. Contrary to Runyon's intention, this emphasis might still end up focusing on the Christian self "feeling its religious pulse."

The Two Poles of Spirituality

For Wesley, as we have seen, love of God and love of neighbor are related. Wesley's interpretation of the Gospel dictum not to "lay up treasures upon the earth" is a good illustration, for it helps us focus on what really matters. The love of God is absolutely central. Yet when Wesley encourages "laying up treasures in heaven," he does not first talk about the utterly transcendent; rather, he immediately points to the neighbor in need.[34] If these words were simply good moral advice, the theological reader could move on. But Wesley's approach brings us back to where we started, at the connection between the human other and the divine Other. The concern for laying up treasures with the heavenly Other makes sense only if it is tied to the human other.

Doing works of mercy or laying up treasures in heaven, by whatever expressions Wesley uses, is aimed specifically at those most in need.[35] In his own way, Wesley arrives at a "preferential option for the poor," taking seriously Matthew 25 and other biblical passages.[36] Recent scholarship exhibits broad agreement that, for Wesley, "the poor are at the heart of the evangel and that life with the poor is constitutive of Christian discipleship."[37] We are now clearer about the theological connections: Any option for the poor must first of all be God's own option for the poor.

Wesleyan theology must deal with two poles: God and the poor. This point reminds us that God's presence in Christ is always tied to specific locations. The encounter with those in need sheds light on our understanding of God. If works of mercy are real means of grace, a neat separation of God's presence from God's identity is no longer possible. That is to say, works of mercy (the encounters with the needy) are channels of God's grace that help us better understand who God is. While works of mercy do not tell the whole story, they do in fact offer a glimpse of God's identity, as Jesus' own story shows.

We meet God and Christ when we respond to the hungry, care for the sick, and work with (not just for) the poor. We do not simply

---

34. See Sermon 28, "Upon Our Lord's Sermon on the Mount, VIII," 26, *Works*, 1:629.

35. The crucial issue of the concrete shape of Wesley's praxis together with his concern for the poor is neglected in Randy L. Maddox's article, "John Wesley—Practical Theologian?" *Wesleyan Theological Journal* 23 (1988): 101-11.

36. Sermon 28, "Upon Our Lord's Sermon on the Mount, VIII," §26, *Works*, 1:629.

37. M. Douglas Meeks, "Introduction: On Reading Wesley with the Poor," in *The Portion of the Poor: Good News to the Poor in the Wesleyan Tradition*, ed. M. Douglas Meeks (Nashville: Kingswood Books, 1995), 9. See also the contributions of the various authors in the volume.

encounter some abstract presence. On the contrary, God shows God's own face. No method of correlation needs to be implied that might assume some inherent quality of the oppressed that would point us to God. Rather, the point is to seek God where God has said God would be.[38] Our thinking about God is no longer adequate without this impulse. Neither the orthodoxy nor the orthopraxis camps have yet paid sufficient attention to this point, and in this light, the contribution of theologies from the margins can no longer be put aside, classified as "special interest theologies." God's own interest in Christ and the Holy Spirit is at stake. The church cannot bypass this fact.[39]

Therefore, the judgment that "modern Methodism . . . must be considered Pelagian, with little spiritual power and very limited intercourse with God" is only true if the classic Wesleyan concern for works of mercy among the poor is misunderstood as a one-way street.[40] Nevertheless, this comment still serves as a warning to Methodist theologians and as a reminder that the relationship between works of mercy and the work of God has now to be seen in the more specific light of the encounter with those at the margins. The ultimate focus of Wesleyan spirituality is not primarily the praxis of the "people called Methodists" but the discernment of, and response to, the triune God's presence and praxis in the world.[41]

God's Praxis

Signs of an increasing awareness of the interdependence of orthodoxy and orthopraxis are evident. A number of recent resolutions of the General Conference of The United Methodist Church could serve as examples of an ongoing attempt to tie together belief and praxis more closely. "Toward a New Beginning Beyond 1992," for

---

38. This is the basic theme of my book *Remember the Poor*.
39. See my essay "Developing a Common Interest Theology from the Underside."
40. Borgen, *Wesley on Sacraments*, 281.
41. As Craig B. Gallaway has pointed out, this is exactly the concern of the Wesley hymns:

The spirituality of these hymns is not political in the sense that it lays down a specific social ethic. But it is political in the sense that it challenges and transforms the way people see themselves in relation to God, and to each other. . . . At the center of this spirituality . . . is the recognition of Christ's continuing presence by the Spirit in history with the community of his people.

From "The Presence of Christ with the Worshipping Community: A Study in the Hymns of John and Charles Wesley" (Ph.D. diss., Emory University, 1988), 226.

example, strives for the interrelation of Christian doctrine and praxis. Yet there are still gaps.[42] The concern for "nurture," "outreach," and "witness" does not go much beyond the old concern for orthopraxis; a call to repentance and the question of what God teaches us in the marginalized other are missing. In this context, the invitation "to meet with local people from racial/ethnic-minority communities in their own setting"[43] might simply produce church people who feel good about themselves and their charities rather than yield genuine conversions.

More recently, the United Methodist bishops have taken an important step toward relating orthodoxy and orthopraxis by asserting that "the crisis among children and the impoverished and our theological and historical mandates demand more than additional programs or emphases. Nothing less than the reshaping of The United Methodist Church in response to the God who is among 'the least of these' is required."[44]

According to the bishops, theology and the church need to be reshaped by working with people on the underside of history. At the same time, the reality of this statement is hardly visible in current Methodist theological reflection. And most of the numerous projects that have sprung from the bishops' initiative revert straight back into programs that try to minister *to* poor children rather than *with* them and forget about reshaping the church altogether.

Various theological models are now available that have grown out of new ways of living the Christian life, beyond orthodoxy and orthopraxis. For Latin America, Gustavo Gutiérrez has created a new paradigm: theology as "critical reflection on Christian praxis in light of the Word."[45] In the North American context, one of the primary models is Frederick Herzog's reconstruction of theology in terms of God-Walk, Theo-praxis, Christo-praxis, and Spirit-praxis inviting Christian discipleship.[46]

---

42. "Toward a New Beginning Beyond 1992," in *The Book of Resolutions of The United Methodist Church, 1992* (Nashville: The United Methodist Publishing House, 1992), 388.

43. Ibid., 390.

44. The Council of Bishops of The United Methodist Church, *Children and Poverty: An Episcopal Initiative* (Nashville: The United Methodist Publishing House, 1996), 7.

45. Gustavo Gutiérrez, *A Theology of Liberation: History, Politics, and Salvation*, trans. Sister Caridad Inda and John Eagleson, 15th rev. ed. (Maryknoll: Orbis, 1988), 11.

46. Frederick Herzog, *God-Walk: Liberation Shaping Dogmatics* (Maryknoll, N.Y.: Orbis Press, 1988). In an instructive article entitled "United Methodism in Agony," Herzog has argued for a constructive interrelation of three concerns that were not yet brought together in The United Methodist Church: the doctrinal mandate, the concern for liberation, and the challenge of the minorities; see *Perkins Journal* 28 (Fall 1974): 1-10. Both Gutiérrez's and Herzog's concerns are developed further in my book *Remember the Poor*.

In any case, Christian practice seems to be ahead of theology, as seen in the United Methodist Covenant Discipleship Groups. These groups, reclaiming the Methodist heritage of bands and classes, tie together four elements: acts of compassion, acts of justice, acts of worship, and acts of devotion.[47] Some theological schools and seminaries that are now beginning to take the field of urban ministry seriously must also be in a good position to provide a new theological consciousness.

In the light of these developments in theology and the church, both the concern for right doctrine and the concern for right praxis can be reconstructed. In order to go beyond frameworks that are caught up in self-referentiality, a basic openness for both the other person and the divine Other must be recovered. While the orthopraxis impasse sheds light on the limits of modernity and the power of the modern self, the orthodox impasse may shed light on the limits of a concern for both God's Otherness and the doctrines of the church, a concern that fails because it neglects the actual plight of the human other.

The encounter with both the needy other and the divine Other, therefore, must lead to a reconstruction of both the moral self (orthopraxis) and the doctrinal teachings of the church (orthodoxy). From this observation, a suggestion for the further development of theology in the twenty first century begins to crystallize. Perhaps the basic point of the theological search is neither our orthopraxis nor our orthodoxy but *God's own praxis* initiating and inviting both the love of God and the love of neighbor.

---

47. See David Lowes Watson, Covenant Discipleship: Christian Formation through Mutual Accountability (Nashville: Discipleship Resources, 1991), 116.

CHAPTER FIVE

Perfection Revisited: Charles Wesley's Theology of "Gospel Poverty" and "Perfect Poverty"

S T Kimbrough, Jr.

Poetry was the primary vehicle of Charles Wesley's theological reflection. Therefore, while his English prosody is generally eloquent and extremely articulate, his lyrics on the subject of the poor are, at times, filled with irony and sarcasm—two literary traits that do not generally characterize the hymns of the Christian church.[1] Charles also emphasizes the common sharing of resources so strongly that one has difficulty knowing how this view resonated and resonates within the Anglican-Methodist traditions, which have never adopted an ethic of complete, common sharing of resources.

---

1. I published a selection of Charles Wesley hymns along with an article entitled "Charles Wesley and the Poor" in a small book, *A Song for the Poor* (New York: General Board of Global Ministries, 1993). The Wesley texts focused on life and ministry with and among the poor. The hymn texts were set to music for congregational singing. The collection resulted from a paper I had presented to the Oxford Institute of Methodist Theological Studies in 1992 and was subsequently published in *The Portion of the Poor*, ed. M. Douglas Meeks (Nashville: Kingswood Books, 1995). I then published a singer's edition, *Songs for the Poor* (New York: General Board of Global Ministries, 1997), in which the hymn texts were musically scored and presented in text blocks. This collection includes the texts that are perhaps the most significant ones for creating the church's memory of its responsibilities to the poor.

There is another group of Charles Wesley texts that had remained unpublished until recently in the second volume of *The Unpublished Poetry of Charles Wesley*, ed. S T Kimbrough, Jr. and Oliver A. Beckerlegge, 3 vols. (Nashville: Kingswood Books, 1990). This group of texts enhances the understanding of Charles Wesley's perspectives on life and ministry with and among the poor. They are primarily reflections on specific passages of the Scriptures but are a part of the corpus of material in Charles's poetical or hymnic literature that may not have been intended for singing per se.

Clearly, however, none of the poetic texts discussed in this paper has been incorporated into the church's hymnic repertory. Nevertheless, these texts are absolutely vital to the theological and historical understanding of the Wesleys and their work with the poor.

The Character and Role of the Poor

(1) *The poor bear the Spirit's character and are marked by distinguished grace*. Charles writes:

> The poor I to the rich prefer,
>   If with thine eyes I see;
> To bear thy Spirit's character
>   The poor are chose by Thee:
> The poor in every age and place
>   Thou dost, O God, approve
> To mark with thy distinguish'd grace,
>   T'inrich with faith and love.[2]

The Spirit of God is the Spirit of grace and love. The poor are chosen by God to bear the grace-filled and love-filled marks of the Spirit's character. These marks distinguish the poor among the people of the earth, for it is God who enriches them with such character. Could this view be why Charles claimed in his *Journal* that the poor "have generally a much larger degree of confidence than the rich and learned"?[3]

(2) *The poor are the body of Christ*. Charles claims that this maxim is something that members of the church should know.

> Members of his Church we know
>   The poor his body are:
> All the goods he had below,
>   They should his garments share.[4]

Even if the members of Christ's church know this truth, Charles says they often act like the soldiers at the foot of the cross who divided Jesus' garments.

---

2. *Unpublished Poetry*, 2:90.
3. *The Journal of the Rev. Charles Wesley*, ed. Thomas Jackson, 2 vols. (London: Wesleyan-Methodist Book Room, 1849) 1:108.
4. *Unpublished Poetry*, 2:67.

> Eager each the whole t'ingross,
> As churchmen never satisfied,
> First they nail Him to the cross,
> And then his spoils divide.[5]

These lines contain revolutionary ideas, though Charles was by no means the first to articulate them. The church had not yet fully absorbed them and integrated them into its faith and practice. The character of the poor is marked by two dimensions of the divine that are mediated through God's action in Jesus Christ—grace and love. These dimensions are perpetually mediated at the sacrament of Holy Communion, making it a means of grace and divine love.

To declare that the poor are the body of Christ is to include them in the family of the faithful and welcome them at the Lord's table. How can this be? The church has never lived this reality. The grace-distinguished poor are precisely the ones who test the grace of the community of faith.

> Yes; the poor supply thy place,
> Still deputed, Lord, by Thee,
> Daily exercise our grace,
> Prove our growing charity.[6]

(3) *The poor fulfill a vicarious role as Christ's representatives on earth.* Those who give to the poor, give to Christ; those who serve the poor, serve Christ.

> What to them [the poor] with right intent
> Truly, faithfully is given,
> We have to our Saviour lent,
> Laid up for ourselves in heaven.[7]

Notice that Charles qualifies the matter of giving to the poor—one lays up gifts in heaven only if one gives to the poor with right intent, that is, truly and faithfully.

In reflecting on Mark 10:40-41, Wesley pens this couplet: "O might I thus thro' life endure, / [and] Serve my Saviour in the poor."[8] His choice of a preposition is most important here. He does not say

---

5. Ibid.
6. Ibid., 2:46.
7. Ibid.
8. Ibid., 2:69.

"through," "with," or "among" the poor. He expresses the desire and prayer of his heart—to serve the Savior who is *in* the poor. They personify the Savior, whom Charles seeks to serve.

When Charles reflects on the act of the woman who did not cease to kiss Jesus' feet (Luke 7:45), he says of her act of humility to serve to the poor:

> Thus may I my faith approve,
>   Lower sinking still and lower,
> Jesus in his members love,
>   Honour Jesus in the poor.[9]

Service to the poor entails self-effacement and total commitment to Jesus. The test of faith in Jesus is whether or not one will take on the form of a humble servant and love Jesus in his members, in other words, honor him "in the poor." Once again, he specifically says, "*in* the poor."

The Responsibility of the Community of Faith

If indeed one serves Christ in the poor, then the community of believers in Christ bears tremendous responsibility for its response to the poor, for it is thereby responding to the Savior. What should be the response of the community of faith?

Much discussion today focuses on the politically correct language relating to all matters that concern the poor. One does not wish to demean the poor but rather acknowledge their full human dignity. While one may be poor in many ways other than economically, in most of these texts, Charles is referring precisely to economic poverty. This propensity is no surprise given the huge economic gulf in eighteenth-century England between the wealthy and the poor.

(1) *The community of faith has the responsibility to preach the gospel to the poor.* With regard to the matter of correct language in referring to life and ministry with and among the poor, Charles unabashedly says,

> Even now, all loving Lord,
>   thou hast sent forth thy Word,
> thou the door hast opened wide

---

9. Ibid., 2:102.

> (who can shut thy open door!)
> I the grace have testified,
>   preached thy gospel to the poor.[10]

Here, Charles writes of the fulfillment of his ministerial office in evangelizing the poor through the proclamation of the Word. In his *Journal* he states, "The poor have a right to the gospel. I therefore preached Christ crucified to them from Zechariah 12:10."[11]

For Charles, there is no question that he can fulfill his ministerial office only by preaching the gospel and the doctrine of perfection to the poor.

> On us, O Christ, thy mission prove,
>   Thy full authority to heal,
> The blindness of our hearts remove,
>   The lameness of our feeble will,
> Open our faith's obedient ear,
>   Our filthy, leprous nature cure,
> Call us out of the sepulchre,
>   And preach Perfection to the poor.[12]

Christ's mission calls us to be healed of our blindness, deafness, and sickened bodies. It calls us out of the grave. Why? That we may "preach Perfection to the poor." This goal becomes a measure by which the effectiveness of our fulfillment of Christ's mission may be judged.

The community of faith unequivocally has the responsibility to preach the gospel—Christ and him crucified—to the poor. The result of the proclamation of the Word will be that many will believe and follow Christ, as John 7:31 states, "Many of the people believed on him." Concerning this passage, Charles wrote:

> God hath chose the simple poor,
>   As followers of his Son,
> Rich in faith, of glory sure,
>   To win the heavenly crown.[13]

---

10. *A Song for the Poor*, 35; from *Hymns and Sacred Poems*, 2 vols. (Bristol: Farley, 1749), 1:312.
11. Charles Wesley, *Journal*, 1:312.
12. *Unpublished Poetry*, 2:100. The poem is based on Luke 7:22.
13. Ibid., 2:240.

(2) *As the servants went into the streets, as recorded in Matthew 22, and gathered the guests for the wedding feast, the community of faith must gather all, including the poor, to feast upon the love of God.* This point of view would seem to be an obvious posture for those who follow Christ, for Divine love knows no limits. Charles was inspired by Matthew 22:10, "So those servants went out into the highways, and gathered together all as many as they found, both bad and good: and the wedding was furnished with guests," and wrote:

> God his grace on them bestows
> Whom he vouchsafes to call,
> No respect of persons knows,
> But offers Christ to all:
> In the wedding-garment clad
> (The faith which God will not reprove)
> Poor and rich, and good and bad
> May banquet on his love.[14]

The "poor and rich, and good and bad" are invited to God's love banquet. No one may be turned away from this feast. No one!

This point of view is the radical social perspective of the gospel of Jesus Christ. It turns all class and societal structures upside down. It leaves no room for prejudice, hatred, marginalization, oppression, or slavery. God's love feast is for all. In offering Christ to all, the banquet of self-giving love begins, and God is the host.

(3) *The community of faith may not neglect the hungry poor, or else it may be guilty of murder.* Based on the conspiracy of the tenants against the vineyard owner's son in the parable from Luke 20:14, "come, let us kill him, that the inheritance may be ours," Wesley writes a scathing indictment of all who would plunder and kill for the sake of personal gain. Such personal gain is precisely what kills the poor by depriving them of the sustenance they need. This action might not entail premeditation of murder but rather mere neglect. Wesley marks the priests of the church who neglect the hungry poor as prime suspects in this conspiracy.

> Ambitious, covetous, and vain,
> Priests who in ease and pleasure live,
> They persecute their Lord again,
> His members vex, his Spirit grieve;

---

14. Ibid., 2:37.

> Souls by their negligence they kill,
>   Jesus afresh they crucify,
> And eat, and drink, and sport their fill,
>   And let the poor thro' hunger die.[15]

The conspiring tenants of Luke 20 foreshadow the priests of the church who, while living in ease, deprive the hungry poor of food thus causing their death. By neglecting the hungry poor, the priests of the church are ignoring members of Christ's body and vexing the Holy Spirit. Those who live in ease and pleasure—who eat, drink, and make merry—crucify Jesus all over again. This poem is a perplexing indictment of the established church and its clergy, but it is as up-to-date at the turn of a new century as it was over two hundred years ago.

The contrast to this behavior is modeled for Charles in the widow of Luke 21:4 who gave two copper coins to the temple treasury: "she of her [poverty] hath cast in all the living that she had."

> God his mighty power displays,
>   God his love to sinners shows;
> Free, and disengag'd by grace
>   Then the poor his all bestows;
> Let his whole provision fail,
>   He his confidence approves,
> Feasts a Friend invisible,
>   One whom more than life he loves.[16]

The widow is free to give what she has, little though it is, because she is a free person. What does Charles mean here? She is free because she has been "disengaged by grace," disengaged from all the trappings of possessions in this world. There is One whom she loves more than all the things of the world, "One whom more than life [she] loves," namely, Jesus Christ, the Friend of sinners. With this life-posture among the community of the faithful, there can be no neglect of the poor, for ease and pleasure, eating, drinking, and making merry can never take priority over commitment to Christ—and commitment to him means commitment to his members, among whom are the poor.

---

15. Ibid., 2:183.
16. Ibid., 2:187.

The Nature of the Community of Faith and the Ethic of Sharing

The fourth chapter of Acts provides models of an ethic of sharing for the community of believers in Jesus Christ to which Charles returns a number of times in his poetry. None of these poems, however, survive in the church for reading or singing. They are uncompromisingly difficult and are unquestionably the basis of an essential difference between Charles and his brother John on economic theory and practice. Charles moves much closer than John to an ascetic view of life that affirms the divestment of all possessions.

(1) *Stewardship of resources and private ownership.* Acts 4 is the occasion for at least three Charles Wesley poems dealing with stewardship of resources.[17] Acts 4:32, 34 reads: "And the multitude of them that believed were of one heart and of one soul: neither said any of *them* that ought of the things which he possessed was his own; but they had all things in common. Neither was there any among them that lacked." Wesley's response to this passage is powerful and eloquent:

> 1. Happy the multitude
>   (But far above our sphere)
> Redeem'd by Jesus' blood
>   From all we covet here!
> To Him, & to each other join'd,
> They all were of one heart and mind.
>
> 2. His blood the cement was
>   Who died on Calvary,
> And fasten'd to his cross
>   They could not disagree:
> One soul did all the members move,
> The soul of harmony & love.
>
> 3. Their goods were free for all,
>   Appropriated to none,
> While none presum'd to call
>   What he possess'd his own;
> The difference base of *thine* & *mine*
> Was lost in charity Divine.
>
> 4. No overplus, or need,
>   No rich or poor were there,

---

17. A poem based on Acts 4:36-37 is discussed later in this chapter.

108

Content with daily bread
Where each injoy'd his share;
With every common blessing bless'd
They nothing had, yet all possess'd.[18]

When life is based on divine charity or love, the distinction of private ownership or possession is removed. This concept remains a foreign message, however, to much of the world. Private ownership is generally thought to epitomize a rugged individualism that is at the heart of capitalism, and the distinction of *thine* and *mine* is fostered as the basis of society. No society in the world operates on the basis of God's love, sharing all in common for the sake of common need and good. However, Charles claims that in the community of faith the soul of the people should be harmony and love. This desire is the singular soul that is to move them. Why? Because the believers have clearly experienced what God has done for them in and through the cross of Jesus Christ. They have been cemented together by this act of divine love and redemption. This unity that binds them together and makes them of one heart and mind is "(far above our sphere) / redeem'd . . . from all we covet here!" Note that Charles placed "far above our sphere" in parentheses. Is he saying that such an ideal "multitude" is so far beyond where we live amid covetousness that it is almost unattainable? Perhaps. But he does see such a reality in the New Testament community as recorded in Acts. For Charles, the ideal for the Christian community includes no rich or poor, and all enjoy their share. "With every common blessing bless'd / They nothing *have*, yet all *possess*."[19]

On verses 34-35 of Acts 4, Charles writes a superb stewardship hymn, which was never included in any hymnbook.

1. Which of the Christians now
    Would his possessions sell?
    The fact ye scarce allow,
    The truth incredible,
   That men of old so weak should prove,
   And as themselves their neighbour love.

2. Of your redundant store
    Ye may a few relieve,
    But all to feed the poor

---

18. *Unpublished Poetry*, 2:295-96 (Acts 4:32); see *A Song for the Poor*, 8-9.
19. This author's italics and change of verb tense.

Ye cannot, cannot give,
Houses & lands for Christ forego,
Or live as Jesus liv'd below.

3. Jesus, thy church inspire
    With Apostolic love,
Infuse the one desire
    T'insure our wealth above,
Freely with earthly goods to part,
And joyfully sell all in heart.

4. With thy pure Spirit fill'd,
    And loving Thee alone,
We shall our substance yield,
    Call nothing here our own,
Whate'er we have or are submit
And lie, as beggars, at thy feet.[20]

Notice how strongly the theme of self-divestment runs through these texts. He realizes, perhaps reluctantly, that "all to feed the poor / ye cannot, cannot give." What, then, do followers of Jesus do? They freely part with earthly goods and "joyfully sell all in heart." They call nothing on earth their own. They fully yield whatever they call "our substance." They submit all that they have and are to Christ. Indeed, they lie as beggars at his feet. What could be more fundamental to the social outreach and policy of the community of believers than these views from Holy Scripture as interpreted by Charles? One does not purchase grace; it is an undeserved and unearned gift of God.

(2) *The community of believers in Jesus Christ does not covet earthly goods and riches*. The church is filled with the problems evoked by covetousness. Not surprisingly, one of the Ten Commandments found in the Hebrew Scriptures admonishes God's children not to covet—anything. But this desire seems to be an essential drive of human nature—to look at something and say *That is mine* or *I want it to be mine*.

Reflecting on Acts 20:33, "I have coveted no man's silver, or gold, or apparel," Charles speaks of the peril not only of possessions but also of assuming God's seat of judgment and of casting dispersions upon those who are rich.

---

20. *Unpublished Poetry*, 2:297-98; see also *A Song for the Poor*, 8-9.

The servant of a Master poor,
Possest of treasures that endure,
Can no terrestrial good desire,
Silver, or gold, or gay attire;
Nor will he judge who riches have,
Limit th'Almighty's power to save,
Or lump them with invidious zeal,
And rashly send them all to hell.[21]

If you serve One who himself was poor and through him you receive eternal treasures that endure, then the things of this world cannot be the object of your desire: silver, gold, or clothing. However, Charles offers a strong caution to all who would indict the rich as not being redeemable by God. God has the power to save even the rich. The community of faith may not condemn them corporately to hell. Within Charles's poetical reflections, then, we meet a tension between how to deal with those who *have* and those who *have not*. At times, he moves closer to an ascetic view of life than his brother John, who, quite pragmatically, encouraged all to earn, save, and give as much as they could and even established possibilities of credit for the dispossessed so that they might have viable economic options. Nevertheless, Charles did not completely forsake the rich. He implored them to share with the poor, but he knew that he must leave their destiny to God's judgment and not to his own.

(3) *The community of faith is marked by grace that cannot be procured by alms for the poor.* Charles finds the foundation for this characteristic of the followers of Jesus Christ in Luke 3:11, "He that hath two coats, let him impart to him that hath none."

Alms cannot alone, we know,
    Cannot grace from God procure,
Yet at his command we show
    Mercy to the helpless poor;
When our sins we truly leave,
    We our neighbour's wants supply,
Till to us the Saviour give
    Food and raiment from the sky.[22]

---

21. Ibid., 2:403.
22. Ibid., 2:87.

Giving to the poor does not purchase God's grace. Charles sees Jesus' admonition as a divine command that requires obedience of Christ's followers. This imperative is not an option. They are to show mercy to the helpless poor. This approach goes a step beyond what rugged individualism is willing to admit. You may give to the poor, but after all, one has a right to expect something in return, namely, that the poor who receive the gift will demonstrate that they are not worthless bums who simply want to soak society of every possible penny on a perpetual basis. Does not society have a right to expect that the poor will want to pull themselves out of the squalor of poverty? Should they not want to better themselves? Should they not want to seek employment so that they rise above the category of the helpless poor? Clearly, John Wesley was engaged in organized activities for economic betterment of the poor, programs that could do precisely these things. But Charles raises an important issue for the community of faith: They have an obligation to the helpless poor. If someone has two coats and the helpless poor has none, then Christ's command is to give one away without qualification or conditions. "Yet at his command we show / Mercy to the helpless poor." By responding in this way, the community of faith supplies its neighbor's wants or needs and leaves its own sins behind, especially the sins of affluence and indifference.

An Ultimate Theological Imperative and an Ultimate Social Principle

A number of additional Wesley texts allow for a cohesive theological and social interpretation of the Christian response to poverty.[23]

(1) *An ultimate theological imperative for the community of faith is "gospel poverty."* In Wesleyan literature, this theological concept is found only in the Charles Wesley text based on Acts 4:36-37. This passage refers to the action of the Levite Barnabas, who sold a field and brought the funds from the sale as an offering. Wesley interprets the text in this way:

> See here an Apostolic priest,
> Commission'd from the sky,

---

23. I have referred to both of these dimensions of life and ministry with and among the poor in *A Song for the Poor* (pp. 5-12) but not explicitly in the sense of an "ultimate theological imperative" and "an ultimate social principle" for the life of the community of faith in its relationship to the poor.

Who dares of all himself divest,
   The needy to supply!
A primitive example rare
   Of gospel-poverty,
To feed the flock his only care,
   And like his Lord to be.[24]

What is gospel poverty? It is not a bereft gospel, one with no enrichment for the community of faith. Rather, it is complete self-divestment. Gospel poverty is daring to give up all in order to supply the needs of others; to have as one's only care "to feed the flock." Once again, Charles does not see this imperative as an option but as "commissioned from the sky." Yet, he clearly understands that it is a rare "primitive example."

The concept of *gospel poverty* is related to that of *perfection*, for personal poverty is a mandate for going on toward perfection.

Thus, thus may I the prize pursue,
and all the appointed paths pass through
   to perfect poverty:
thus let me, Lord, thyself attain,
and give thee up thine own again,
   forever lost in thee.[25]

Self-divestment receives a further interpretation and emphasis in another text from *Short Hymns,* where personal poverty, or gospel poverty, is specifically related to perfection.

"Ye shall be perfect" here below,
he spoke it, and it must be so;
   but first he said, "Be poor;
"hunger, and thirst, repent and grieve,
"in humble, meek obedience live,
   "and labor, and endure."[26]

According to Charles, Christ's mandate, "Ye shall be perfect," has a prerequisite, namely, "Be poor." These two are mutual imperatives.

---

24. *Unpublished Poetry,* 2:298-99; this author's italics.
25. *Songs for the Poor,* no. 7; from *Short Hymns on Select Passages of the Holy Scriptures,* 2 vols. (Bristol: Farley, 1762), 2:140. Here Charles Wesley expands the concept of *gospel poverty* to *perfect poverty.*
26. Ibid.

All the requirements—hungering, thirsting, repenting, grieving, and living in humble, meek obedience, laboring and enduring—all are the marks of gospel poverty in the lives of Christ's followers. They describe the life-posture and lifestyle of the faithful who are going on to perfection, to perfect poverty. This perspective signals a radical departure from a mere spiritualized concept of the doctrine of perfection. Charles is saying that perfection is directly related to the social location of the individual in his or her context. If one is not willing to divest oneself of worldly things that inhibit perfection, that starve and deprive the hungry, then one cannot experience gospel poverty or perfect poverty. Indeed, one will have an extremely difficult time going on to perfection. These mutual imperatives are but two ways of expressing the same theological idea.

One additional Charles Wesley poem, only recently published, provides an interesting dimension to the interpretation of the relationship of *perfection* and *the poor*. The work is based on Luke 14:34, "If the salt have lost his savor, wherewith shall it be seasoned?" The passage precipitates a prayer that Charles eloquently composed and that Christ's followers should always be praying:

> O may I ever be
>   The least in my own eyes,
> Retain my poverty,
>   And labour for the prize,
> And always dread th'apostate's doom
> And watch, and pray, till Jesus come![27]

As Wesley clearly states in the previously cited poem, the first summons or mandate that precedes hungering, thirsting, repenting, obeying, laboring, and enduring is "be poor." You cannot go on to perfection unless you are willing to be poor. Hence, it is not surprising that he prays, "O may I ever . . . retain my poverty."

Is this view not a spiritualized concept of *poverty* and *the poor*? Indeed, but it is more—it is also a socialized concept of *gospel poverty* that affects how the individual Christian and the faith community care for one another and help the helpless poor, how they share, labor, and endure. The world has yet to experience a Christianity that lives in full measure according to Charles Wesley's concept of *gospel poverty*, which, according to his interpretation, is authentically biblical in its

---

27. *Unpublished Poetry*, 2:152; this author's italics.

foundation. Christianity and the world do, in fact, have the examples of St. Francis of Assisi, Mother Teresa, Albert Schweitzer, and many unsung heroes and heroines of the faith who are examples of gospel poverty, of true self-divestment for Christ and the gospel. But the church of Jesus Christ, be it in the East or West, North or South, has yet fully to commit its life and resources to gospel poverty.

(2) *One of the ultimate social principles for the community of faith articulated by Charles Wesley is, "Help us to make the poor our friends."*[28] The community of faith is to be characterized by the reality that it makes friends of the poor. It does so following Christ's example.

1. The poor as Jesus' bosom-friends,
      the poor he makes his latest care,
   to all his followers commends,
      and wills us on our hands to bear;
   the poor our dearest care we make,
   and love them for our Savior's sake.

2. Whate'er thou dost to us entrust,
      with thy peculiar blessing blest,
   O make us diligent and just,
      as stewards faithful to the least,
   endowed with wisdom to possess
   the mammon of unrighteousness.

3. Help us to make the poor our friends,
      by that which paves the way to hell,
   that when our loving labor ends,
      and dying from this earth we fail,
   our friends may greet us in the skies
   born to a life that never dies.[29]

The first stanza is based on Acts 20:35-36: "I have shewed you all things, how that so labouring ye ought to support the weak, and to remember the words of the Lord Jesus, how he said, It is more blessed to give than to receive. And when he had thus spoken, he kneeled down, and prayed with them all." The second and third stanzas are based on Luke 16:9, "And I say unto you, Make to yourselves friends of the mammon of unrighteousness; that, when ye fail, they may receive you into everlasting habitations."

28. This Charles Wesley text is also cited in *A Song for the Poor* (p. 8), in the sense of a vocation rather than as an ultimate social principle.
29. *Songs for the Poor*, no. 3; see *Unpublished Poetry*, 2:157, 404 (the final couplet of stanza 1 is this author's alteration of the last four lines of an original eight-line stanza; cf. 2:404).

To aid the helpless poor is one thing, but to make them your friends is quite another. The faith community has the model of Jesus as its guide: Jesus makes the poor his "bosom-friends." They are his latest care, in other words, his most vital care, and he commends those who follow him to make the poor their "dearest care." What can be more important to the faith community? What is dearer than the believers' dearest care? In the spirit of the gospel message, Charles affirms friendship of and care for the poor as top priorities for those following Jesus. When they love the poor, they are loving Jesus. Faith communities in the Wesleyan tradition and other traditions have often sung the refrain of the gospel hymn, "There is a name I love to hear":

> O how I love Jesus,
> O how I love Jesus,
> O how I love Jesus,
> because he first loved me.

But they have probably not thought that this was synonymous with saying or singing,

> O how I love poor folk,
> O how I love poor folk,
> O how I love poor folk,
> because Jesus first loved them.

Yet, for a church that would follow Holy Scripture and Charles Wesley's interpretation of it, this parallel theological concept is precisely what should imbue its life and witness.

Loving Jesus and loving the poor are mutual imperatives, and such love articulates in word and deed an ultimate social principle for all who follow Jesus. These imperatives evoke the constant prayer, individually and corporately, that Wesley has created for private devotion and corporate worship: "Help us to make the poor our friends." The ultimate reward is that these are the friends who will greet us in heaven.

A Word of Caution

A discussion of the poor may easily tend to be one-sided, as though there is no redemption for the wealthy and as though Jesus

116

and the Wesleys have no concern for either their salvation or their viable integration into the community of faith as active and faithful participants. Nothing could be further from the truth. The rise of liberation theology and other dimensions of theological concern have quickened the church's sensitivity to this indispensable arena of faithful Christian witness and service, namely, life with and among the poor and the common sharing of resources. With this development, one may easily succumb to a singular emphasis that lacks balance. James H. Charlesworth, Professor of New Testament Language and Literature at Princeton Theological Seminary, shapes this word of caution eloquently.

Many persons interested in missions are rightly confused by liberation theology. It is marvelous to see systematic theologians, like Gustavo Gutiérrez, take the Bible seriously in a way unparalleled by such specialists in Europe and America. But as Norbert F. Lohfink, states, the liberation theologians have not represented all the challenging ideas on poverty and the rich preserved in our Bibles.[30] God is certainly on the side of the poor and the oppressed, but as Mother Teresa stated and showed, the rich often are more hungry for God than the poor. Is the Good News not for them also? Moreover, Jesus did not commence a movement among the poor, as Deissmann thought.[31] Recent sociological and anthropological studies indicate that Jesus attracted all segments of society.[32] I cannot find one of his Twelve who was poor. James and John, the sons of Zebedee, were well-to-do if not wealthy. Judas certainly was not one of the poor, if he was in charge of the money of the Twelve, as reported in the Gospel of John. Peter and Matthew were probably moderately wealthy. Jesus came to speak to the needs of all, whether they were poor or wealthy.[33]

---

30. See N. F. Lohfink, *Option for the Poor: The Basic Principle of Liberation Theology in the Light of the Bible*, Berkeley Lectures Series 1 (North Richland Hills, Tex.: Bibal Press, 1995). Also see Lohfink's *God on the Side of the Poor: Biblical Investigations in Liberation Theology*, in preparation.

31. Adolf Deissmann, *Licht vom Osten*, 4th ed. (Tübingen: J. C. B. Mohr, 1923).

32. For example, when Jesus called James and John, the sons of Zebedee, they left their father and the hired servants in the boat (Mark 1:20). See esp. A. Malherbe, *Social Aspects of Early Christianity*, 2d ed. (Philadelphia: Fortress Press, 1983); Wayne A. Meeks, *The First Urban Christians: The Social World of the Apostle Paul* (New Haven, Conn.: Yale University Press, 1983); P. Lampe, *Die stadtrömischen Christen in den ersten beiden Jahrhunderten: Untersuchungen zur Sozialgeschichte* (WUNT Reihe 2.18; Tübingen: J. C. B. Mohr, 1989); Bengt Holmberg, "The Social Level of the First Christians," in his *Sociology and the New Testament: An Appraisal* (Minneapolis: Fortress Press, 1990), 21-76.

33. Text and footnotes from James H. Charlesworth, "Evangelization, Creation, and Christian Origins," unpublished paper presented at "Evangelization and Creation: the Meaning of Redemption," a missions and evangelism consultation in Leesburg, Florida, 15 January 1998.

Without question, the Wesleys reached out to the well-to-do and well-educated of eighteenth-century England, though it would be wrong to suggest that the Methodist Societies were overflowing with them. The London "West-end connection" should not be forgotten—the people who parked their carriages in Drury Lane and frequented the best cultural events of London including performances at the Covent Garden Opera House. George Frederick Handel, famed composer of the oratorio, *Messiah*, and head conductor at the opera house, was moved to set at least three of Charles Wesley's hymn texts to music. John Lampe, composer and first bassoonist of the opera house orchestra under Handel, probably became a Methodist and, in 1746, published the folio volume *Hymns on the Great Festivals and Other Occasions* containing his own musical settings of twenty-three Charles Wesley hymns and one of Samuel Wesley, Jr.'s hymns. The associations with the Countess of Huntingdon, Lady Hotham, and many others are well known from the diaries and journals of John and Charles, and the latter pays tribute to a number of nobility in his death poems.

The voluminous repertory of literature written and edited by John Wesley also helps foster a balanced view of the outreach of the eighteenth-century Methodist movement. For whom was he preparing grammar textbooks of English, French, Latin, Greek, and Hebrew; a compendium of logic; and works on world history and electricity?[34] He believed that all people who had committed their lives to the God of creation should seek to learn all they could about creation. Hence, much of what he wrote and edited was designed to provide a broad spectrum of literature to all, both rich and poor.

While it is not my purpose to discuss extensively the Wesleys' outreach to the wealthy and well-educated, one should keep a balanced view of both their ministry with and among the poor and their outreach to all people regardless of their economic or intellectual status.

Conclusion

We indicated at the outset that most of the poetical texts cited here were probably written more for theological reflection than for corporate song. Nevertheless, Charles Wesley's telescopic way of focus-

---

34. See *Works* (Jackson), 14:1-189.

ing the character and nature of the poor, the vicarious role of the poor in the world, the nature of the community of believers and its mutual sharing of resources, and particularly the powerful concepts of *gospel poverty* and *perfect poverty*, can help individual Christians and the corporate body of the church in the new millennium to discover a viable life with the poor and hence with Jesus Christ, the Savior. In fact, Charles can help all Christians learn that to seek perfection without both self-divestment and life with and among the poor may indeed be futile. Yes, without these actions, life with Christ and the way toward perfection may not be possible.

CHAPTER SIX

Eighteenth-Century Methodism and the London Poor

Gareth Lloyd

We are fortunate that two particularly important sources of information have survived to allow for a careful examination of outreach to the poor by the London Methodist Society from 1760 until the end of the eighteenth century. The Poor Fund account book of West Street Chapel from 1764 to 1796 and the London Society account book from 1766 to 1802, which have not been used to any great extent by scholars, contain a wealth of detail.[1] Their detailed contents must be understood within the context of the broader view of Methodism in the capital during this period.

London Methodism

The London Society was the most important Methodist Society in Great Britain and had been so since the birth of the Methodist revival at the end of the 1730s. By December 1743, total membership in the city stood at 2,200; by 1760, it had risen to just over 2,500.[2] While the London Society had the highest membership of any in Britain throughout the eighteenth century, the city was not, and indeed

---

1. Both are on deposit at the Methodist Archives and Research Centre, John Rylands University Library of Manchester.

2. George Stevenson, *City Road Chapel, London, and its Associations, Historical, Biographical and Memorial* (London: Methodist Book Concern, 1872), 28, 49.

never has been, what one would term a Methodist stronghold. This apparent contradiction is explained by looking at membership as a percentage of the population. When viewed in this way, London lagged considerably behind other urban centers particularly in the North of England. For example, the Methodist Society in Manchester had a membership of 2,050 in 1791 compared to 2,950 for London despite the fact that London's population was at least twelve times greater.[3] Even the small Yorkshire town of Birstal had 1,230 people in the Society that year.

The importance of the London Society was not based on its size but on the city's place at the center of national life. The leadership of Methodism may have been peripatetic to a large degree, but if there was a national headquarters, then it was the Foundery in the Moorfields District of the city. From there (and later from City Road Chapel) John Wesley planned his movements, and Connexional activities such as publishing and book distribution were also concentrated there.[4]

The Foundery was the first specifically Wesleyan Methodist building in London, adapted for that purpose during the winter of 1739–40.[5] From then until its supercession by City Road Chapel in 1778, it was the largest and most important building in British Methodism, with seating for fifteen hundred people and sufficient space to permit a wide range of services including a medical dispensary, school, alms houses, and accommodations.[6]

Such was the success of Methodism in the early years that in the spring of 1743, Wesley acquired the lease on his first consecrated building, a former Huguenot church on West Street in the area known as Seven Dials.[7] The Methodists used this building until 1798 when the congregation moved to a new location on Great Queen Street. Unlike the Foundery, the West Street building still stands as commercial premises.

In the same year that West Street opened, the Wesleys were offered a third preaching house at Snowsfields, south of the river Thames. To these was added Spitalfields on Great Eagle Street, which

---

3. *Minutes* (Mason), 1:251-52. The population of Manchester in the census year of 1801 stood at just over 70,000 while that of London was 900,000.

4. Frank Cumbers, *The Book Room* (London: Epworth Press, 1956).

5. Richard P. Heitzenrater, *Wesley and the People Called Methodists* (Nashville: Abingdon Press, 1995), 109.

6. J. Henry Martin, *John Wesley's London Chapels* (London: Epworth Press, 1946), 25-26.

7. Ibid., 47-49.

Methodist historians record as opening in 1750.[8] Interestingly however, Roque's map of 1746 specifies that there was already a Methodist meeting house in that precise location, representing a puzzle for which there is no ready solution.

Work commenced on a Methodist preaching house in Westminster in about 1750,[9] and although the building has left little trace in the secondary sources, it was important enough to be listed in the London steward's book until 1780. During its last three years, however, it did not render any accounts, indicating that while it retained a worship function, it had no control over its own affairs. One other Methodist building, Wapping Chapel in the East End of the city, opened in 1764.[10]

These preaching houses are the only ones listed in the steward's book of the Society. There were others that were certainly in existence such as Deptford and Poplar, which were built in 1757 and 1772 respectively.[11] It is curious that the steward's book does not mention all of the Methodist locations in the city. It may be, that for administrative reasons, certain ones were grouped together. Certainly much work remains to be done on the detailed organization of Methodism at the grassroots level. London was unique in having more than one preaching house. Even in cities like Manchester and Bristol, second and third Methodist chapels were not built until the closing years of the century.

Methodist Social Concern

The practical expressions of Methodist social concern can be divided into two groups: giving that was channeled through the Society and therefore appears in the accounts and additional acts of generosity by individual Methodists. The latter included some of Wesley's wealthy followers, the banker Ebenezer Blackwell being a well-known example.[12] The obituaries in Stevenson's *City Road Chapel* invariably mention their subjects' generosity and involvement with charitable organizations. One particularly noteworthy philanthropist was William Marriott, who acted as the City Road Steward in 1788

---

8. Ibid., 52.
9. Ibid., 51-52.
10. Ibid., 54.
11. Ibid., 55-56.
12. *The Encyclopedia of World Methodism*, ed. Nolan B. Harmon, 2 vols. (Nashville: The United Methodist Publishing House, 1974), 1:282.

and collected the money to pay for Charles Wesley's funeral.[13] Marriott lived a simple lifestyle and devoted his considerable wealth to worthy causes. His giving was often anonymous, transacted through third parties. After his death in 1815, it was revealed that in one three-year period alone, he had given away more than £16,000.[14]

Methodists have traditionally been active in establishing charities. One of the most important was the Strangers' Friend Society, founded in 1785 by the London Methodist, John Gardner, to "look after the 'destitute sick poor, without distinction of sect or country, at their own habitations.' "[15] Within a few years, the Society had branches as far afield as Manchester and Dublin.[16] On a more local level, chapels often had specific funds attached to them, such as the Friendly Union Benefit Society, which was set up at West Street in 1756.[17] Contributions to such causes were sometimes made from chapel or Society funds, but in most respects, they appear to have been operated separately.

Direct Relief to the Poor

The provision of direct relief to the poor is reflected in the London Society accounts. The official who would have been responsible for their compilation was the steward, whose duties were laid down by the first conference of 1744 and included the following:

1. To manage the temporal things of the Society.
2ndly. To receive the weekly contributions of the leaders of the classes.
3rdly. To expend what is needful from time to time.
4thly. To send reliefe to the poor . . .
6thly. To keep an exact account of receipts & expenses.[18]

The stewards, as the financial officers of Methodism, would have been the officials with the greatest personal involvement in giving to the poor. Because of the weight of the stewards' responsibilities, the Lon-

---

13. Stevenson, *City Road Chapel*, 94.
14. Ibid., 573.
15. *Encyclopedia of World Methodism*, 2:2261.
16. Leslie F. Church, *More about the Early Methodist People* (London: Epworth Press, 1949), 194.
17. John Telford, *Two West End Chapels: Sketches of London Methodism from Wesley's Day* (London: Wesleyan Methodist Book Room, 1886), 71.
18. John Bennet, MS Minutes of the First Conference (Methodist Archives and Research Centre, John Rylands University Library of Manchester), 19.

don Society required sixteen of them during the early 1740s, although this number was reduced to seven by the end of the decade.[19]

Among the rules governing the stewards' conduct was the injunction that expenditure had to be balanced by income and that the Society's accounts were to be done on a weekly basis. Of particular interest is the warning that they should not give an ill look or word to anyone asking for relief—"Do not hurt them if ye cannot help them."

In the West Street Chapel Poor Fund ledger, the left page lists income from various sources. By far the greatest proportion of this was from the weekly penny contribution made by class members. There does not appear to have been any uniformity of practice in British Methodism with regard to the disbursement of this money. In some areas, it was used to help finance such things as the construction of a chapel while in others it was earmarked to provide for the maintenance of traveling preachers.[20]

Other sources of income included donations in the poor box and money raised by special collections on occasions such as Easter and Whitsunday. The ledger also contains records of personal gifts made by named individuals or from legacies. The amount raised by collections could vary considerably, depending to some extent on the occasion. The collection made at the Watchnight service on August 6, 1784, apparently raised nothing while the special collection made at the end of that month for the support of preachers in America raised the substantial sum of £13 6s.

The right page lists some of the ways the money was spent. The West Street stewards had a broad definition of who constituted *the poor*, for example the housekeeper who was given five shillings and three pence at Christmas and the American preachers who were given money from a collection. These examples are simply another reflection of Methodism as, overwhelmingly, a poor person's church. The appearance of the simple notation, "To poor," hides a wealth of activity. We know from other sources that, in London, the leaders brought in the money collected from the class members and also participated in the distribution to deserving people.[21] Considerable effort would have been expended by the class leaders and other Methodists in finding out who was in need and responding in a timely and effective

---

19. Stevenson, *City Road Chapel*, 40.

20. Gordon Rupp and Rupert Davies, eds., *A History of the Methodist Church in Great Britain*, 4 vols. (London: Epworth Press, 1965–1988), 1:227.

21. Richard Viney's diary of 1744, cited in Rupp and Davies, *History*, 1:227.

fashion. The recorder also made a careful distinction in the accounts between those who were helped on a weekly and on a monthly basis.

Sometimes specific cases are recorded in the ledger by name, such as the four shillings given to Brother Barham for bread and the money collected for Kingswood School and for the benefit of Charles Wesley's poor, presumably individuals in whom Charles took a personal interest. Occasional administrative costs are also recorded, such as advertising for a charity sermon in February 1776. Most of the money, however, would have been spent directly on people in need.

Attitudes Toward Poverty

John Wesley expected a great deal from his followers in terms of commitment, not just spiritual but also material. He had a strict definition of wealth, namely, the possession of money beyond what was needed for food and clothes with a little left over.[22] He also declared that retention of such surplus sums for personal use amounted to theft from God. Wesley, therefore, saw nothing wrong in expecting his followers to give unsparingly, even when most people would have regarded them as poor themselves.

His uncompromising attitude led to criticism. In one letter of March 1760, his brother Charles writes scathingly of John's expectations with regard to his London followers:

How many collections think you has my brother made between Thursday evening and Sunday? No fewer than seven. Five this one day from the same poor exhausted people. He has no mercy on them, on the GIVING poor I mean; as if he was in haste to reduce them to the number of RECEIVING poor.[23]

John, of course, set a rigorous personal example. He took pride in the fact that when staying at the Foundery, he and his preachers ate at the same table and from the same food as the poor.[24] It is hardly surprising that the Methodists held their leader in high regard, despite his demands, or that they responded as best they could.

22. Sermon 131, "The Danger of Increasing Riches," I.1, Works, 4:179.
23. Charles Wesley, MS letter to his wife, Sarah, 2 March 1760, Methodist Archives and Research Centre, John Rylands University Library of Manchester.
24. "A Plain Account of the People Called Methodists," XIII.2, Works, 9:277.

London Society Book

The London Society book contains comprehensive details of income and expenditure from all quarters of the Society in the city and, therefore, has a wider interest than the West Street poor account, which relates specifically to that chapel.[25] Careful examination of the Society book provides a number of valuable insights into the inner workings of Methodism. For example, the sacramental collections at the Foundery raised significantly less money than those at West Street and Spitalfields. The probable explanation is that the latter were consecrated buildings and for this reason were favored for sacramental services. John Bowmer expressed doubt that the Foundery was used for communion at all during the early years, although he was unaware of when that policy changed.[26] The Steward's book reveals that sacramental collections at the Foundery commenced in 1768.

Such evidence reveals that in important aspects, the spiritual focus of the movement in London was not at the Foundery despite its administrative significance. The Foundery, an unconsecrated building, was not regarded as a chapel. With the opening of City Road Chapel in 1778, built as a sacramental structure, Methodism in the city experienced a major change. Income at Spitalfields in particular was reduced to a fraction of what it had been, indicating a shift in importance to City Road, along with a part of the congregation. Spitalfields was less than a mile from the new building on City Road, whereas West Street, which seems to have survived the opening of the new chapel much better, was about twice the distance.

Among the sources of income listed in the Society Book were collections for the furtherance of the Gospel, seat rents, class and band money, and the Poor Box, which for unknown reasons only appeared under the listing for the Foundery despite the fact that we know from the West Street Poor Fund records that there was also one at that chapel. The largest single source of revenue was again the class money. In 1775 this source accounted for £443 at the Foundery and represented over half of the congregation's income. In contrast, the

---

25. The exact relationship between these two documents is unclear. The records do not immediately reveal whether the two accounts were strictly separate or whether the West Street fund was incorporated into the Society account. Clarity in this matter would require a more detailed examination of the actual figures than is possible here.

26. John Bowmer, *The Sacrament of the Lord's Supper in Early Methodism* (London: Dacre Press, 1951), 67.

bands accounted for just under £19, underlining the fundamental importance of the class as a unit of organization.

The expenditures listed on the right page encompass the running costs of the Society. Here again, one can see the paramount place of the Foundery. The costs of housekeeping alone amounted to £281, more than three times the bill for the other London chapels put together. Perhaps most illuminating of all is that the Foundery was the only Methodist site in London with a budget for stationery and furniture. Of course, the Foundery was also a center for spiritual activities—it was, for example, the principal venue in London for Love Feasts, as shown by the fact that of £15 16s spent on buns in London, £13 8s was accounted for by the Foundery.

The records of the allowances paid to the preachers are also revealing. Charles Wesley was paid the largest amount as the most senior ordained minister in permanent residence in London. The itinerants received varying amounts of money depending on their family circumstances. Separate provision was made for the wives of three named preachers.

The largest item of expenditure was that for the poor. In 1775, this amount was over £784 for the Society as a whole, more than a third of the annual expenditure. At individual chapels, the proportion could be even higher—in 1769, for instance, the West Street congregation spent £49 12s on the poor, out of an income of just £92 9s 7d. Additionally, money was spent on what might be termed *causes arising from the institutional poverty of Methodism*: £21 11s spent on the funeral of the preacher John Downes and £15 4s collected in 1773 for the Lending Stock. Clearly, eighteenth-century Methodism represented the poor helping the poor. Aside from individuals like Marriott and Blackwell, the Methodists as a group were not wealthy, a consideration that renders the sheer extent of giving even more impressive.

Money given to the poor does not appear to have come from a single source. The class money or the sacramental offerings within the Society were not earmarked for such a purpose. The money spent on helping the poor was far in excess of any single source of revenue. And within the strict proviso that expenditure had to be balanced by income, there was considerable flexibility in the Society's response to various needs. As an institution, Methodism responded to Wesley's demand that anything left over from providing for necessities should be given to help others. Wesley was concerned that societies not overextend themselves financially, for example by incurring a large chapel-building debt. If the London Society can be regarded as typical, money that was saved by the exercise of strict financial prudence was normally devoted to charitable rather than institutional purposes.

These financial records also reveal that while Methodism in London consisted of several constituent congregations, the sense of identity as one Society was very strong. Expenditure at the Foundery exceeded income by the considerable sum of £326. This shortfall was covered by West Street and Spitalfields, where the balance sheet showed a healthy surplus. This sense of community was also reflected in worship. While the Foundery was favored for Love Feasts, the sacramental services tended to be held elsewhere. It must have been common for London Methodists to have worshiped at sites in the city other than their usual chapel. It would be interesting to know if this was a deliberate policy on Wesley's part.

Changing Priorities at the End of the Century

Toward the end of the century, prioritization of expenditure began to change, which had an impact on the provision of direct relief to the poor. The Society accounts for the 1790s reveal an interesting pattern, which is illustrated in the following table by the figures for 1800. The records reveal an increased number of demands on Methodist funds. Overseas missions, Sunday and day schools, and particularly ministers and preachers and their families began to gain considerable attention. At both Great Queen Street and City Road Chapels, the largest single source of expense in 1800 was the allowances paid to ministers. At City Road, this expense amounted to £841[27]—over half of the total expenditure for that year—compared to the £332 that had been spent on the preachers at the Foundery in 1775. [28]

At the same time, money given directly to the poor amounted to £429, representing a considerable reduction compared to the earlier period. It could be argued that causes such as Sunday Schools were primarily devoted to the poor in any case. But it appears from this evidence that money given in direct relief—the actual putting of bread on the table and clothes on the back, which would of course have been of great importance to the destitute as opposed to those who were merely "poor"—was being drastically reduced. This tendency

---

27. The money was spent on furnishings, stationery, salary, family allowances, medicine, and traveling expenses.
28. This figure takes into account changes in accounting.

is made clear by the following table, which shows figures extracted at approximate five-year intervals from the Steward's book. The proportion of money given to the poor in 1775, expressed as a percentage of Society income, was 36 percent. By 1802, the last year of the Steward's book in this particular volume, it had fallen to just 14 percent.

Year	Society Income/Expenditure	Direct Relief to Poor	Percentage
1770	£2,464	£760	31%
1775	£2,212	£784	36%
1780	£2,129	£763	36%
1786	£3,389	£645	19%
1790	£3,256	£659	20%
1795	£2,189	£540	25%
1800	£3,537	£559	16%
1802	£3,767	£528	14%

These percentages are reflected to a certain extent in the figures for the West Street Poor Fund. In 1775, the fund spent about £230; by 1795, this figure had fallen to £148. And from 1788, class money no longer appears as a source of revenue in the West Street accounts, having been replaced by collections and gifts. It is surely of symbolic significance that the former most important source of revenue should have been diverted to other purposes.

Such statistics at the end of the century display the opening of a gulf between the Methodist Church (as it had now become) and the people with whom it had once been primarily concerned. One might say that a major difference between Methodism as a revival movement and Methodism as a church was the greater awareness of institutional needs by the latter. In his closing years, John Wesley seems to have been aware of and hated this change in priority.[29] The Steward's book seems to indicate that his complaints regarding the younger generation of Methodists were more than an old man's nostalgia after a golden age.

Two important questions remain: (1) How typical of British Methodism was the London Society in this respect? (2) Are these accounts, taken in isolation, an accurate reflection of what was happening in London? The fact that we are probably unable to give answers highlights the need to give more attention to the study of Methodism in the area where it made the most impact, namely, in the lives of ordinary people.

---

29. This point is discussed at length by Theodore Jennings in chapter eight of his book *Good News to the Poor: John Wesley's Evangelical Economics* (Nashville: Abingdon Press, 1990).

CHAPTER SEVEN

Friends of All?
The Wesleyan Response to Urban Poverty in Britain and Ireland, 1785–1840

Tim Macquiban

The Strangers' Friend Societies were established in London and provincial cities to engage in mission alongside the urban poor. An examination of the Societies' work also reveals a great deal about the attitudes of British Methodism toward the poor from the 1780s to 1840—how Methodists received and developed the "evangelical economics" of Wesley's teaching and praxis.[1] While the theological and social rationale for their work did not significantly differ from prevailing Anglican social thought, the place of lay people of lower social status within the movement and their hands-on approach to the poor was in marked contrast to the paternalistic attitudes of other Church people. The reasons and motivation for the Societies' work were a mixture of concerns for the spiritual welfare of all. A warm humanitarian spirit was modified by both hardening social attitudes that stressed the "reformation of manners" and the nature of the Societies' role as an agency of social control more than social concern. The Strangers' Friend Societies' (SFS) own development and decline mirror the distancing of Wesleyan Methodism from the urban poor of Britain and Ireland and the concentration of resources more on overseas than on home missions.

---

1. In my recent studies in this area, I have made extensive use of Methodist sources—printed sermons, ministers' writings, and Conference publications—and have also looked closely at the work of the Strangers' Friend Societies.

The Social Context

At the beginning of this period, London had a population of nearly one million people. Forty years later, the population had almost doubled. With wars and economic fluctuations, this period was a time of social and political unrest exacerbated by food crises and years of trade depression.[2] At least one tenth of the population was reduced to beggary. Yet thousands continued to flock to the metropolis in search of work, creating a city of marked contrasts between wealth and poverty in which the "poor districts became an immense *terra incognita* periodically mapped out by intrepid missionaries and explorers who catered to an insatiable middle-class demand for travellers' tales."[3] The churches were among the social agencies that addressed the condition of poverty and the poor, with a missionary zeal for the conversion of England as well as the amelioration of the physical needs of the poor.

Antecedents, Origins, and Development of the SFS from 1785

The Strangers' Friend Society was established in London by John Gardner and other members of the City Road Methodist Society in 1785, with the approval of John Wesley, as an arm of social outreach to the poor, complementing the work of the Sunday schools. From the beginning, the SFS relied on lay initiative and leadership, both in the Committee and through the Visitors who sought out the poor in their miserable attics and cellars in the surrounding districts of Spitalfields and the East End. The Society began as a small-scale operation with regular subscriptions to aid those who were friendless, especially the unemployed and widowed. The members were not required to be Methodists. The group quickly expanded through the encouragement and patronage of Adam Clarke, not only within London, in terms of branches established by the parent body, but also to provincial cities and towns in Britain and Ireland. The Society extended its scope and organization: It gave aid to thousands of families and individuals every year, with the influential backing of prominent lay members such

2. F. H. W. Sheppard, *London 1808–1870: The Infernal Wen* (London: Secker and Warbury, 1971), 19.
3. Gareth Stedman Jones, *Outcast London: A Study in the Relationship between Classes in Victorian Society* (Oxford: Clarendon Press, 1971), 14.

as William Marriott and Joseph Butterworth. The greatest impact of the Societies was found in the 1820s. After 1840, the scope of the giving—extended in later years to benefactors beyond the bounds of Methodism—declined, as did the involvement of Methodists in the weekly visitation to the homes of the poor. The contribution they made to the welfare of the poor was generally recognized not only within Methodism but also within British society thus explaining the measure of support given to the work by Evangelical Anglicans and others who saw it as an effective way of reaching the poor. There were many examples of Methodists who had climbed the social ladder, plowing back into the community the fruits of their substantial gains in an extraordinary outpouring of the philanthropic spirit not quenched by the rising tide of skepticism of welfare measures and fear of the poor.[4] And there were many reasons for Methodist involvement with the poor, as exemplified by the work of the SFS.

Reasons and Motivation for the Work of the SFS

In the 1830s, John Thom of Liverpool questioned the motives of the Visitors, many of whom considered the poor "very ungrateful for not being overpowered by their kindness."[5] Was there any value in visiting the poor? Did the Societies propagate the very evils they intended to counteract (presumably of idleness and vice)? Did they create a source of dependency and degradation among the lower levels of the poor? What were the motives behind the investment of so much time and money in such a program of poor relief? An examination of London and provincial SFS documents reveals some of their motives.

The general remarks at the beginnings of annual reports indicate that the Committee recognized the mixture of motives and imperatives in the work of the SFS—that their desire for the physical welfare of the Christians' neighbors was not exclusively directed "to a supply of temporal necessities." In the course of the distribution of money to buy food and other things to save the bodies of the poor, they were also expected to visit great numbers of people whom they found "in a most lamentable state of ignorance." They recognized the enormity

4. Wellman Joel Warner, *The Wesleyan Movement in the Industrial Revolution* (London: Longmans, Green and Co., 1930), 192.

5. David Owen, *English Philanthropy, 1660–1960* (Cambridge, Mass.: Harvard University Press, 1964), 138.

of their task, for "to gain access to the minds of such is extremely difficult." Nevertheless, education was an appropriate role of the Visitors, to "bring them to proper reflection . . . ; to convince them that they are accountable to God . . . , that they as sinners are exposed to his displeasure . . . , to teach them the need for repentance and reformation and the humble reception of the great truths of Christianity."[6] This great opportunity of bringing physical relief, which gave them entrance into the homes of the poor, meant that they could also offer spiritual nourishment as well. Seeing this connection is the key to understanding the rationale of the work of the SFS.

In that "Age of Atonement," such middle-class values and piety would, it was hoped, foster new concepts of public probity and national honor as well as the more individual ideals of economy, frugality, morality, and financial rectitude. Such virtues were the badges of vital religion, which was a religion of the heart that responded to a world in a state of alienation from God, lost in depravity and guilt, and waiting for redemption.[7] A variety of humanitarian and spiritual motivations contributed to the philanthropic impulse of those who gave time and money to the SFS.

Desire for Spiritual Welfare

The general comments contained in the annual reports reveal an eagerness to deny that the SFS was guilty of the dreadful accusation of proselytism. The Society was keen to dissociate itself from such criticism while still acknowledging the general religious principles behind its work. In this regard, the Society had an advantage over some of the other evangelical societies that were more openly denominational in outlook and evangelistic in approach. After outlining the practical help given to recipients of relief, the first report highlights the conveying of religious instruction as a benefit, supplemental to the "pecuniary assistance," designed to remedy the ignorance of the poor and to reinforce an understanding of their "duty to God and to their neighbours." This instruction is not to be seen as proselytism, since "their desire is only to communicate religious instruction consistent with the New Testament, [and] the liturgy and Articles of the

---

6. London Strangers' Friend Society Annual Report (hereafter: LSFSAR), 1814.
7. Boyd Hilton, *The Age of Atonement: The Influence of Evangelicalism on Social and Economic Thought, 1795–1865* (Oxford: Clarendon Press, 1988), 7.

Church of England"; nor is such instruction distinctive "on account of the nation, sect, or party to which the sufferer belongs."[8]

The Christian conservatism of Edmund Burke was more to the taste of many Methodists than any Jeffersonian ideas of liberty and equality.[9] The prevailing mood of Wesleyan Methodism was expressed at their 1792 Conference in an exhortation to "honour the King and fear God." This perspective, however, did not necessarily entail political neutrality. When Lord Sidmouth's bill gave indications of government repression and restrictions on preaching, resistance was fierce. The Methodists insisted that their teaching, far from being seditious, encouraged the poor to be like themselves: "frugal, thrifty, and hardworking."[10] Thomas Allen, a Methodist local preacher, solicitor, and prime mover in coordinating resistance to the Sidmouth initiative, protested that Methodist local preachers "'would only officiate in the workhouses and small chapels, delighting mostly to address Gospel truth to the poor, the aged, the infirm, the friendless and the afflicted.'" They would not infect the disaffected with radical ideas subversive to the state.[11]

The primary desire for the spiritual welfare of the poor was evident in many of the comments of the Visitors and in the assistance they gave. This desire was also manifest in other ways. The SFS distributed Bibles and tracts. They were also involved with the Sunday school movement. The SFS pleaded to all who approved of giving religious instruction to the poor and ignorant to send books and tracts to the district officers. Some of these materials were no doubt obtained from the British and Foreign Bible Society. Where the SFS were unable to supply the books themselves, they gave money directly to the poor to pay the weekly penny subscription that the Bible and tract distributors collected.[12] In the 1830s this policy was given an added impetus by a generous donation from the Bible Society, which recognized the value of the distribution network of the SFS.

The Societies also made contact with the poor in order to get children into the growing numbers of Sunday schools. The *Annual Report* of 1816 reports on the improvement in the moral condition of the poor

8. LSFSAR, 1803.

9. J. M. Turner, *Conflict and Reconciliation: Studies in Methodism and Ecumenism in England, 1740–1982* (London: Epworth Press), 117.

10. "On Evangelical Sects," *Quarterly Review* (Nov. 1810): 489-90.

11. W. R. Ward, *Religion and Society in England: 1790–1850* (London: Batsford, 1972), 57.

12. Thomas Evans was assisted in 1814 and given money that helped him subscribe to a "Bible Association for a copy of the Holy Scriptures." LSFSAR, 1814.

thus: "Multitudes of children brought up in a state of total ignorance have been sent to Sunday Schools for the habit of regularity and acquaintance with the Holy Scriptures which inculcate their various duties to God and man."[13]

Sunday schools were not primarily designed for the advancement of working class literacy, for many people feared the consequences of educating the poor. Rather the goal of the schools was to enforce a "sense of religious obligation to the aid of Industry."[14] Such an emphasis has led E. P. Thompson and others to charge that the Sunday school movement was nothing more than a form of religious terrorism in which evangelicals indoctrinated the children of the poor in forms of moral instruction in order to make them good and obedient citizens.[15] Examples abound of the Visitors' assistance encouraging attendance at Sunday schools even though continued poverty could present a difficulty for some. Ann Howell was assisted upon the birth of her third child, her husband being a tripe man out of work. Meanwhile, their six-year-old son "went regularly to the Sunday School, till being barefoot he was obliged to stop away."[16]

Sometimes the work of the SFS clearly paralleled the efforts of the churches as with Sunday school work and tract distribution. The *Wesleyan Methodist Magazine* for 1822 reports the work of George Marsden in raising a sufficient sum of money to buy 30,000 religious tracts for distribution. Seventy people were recruited as Visitors, covering thirty-four small districts. They were to visit homes on the Lord's Day, to leave a tract, to enter into conversation with the families about "spiritual and eternal concerns," and to invite them to the "house of prayer."[17]

Such a description might seem to lend weight to J. D. Marshall's claim that the work of evangelicals in Manchester—distributing tracts and encouraging Sunday school attendance—"reinforced moral controls in education with spiritual inspiration and materials for recalling the poor to their submission to religious authority."[18] That allegation, however, is as crude as his assertion that such work was intended merely to offer the blessings of heaven to compensate for

---

13. LSFSAR, 1816.
14. John Rule, *Albion's People: English Society, 1714–1815* (New York and London: Longman, 1992), 147.
15. E. P. Thompson, *The Making of the English Working Class* (London: V. Gollancz, 1963), 376.
16. LSFSAR, 1818.
17. *Wesleyan Methodist Magazine* 45 (1822): 230.
18. John D. Marshall, *The Old Poor Law, 1795–1834* (London: Macmillan, 1968), 73.

their earthly sufferings. While evangelicalism might not have greatly extended the work of institutional religion among the poor, the SFS certainly did exhibit a genuine empathy for the plight of the poor.

Desire for a Good Death

Instruction was provided not merely to encourage reading of the Scriptures and attendance at chapels and Sunday schools. It had a greater urgency in most cases. The primary motivation was to save souls that were close to perishing, especially to help the poor die a good death. After all, John Gardner was initially persuaded to establish the Society in London in 1785 by the sight of a man dying of a fistula. As he lay on the floor dying, covered only in a sack, he exclaimed with despair, "I must die without hope." Gardner reflected, "It was to little purpose to offer comfort to the soul when the body was the subject of gnawing hunger."[19]

Frank Prochaska regards the common preoccupation with death as the "great stimulus to religious and charitable practice," born out of a desperate evangelical fear of not being converted before death.[20] This fear was a powerful theme of many reported cases and mirrors the morbid interest of the evangelicals in the need for repentance and faith before meeting God. They regarded the world as a probationary period for the soul. Heaven was the true believer's home. Earthly happiness was irrelevant by comparison. In the midst of such misery, one had to look to God for true happiness and eternal bliss. Deathbeds, Doreen Rosman suggests, had an almost sacramental function in the evangelical experience, with the recitation of faith in the saving grace of God through Christ perhaps the equivalent of the Catholic reception of the last sacrament as a rite of passage. The deathbed provided a supreme moment of opportunity to witness to the truth of the Christian gospel—an experience that should be shared with others.[21] Visitors of the SFS were in a privileged position to accompany the poor and help them realize the rewards denied them in earthly terms.

19. John Gardner, *The Grain of Mustard Seed; or, An Account of the Rise, Progress and Extensive Usefulness of the Benevolent or Strangers' Friend Society, founded 1785* (London: Christie, 1829).

20. F. K. Prochaska, *Women and Philanthropy in Nineteenth-Century England* (Oxford: Clarendon Press, 1980), 123.

21. Doreen Rosman, *Evangelicals and Culture* (London: Croom Helm, 1984), 16.

Desire for Reformation of Manners

In the assumption that many recipients of relief, both spiritual and physical, would recover, the Visitors maintained an ardent hope that ignorance would be replaced with an increased understanding of the truths of Christianity, which would then produce a new lifestyle in conformity to that of the Visitors and subscribers. This mixture of the need both to create the conditions for a good death and to achieve reformation of character is powerfully stressed in some of the annual reports of the SFS such as that for 1808:

> Many, before they were thus visited, had lived lives in habitual vice and wickedness; but they have been brought to serious reflection and turned from the error of their ways. Several of them are now useful members of society; many others have died praising God for those who pointed out to them the only remedy for the disease of their immortal souls.[22]

If indigence was seen as a result of moral failing, then, as Prochaska points out, the religious and social skills of women were ideally suited to this crusade of moral reformation. Women saw themselves as agents of social improvement, with much more time on their hands and more sympathy than the men could dispense in a work of self-sacrifice and compassion.[23] "Back to health" and "back to work" were the cornerstones of the SFS, which was influenced by the contemporary attitude that the poor were an affront and a danger to society. Women, too, had a unique role at this point, for they could bring to the philanthropic task the application of domestic skills that taught "outcast women and children the habits of honest labour." Finding jobs for girls was one aspect of this reformation of manners.[24] Religious instruction and moral reformation were the twin planks of such visiting. To befriend the poor was very much in the tradition of the Wesleyan response to poverty—to gain an intimate familiarity with their conditions of life, however sordid and remote from their own experience, and to bring relief to those who seemed to merit help. Their goal was *metanoia*—a turning around, a reformation of manners.

---

22. LSFSAR, 1808.
23. Prochaska, *Women and Philanthropy*, 7.
24. Ibid., 149.

Desire to Reward the Deserving Poor and Rich

With so many poor people in need, where was the SFS to start? With the growing debate about the nature of poverty and the right response of society, the SFS (along with others) drew back from indiscriminate relief and focused its attention on the "deserving poor," those who perceived their own need and were prepared by their own efforts to work at such a reformation of life. The strong interventionist policy of the Visitors implied that the poor were not to be entirely trusted to be able to redeem the situation for themselves. And yet, the truism "God helps those who help themselves" appears to have been a very strong motivation in choosing those for whom relief was felt appropriate—if they were prepared to do something about it themselves with suitable instruction. For example, Mary Watson's husband, a shoemaker in the army as a private, was given relief to help her in her illness because "they will again be enabled to earn their bread by honest industry . . . ; they are led seriously to fear [the Lord's] name, to reverence his laws, and to seek his salvation."[25]

But who, in the midst of so much want, was to receive such relief? Clearly, despite the claims that all were eligible, the SFS's motives necessarily dictated that the Visitors should avoid some and seek out others. The principle seems to have been to ignore the pleas of those who actively and sometimes aggressively sought relief and to reward the silence and invisibility of the more deserving poor. The nation had a general hostility toward street begging; such actions were to be ignored or suppressed. Visitors were encouraged to resist all attempts of solicitation by the poor. The visitation in the homes was intended to achieve a reformation of character that would reduce the likelihood of recourse to mendicancy.

Dislike of the Poor Law System

The more public provisions were made for the poor, the less they provided for themselves, and of course became poorer.
—*Benjamin Franklin.*[26]

Marshall and others have demonstrated how, at the end of the eighteenth century, the Old Poor Law system broke down. The poor laws had worked more or less efficiently in a rural setting, where a

25. LSFSAR, 1806.
26. Benjamin Franklin, "On the Price of Corn, and Management of the Poor," *The London Chronicle* (London, 1766).

personal service could be offered in smaller units on the basis of knowledge of the immediate needs of the poor. But the system broke down in the "crowded and impersonal" urban parishes of the big towns and cities. The cost of poor relief rose dramatically in the period following 1780, not merely because of a series of food crises and trade slumps. Attempts to bring in government reform met with stiff resistance and public debate as to the appropriateness of such support. John Rule comments that it was the end of a period of "sympathetic paternalism towards the poor."[27]

The 1818 *Annual Report* of the London SFS seems to exhibit a new edge and impatience with the limitations of the system for relief of the poor, which had been in place since the sixteenth century. That year, the report stated, was important for the consideration of the "indigent and destitute." "The subject has excited an interest proportioned to its acknowledged importance," putting existing modes of relief under careful examination, for which some were "freely condemned as not only useless but injurious." The Committee observed that nothing highlighted in the government reports had lessened their own confidence in the principles and practices of the SFS: "The object of the Strangers' Friend Society is not the relief of general indigence, or parochial poor, but of casual distress, occasioned by the pressure of sickness or by some other unforeseen calamity."[28]

The comments of Visitors from time to time illustrate the impatience they had with a system that had clearly broken down in its scale and operation. Many were encouraged to both give to the SFS and serve as Visitors because of their dislike of the system of poor relief, composed of compulsory rates and indiscriminate and wasteful outdoor relief by incompetent parish officers. Again and again, the targeted approach of the SFS was underlined, as seen in the rules of the Dublin society: "money . . . not for street beggars or common paupers but for the relief of distressed strangers and the resident sick and industrious poor of good character."[29]

Dislike of Indiscriminate Aid to Beggars

There were many beggars on the streets of London. Many observers saw a direct link between this visible poverty and the high

---

27. Rule, *Albion's People*, 121-29.
28. LSFSAR, 1844.
29. Dublin SFS, Rules, 1844.

incidence of metropolitan crime. This correlation was particularly evident in districts such as St. Giles and Shoreditch, with their notorious lodging houses that were reputedly centers of vice, prostitution, and organized crime.[30] The SFS appealed to the common feeling of dislike toward transient begging by the able-bodied. Its Committee was quite strong in its policy of not giving to street beggars, for they were "not suitable objects of charity." Citing the recent report of the Committee of the House of Commons on the state of mendicancy in the metropolis, they came down on the side of those refusing to give beggars relief, branding them imposters who "spend their idle games in habits of gross profligacy." The SFS Committee pointed to the necessity and advantage of personal visits and inquiries that would probe the circumstances and determine the "real" cases of poverty that deserved the benevolence of the SFS. The Committee reported fully on one artful case of deception by which, through the recommendation of a person of high rank, a family obtained £14 from an individual visitor who had heard of their "extreme distress." He returned to their house one Saturday evening to find the man and his wife and various associates in a state of intoxication, "regaling themselves on a fine piece of pickled salmon with plenty of porter and a bottle of gin before them, and on a side table a large sirloin of beef intended for their Sunday dinner." Such an extreme case was reported in order to remind benevolent individuals to give their donations through a far more just and efficient administration such as that offered by the SFS Visitors, who were required to visit the homes of the poor rather than "bestow alms merely from the unauthenticated representations and importunities of the objects themselves," whose word was all too often not to be trusted.[31]

Fear of Revolution and Anarchy

Perhaps the most difficult motive for which to find evidence is that of social conservatism and the counterforce to radicalism. Was the SFS an instance of Methodism's support for religion as a bulwark of the state against revolutionary forces in society? Did, as Ian Christie asks, the Evangelical movement absorb the kind of revolutionary drive and zeal that elsewhere produced political breakdown,

---

30. Rule, *Albion's People*, 231.
31. LSFSAR, 1816.

by providing spiritual consolation and physical relief, which created good and loyal citizens?[32]

In the climate of fear of revolution spreading across the English Channel, some of the lower classes were drawn to Dissent and Methodism because they saw it as "an attractive alternative to the dominant Anglican vision of society" seen as ordered and ordained by God in a hierarchical fashion that preached obedience and subservience. James E. Bradley comments that "Nonconformity functioned as a midwife to radical political behaviour."[33] Those who engaged in philanthropy from churches rarely shared the radical vision of a reformed society; rather, they worked for the radical reform of individuals through moral persuasion and action. For evangelical Visitors, part of the motivation of their work was to neutralize the activities of men of infidel principles. Those who were sent out to combat such infidelity were

> pious men, zealously and conscientiously attached to their King, their country, and its constitution; taking the Bible as the guide of their lives and the rule of their conduct, in the intercourse with the poor they constantly enjoin upon them, in its authoritative language, the duty of submitting to every ordinance of man for the Lord's sake; that honour is rendered to whom honour is due, and tribute to whom tribute; that to fear God and honour the King, is the imperative command of Holy Scripture; and to avoid all meddling or association with those who are given to change, one of its most salutary cautions.[34]

Such a spirit of subordination was clearly one strand of Wesleyan Methodism's response to the political climate of the 1790s, expressed in its Conference resolutions and the sermons of its most noted preachers. The poor should be taught to submit to God's will, carefully guarding against unkind or envious feelings toward the rich and those set over them in God's order for society. The noble excellency of religion, "which can sweeten every lot in life," should teach them contentment and happiness even in the midst of abject poverty.

The work of the SFS was a consciously active participation in the well-being of the state by creating good citizens who accepted their

---

32. Ian Christie, *Stress and Stability in late Eighteenth-Century Britain* (Oxford: Clarendon Press, 1984), 204-5.

33. James E. Bradley, *Religion, Revolution, and English Radicalism: Nonconformity in Eighteenth Century Politics and Society* (Cambridge: University Press, 1990), 423.

34. LSFSAR, 1819–1820.

lot with cheerfulness rather than turning to dissent and revolt. The Visitors were to "inculcate gratitude and respect towards the higher orders of society" so that the industrious poor should become aware of the favors they had received.[35] Thus the Visitors could, as part of their moral and religious duties, counteract the "mischievous attempts that have been made by men of infidel principles to take advantage of the prevailing distresses of the times, to excite among the poor a spirit of disloyalty and insubordination."[36] These words were written on the eve of the Peterloo massacre in Manchester, where between three and four hundred radicals were injured by the Lancashire militia.[37] The dangers of the times were all too evident.

Biblical Imperatives: the Commands of Jesus

On the first title page of every Annual Report was printed a text from Matthew 25:35-36, "I was a stranger, and ye took me in: Naked, and ye clothed me: I was sick, and ye visited me." Prochaska suggests that this text was a powerful influence on women for whom the urge to be benevolent and to help the poor was a product not only of their own conversion and their desire to convert others but also of the profound anxiety of souls needing to demonstrate that they were indeed saved. The example of Christ meant that they, too, must submit to Jesus and obey his commands and moral laws in order to lead the world to salvation through service and self-sacrifice.[38] Yet, apart from this obvious citation of the parables of Jesus, there is little evidence of the primary religious motivation of the work of the SFS. Instead of being expressed through explicit comment, most of the theological reflection is evident in the Visitors' and donors' active involvement with the SFS, working alongside or for the poor. Most of their attention was focused on the effect of their religious instruction on the poor: to make them better, happier people whose souls have been saved and whose lives have been enriched by the gospel action taken on their behalf. Whatever the humanitarian aspects of the work of the

---

35. LSFSAR, 1814.

36. LSFSAR, 1817.

37. "On August 16th [1819] a mass meeting was arranged by the Manchester radicals to hear Henry Hunt, a speaker who advocated annual parliaments, universal suffrage, and the ballot. A crowd gathered in St. Peter's Fields, and trouble arose between it and the Lancashire militia who were present on the plea of preserving order. The troops charged and killed several persons, to the intense indignation of radical sympathizers in every part of the island." See www.fordham.edu/halsall/mod/1819peterloo.html.

38. Prochaska, *Women and Philanthropy*, 14.

SFS, the religious motives, while not overstressed, were clearly visible in many of the public aspects of the work. Many people were motivated to offer their services in order to gain members for the growing Methodist movement and to share the benefits of an evangelical gospel, as much as for the delight of helping the poor.

Sometimes the reflections of the SFS Visitors or their recipients contain echoes of Scriptures that underline these traits, as in the case of Sarah Brazier. Her husband, a servant, died of cancer in Guy's Hospital, leaving her a widow with five children and another expected. The Annual Report noted that in the Visitor's action of giving relief, it was revealed that "The Lord has been the husband of this poor widow, the father of these poor helpless orphans," with echoes of Old Testament stories that recount the fatherhood of the all-providing God who cares for his people.[39]

The explicit intention of the Committee was that the role of the Visitors was to participate in the revelation of a message that could bring life and refreshment for bodies and souls, "the seed of eternal life which the Visitors are anxious to sow in the hearts of all they visit." When describing those whom they visited as being snatched from the jaws of death (and by implication, hell besides), their imagery is powerful and reflects the language of the Psalms. This fear of judgment emerges in the Annual Report of 1824, in which the SFS Committee undertakes not to bury the God-given talent entrusted to them, "lest the poor and needy should rise up in judgment against them, and lest the Judge of the whole earth should cast them out as unprofitable servants."[40] The humanitarian response to this religious motivation, nevertheless, is still evident. The tenderheartedness that comes from God's generosity to fallen humankind and "the feeling which prompted the Good Samaritan to relieve the wounded Jew" enable the Visitor or benefactor to acknowledge that many of the poor regard their activities as God-given opportunities for spiritual salvation and social survival. The reciprocity of giving and receiving is experienced in the shared blessing.[41]

For most Visitors, their activities must have been a source of immense pleasure that allowed the good experiences to make up for the bad. What did they actually feel as a result of their encounters with the poor? Prochaska suggests that they obtained a sense of self-

---

39. LSFSAR, 1819–1820.
40. LSFSAR, 1824.
41. LSFSAR, 1828.

esteem, to be known and respected by one's neighbors. Their work gave them opportunities to break the monotony of domestic routine by meeting a variety of those for whom no such break was likely. Such activity "represented basic human urges: to be useful, to be recognized, to be informed, to be diverted, to 'keep up with the Joneses,' to gossip, to be loved."[42] Mike Martin locates such feelings among the mixed motives of most people when they engage in philanthropy. The external rewards—of social recognition through increased personal esteem and religious gains and of helping others obtain salvation—are present in the work of the SFS. Also present are the internal rewards—of experiencing pleasure in helping others or relieving their anguish, of the self-respect restored to others as well as the demonstration of one's own living up to Christian ideals, and of thus avoiding guilt in seeing others suffer.[43] The good death that often came to the poor stranger was the reward for the Visitors' efforts. A further source of satisfaction was the knowledge that the family might have learned from their instruction and been helped by their generosity. This perspective was part of the evangelical ethos that waged war on sin, fought for victory over death, and sought the moral and spiritual reformation of lives in conformity to the new vision of society that they offered in contrast to the prevailing social mores of their day.

Significance of the SFS Organization and Work

The SFS was the largest of the benevolent societies in early–nineteenth-century Britain and had the widest distribution of relief. Having first been used by both state and church as an agency, the Society was increasingly supplanted by both, through Poor Law provisions and the creation of rival societies. Nevertheless, the Society became a pattern for other groups in the voluntary sector both in their methods of administration and their rationale for private charity.

Among the major contributions of the SFS to the problem of pauperism was the efficiency of its organization, based on voluntary labor and district visitation. The Society relied largely on existing religious groups that identified, through careful casework, specific cases of real need. Poor relief was regarded as safe in the hands of the SFS.

---

42. Prochaska, *Women and Philanthropy*, 125.

43. Mike W. Martin, *Virtuous Giving: Philanthropy, Voluntary Service, and Caring* (Bloomington: Indiana University Press, 1994), 124-28.

Their assistance extended beyond simple humanitarian aid by adding, as useful adjuncts, moral reformation and religious instruction. Nevertheless, they felt that the primary human virtue and duty of every Christian was to visit and care for the poor. This perspective was very much a Wesleyan view found in all Strangers' Friend Societies: to befriend the poor, to gain familiarity with their conditions of life, and to provide relief to those who merited it. The records of their work reveal this equal regard for physical and spiritual welfare.[44]

Analysis of Theological Themes

An examination of the sources, sermons, and other writings of the period raises several questions. To what extent do common attitudes to poverty run through all Methodist preachers and thinkers? How different were these perspectives from the prevailing Anglican social thought of the time? Was there a distinctive Methodist ideology? Or were they merely absorbing the Anglican heritage and the current vogue for political economy? To what extent was poverty viewed as a result of sin? Or to what extent was poverty seen as an unavoidable misfortune or a divinely ordained station in life to be accepted with resignation and patience?

Branislaw Geremek judges that poverty, in nineteenth-century thought and criticism, was treated as "the shameful disease" of modern society: Philanthropists and Christian social doctrine emphasized the moral degradation that poverty brought into people's lives. He observes that "prejudice towards immigrants . . . , despite being relatively unimportant in itself, can and does preserve, culturally and ideologically, the stigmatizing effect of poverty." Given that much of the work of Methodists was with marginalized groups—the strangers, women, children, and those who fell through the safety net of the welfare system—one might ask whether their work was a pragmatic response based on the Wesleyan legacy of work with the poor rather than a sustained re-definition of the place of the poor and pauperism in society.[45]

From the SFS records and sermons examined, a pattern emerges that is different from the prevailing Anglican social thought of the time.

44. Margaret Bayne Simey, *Charitable Effort in Liverpool in the Nineteenth Century* (Liverpool: University Press, 1951), 7.
45. Bronislaw Geremek, *Poverty: A History* (Oxford: Blackwell Publishers, 1994), 1-6. Geremek poses two fundamental questions about poverty: *What causes poverty?* and *How is it to be eradicated?*

The Methodist attitudes can be summarized in four areas: (1) The Methodists' view of society and theological framework, (2) their expressed views of wealth and poverty, (3) their proposed program for the poor, and (4) their expectations of response by the poor.

The View of Society

The homiletical evidence of the time reveals that the Methodists were working with a traditional hierarchical view of society in which both wealth and poverty were ordained by God. In this divinely ordered society, each rank had its place. One of Jabez Bunting's sermons in 1832 gives a clear description of this worldview. God decides the level of "worldly goods" each person has, "consistent with our spiritual and eternal welfare." He condescends "to order our lot and condition in life." Humanity has no absolute right to happiness or goodness: One's lot comes as a gift of God to be received with thankfulness or borne with fortitude.[46]

Therefore, one recognizes and accepts the inequalities in life—some are rich; others are poor. As John Stephens points out, there is a "perpetual existence of a class of poor people in the world." Some fluctuation may occur between the two, but the "poor [are] always more numerous . . . ; we know that must be so." The lot of the poor is ordained by God so that they necessarily depend on his goodness and kindness for their well-being. Any leveling and redistribution of wealth could only lead to anarchy and further poverty. The gospel is needed in order to reduce the ignorance, insubordination, and ingratitude of the lower orders.[47]

But in two ways there is equality. Stephens's son, Joseph Rayner Stephens, says there is equality of temptation—temptation for the poor to feel envy and for the rich to feel greedy. A number of sermons make a similar point that there is also equality of need: Both rich and poor need salvation. However, both face the prospect that it might be more difficult to be saved if (1) you have riches and desire more, or (2) you are poor and cannot accept your lot.[48] Methodists stressed equality in the sight of God and stated the point bluntly in a manner

---

46. *The Wesleyan Preacher, containing Sermons by the Most Eminent Ministers in the Connexion* (London: A. Northcote, 1832–39), no. 3 (1835): 85.

47. John Stephens, *The Mutual Relations, Claims, and Duties of the Rich and the Poor* (Manchester: Stephens, 1819), 8.

48. Mr. Bowes, in a sermon at Wilderness Row, 1832; in *Wesleyan Preacher* 1 (1831): 397.

rarely found in Anglican sermons. God loves the poorly clad beggar just as much as the "greatest personage in the world." Everyone is a sinner who needs to be taught the way of salvation.[49]

From what do the sermon writers derive this theological view-point? Not explicitly from reason, but rather from revelation—the majority of sermons are expositions of scripture texts. The person of Christ is central as the example of God's generosity and condescension. George Steward talks dramatically of a Christianity whose "God was peasant, houseless, moneyless, derided, dying the death of a slave," while Joseph Benson refers, rather less radically, to the Christ as the exemplar for all the merciful—the "tender hearted, the compassionate and kind Jesus."[50] In the main, the early–nineteenth-century exhibits more of the latter view. The gospel imperatives, especially the often-quoted verses in Matthew 25, require Methodists to view Christ as one who, "though he was rich, yet for our sakes became poor"—a Christ who is identified with the poor in a way that requires similar sympathy and action on the part of his followers, who are to show that same tenderhearted, compassionate attitude to the poor.

The View of Wealth and Poverty

Methodists did not have a very sophisticated or developed view of wealth and poverty beyond that determined by the theological framework within which they operated. Little awareness of the contemporary debate on "political economy" percolated through to the sermons of the period. Their views were guided by Scripture. Wealth is almost universally regarded as a millstone around the neck of believers—what Samuel Warren calls an "insuperable obstacle."[51] Adam Clarke, in his *Prayer of Agur* sermon, states that the extremes of both wealth and poverty are dangerous to the immortal destiny of man. Wealth can lead to temptations, to enjoy a "life full of sensuality" and "frippery fashions."[52] The gospel warning is therefore "lay not treasures upon earth," for they seriously damage your opportu-

---

49. Joseph Entwisle, in a sermon at Lambeth, 1832; in ibid., 237.
50. George Steward, *The Duty, Honour, and Blessedness of the Bounty to the Poor* (Newcastle-upon-Tyne: Northern Advertiser, 1843), 22; Joseph Benson, *Sermons on Various Occasions* (London: Mason, 1836), 338.
51. Samuel Warren, *Sermons on Various Subjects* (London: Simpkin & Marshall, 1833), 53.
52. Adam Clarke, *Discourses on Various Subjects* (London: Clarke, 1836), 283.

nities for salvation.[53] By contrast, poverty is regarded as something less than shameful, though its misery is well-recognized and pitied. Clarke says that the absolute state of dependence can be an uncertain and uncomfortable place.[54] While poverty is well-defined in terms of human needs, the causes of poverty are also hinted at in some sermons that seek to draw a distinction between the deserving and undeserving poor. Joseph Entwisle, after describing the other cases of poverty that deserve relief, points to "those who are involved in sickness and poverty . . . by their own improvidence and wickedness." Even so, he rather uncharacteristically and daringly declares that "they also deserve our compassionate consideration."[55] This statement represents another example of the Methodist egalitarian spirit that breaks through barriers to benevolence.

The devastating cholera epidemic of the 1830s sharply challenged the softened humanitarianism of the Methodists as they struggled to understand the nature and development of the disease. Cholera was interpreted as a massive demonstration of both the power and the mercy of God, both to confound science and to underline the dependence of humanity on God. Methodists often saw this devastation as a direct consequence of sin, noting particularly how it affected those prone to alcoholic drink. God was selective in targeting the victims of the disease. God used cholera as a scourge toward unrepentant sinners for their sins of infidelity and sectarian animosity as well as drunkenness: "Every victim is selected by infinite wisdom, acting under the direction of mercy and justice."[56] Within this powerful interventionist framework, God's providence was manifest not only in his choice of who was poor but also in the level of their material possessions and their physical condition.[57]

The Methodist Response to the Poor

Three main themes emerge as descriptions of an appropriate response to the needs of the poor. That one should do nothing was rarely suggested. The responses were framed in terms of (1) mutuality

53. Robert Newton, in a sermon at Hinde Street Chapel, 1832, in *Wesleyan Preacher* 2 (1833): 216.

54. Clarke, *Discourses*, 278.

55. *Wesleyan Preacher* 1 (1832): 236.

56. *Wesleyan Methodist Magazine* 55 (1832): 21.

57. Robert John Morris, *Cholera, 1832: the Social Response to An Epidemic* (London: Croom Helm, 1976), 131.

or brotherhood, (2) visitation and personal engagement with the poor, and (3) working on behalf of those deprived of rights and liberties.

The prevalent view of society included an understanding that rich and poor are not set against each other in mutual opposition; rather, they are mutually interdependent. As Stephens says: "Men are not formed for a state of perfect equality and independence in life. God has made us for one another." All parts of society are bound together by mutual duties, obligations, and affections. The poor have a perpetual claim on the rich for "protection, benevolence, and kindness." "Let the rich help the poor" is a constant refrain of Conference and pulpit in Methodism. The continuing presence of the poor presents a test for the faithfulness of the rich in their response, "a means of giving exercise to the benevolence of the rich."[58] The poor can be a "means of grace to your own souls," especially when personal engagement takes place.[59]

Why bother with the poor, especially when they are unknown? And, if convinced of the futility of the exercise, one could make many other excuses. In answer to such excuses, Methodists were urged to be economical, not only with money but also with time, in order to be generous. By this method, they could provide a better life for the poor and find opportunities for evangelism. Benevolence to strangers has a long history in Christianity. And charitable giving of surplus goods has an honorable place in the Methodist tradition. Following in Wesley's footsteps, Adam Clarke suggested that they "give what is not absolutely necessary for one's own support to the poor."[60] And Alexander Bell, in a sermon at Battle Bridge in 1833, noted that brotherly love is a good and Christian thing to exercise, particularly through hospitality and visitation, showing "sympathy, care, and concern."[61] "Mercy respects the miserable," said Joseph Benson, and is a sign of our response to God's commands to "love one another" with an active, not a passive, love.[62]

This aspiration could be achieved, in part, through the church speaking for and acting on behalf of those who are voiceless and powerless. This approach supported the work of John Howard in penal reform and of William Wilberforce in the anti-slavery move-

---

58. Stephens, *Mutual Relations*, 19, 31.
59. *Wesleyan Preacher* 1 (1832): 237.
60. Clarke, *Discourses*, 278.
61. The sermon bears the note, "In aid of the funds of the Strangers' Friends' Society"; *Wesleyan Preacher* 3 (1835): 172.
62. Benson, *Sermons*, 329.

ment. This method was also implicitly critical of the lack of political involvement of Methodists in a wide range of social issues. For John Stephens, it meant protecting the poor from themselves and their inclination to be led into radicalism and social unrest. For his son, it meant becoming the voice of the voiceless against the authorities of the day who were exploiting and oppressing the poor. The Bible as "Bill of Rights" could be read in many ways either conservatively or radically. Despite the apparently harsh attitude of Methodists in the cholera epidemic, Robert John Morris judges that

> the Wesleyans were one of the few groups to suggest that "the sufferings of the labouring poor in England", especially their inadequate level of wages, might be a cause of just anger from God, for their situation was "such as to seriously interfere with their spiritual interests".[63]

The Response of the Poor

In the main, the Methodists preached acceptance of the status quo and resignation, with patience, to the lot of poverty and affliction. A Letter of Conference in 1812 addressed the poor: "Be ye therefore patient" and rely on the generosity of the rich in alleviating distress.[64] To others, poverty and sickness are regarded as evils. But to those who are meek, they are opportunities to yield entirely to God in trust and obedience. Such resignation will remove the abhorrence, fear, sorrow, and hatred that afflict those who are not meek.[65]

Poverty itself is seen as a potential source of blessing, and if the poor are resigned and patient, they will certainly be blessed by God. Their reward will be two-fold: knowing that they have been the source of blessing to those from whom they have received much and knowing that the rewards ultimately are not earthly but heavenly. Though they die, yet they will be "happy beyond the reach of misery."[66] They will then dwell in "everlasting felicity and joy."[67] The poor must be thankful that all tribulations are ultimately ended for the faithful.

The warm humanitarianism of the late eighteenth century was somewhat disturbed in the first three decades of the next century by

---

63. Morris, *Cholera*, 133.
64. *Minutes* (Mason), 3:304.
65. Benson, *Sermons*, 325.
66. Alexander Bell, in a sermon at Battle Bridge, 1733; in *Wesleyan Preacher* 3 (1835): 176.
67. Benson, *Sermons*, 325.

the ascendancy of "political economy" and the debate within church circles of the impact of T. R. Malthus's views of the poor, a harsh and pessimistic attitude that mirrored the uncertainties of the times. The problem of poverty and the proliferation of the urban poor were major concerns of political economy advocates.[68] Of these, Thomas Chalmers appears to have had the most effect on the Methodist viewpoint, transfusing political economy into the lifeblood of evangelicalism through his friendship with Bunting and members of the Wesleyan leadership. But his influence was also felt more widely. His position was aligned with the hostility of many churchmen to forms of public relief. They preferred local programs that matched the increasingly discriminatory way in which private voluntary charity was operated by the SFS and others.

Jennifer Hart has illustrated the way in which such developments slowly affected Anglican preaching about the poor in the period 1830 to 1880. She has demonstrated that there was still an adherence to a divinely ordained hierarchical society in which the poor had their allotted place in life. To tamper with this was to court disaster. Each class had its own sphere, even though within the sight of God all were equal. Poverty was a consequence of the Fall, a curse and a necessary element in earthly life, a hallowed state enjoyed, and given grace and dignity, by the Savior who came to redeem all from the curse. The poor would find it easier to inherit the kingdom of God, for they were made humble and attentive to the need for God in a way that the rich found difficult. The rich needed the poor as the source of their morality, the cause of their ministry, and the test of their faithfulness. In the end, wealth and riches were trifles—the immortality of the soul was all-important. The rich should be generous. And the poor should accept their lot with resignation and patience, firm in the knowledge of God's power and goodness to reward those who were faithful.[69]

Most of these elements are also found in the Methodist material. Some are perhaps more pronounced in the Anglican sources. The Anglican sermons place more emphasis on the need to pity the poor, who are most often poor through no fault of their own. They talk less, however, of the poor as deserving to suffer because of wickedness.

68. R. A. Soloway, *Prelates and People: Ecclesiastical Social Thought in England, 1783–1852* (London: R. Routledge & K. Paul, 1969), 93.

69. Jennifer Hart, in A. P. Donajgrodzki, ed., *Social Control in Nineteenth-Century Britain* (London: Croom Helm, 1977), 108-18.

The Anglican material also lacks an emphasis on the prophetic nature of the role of the church speaking out in defense of the rights and privileges of the poor. The Methodist sermons stress equality before God but have less emphasis on the stratified nature of society. The Methodists recognize the need to be benevolent to the poor as a proper response to the ministry of Jesus, who exhibited the qualities that God would have his followers display. The person of Jesus is far more central to the Methodist understanding of proper theological exposition than the Anglican view of God as a forbidding figure of justice and mercy set over his subjects to instill fear, reverence, and obedience in the properly ordained powers of Church and State.

Power and Authority

The evidence displays an inherent contradiction that has fed different interpretations of Methodism's place in religious developments of the period. The people called Methodists had a particular appeal for the poor and gave them a place and sense of purpose within the organizational framework of the movement through the educational opportunities afforded by the classes and the Sunday schools. And yet, many Methodists feared they should not interfere with, much less upset, the God-given social equilibrium. *"The powers that be" were ordained by God, and woe to them "that meddle with change"* was a constantly recurring theme of Conference pronouncements. Such conservatism was at odds with the innovative ways in which Wesley and his followers had challenged both the structures of organized religion and the Anglican hegemony of the spiritual well-being of all citizens. Their attempt to reform the Church of England had failed, but now, in alliance with Evangelicals within that church, the Methodists joined in the attempt to reform the manners of the nation in a moral crusade that earned the backing of the rich and powerful. The price to pay for this support was the social conservatism and control that Jabez Bunting and others so vigorously defended as the church's divine destiny. The price also for Methodism was condemnation to an "age of disunity," as revivalists and radicals were successively expelled or excluded.[70] From a sociological point of view, one might say that the poor felt less inclined to join the upwardly mobile Wesleyan Methodists and more inclined to join the Primitive

---

70. J. H. S. Kent, *The Age of Disunity* (London: Epworth Press, 1966).

Methodists, Bible Christians, and others who were able to share far more effectively the leadership of their denomination across the social spectrum. At the beginning of the period, 1785, there was but one Conference. By 1840, British Methodism was divided into many parts. The internal battles over the years diverted much of the effort of Methodists away from a generous engagement with the poor toward competition and survival in the harsh economic realities of the chapel-building craze.

The SFS can be viewed as the fulcrum of these tensions between opposing forces in Methodism, between social control and social concern, between an evangelistic missionary movement and pietistic societies, between ensuring that the poor were converted and became good citizens in a structured and orderly society, and enabling the poor to take their place and make their contribution to that society as equals. Within the SFS, there was increasingly an opportunity for laymembers to do work that reflected the enhanced social status of Methodists in society, which thereby, gave them a chance to exercise forms of patronage. This transition occurred in spite of Wesley's more egalitarian spirit that despised the patronage of those well-placed in society to offer him help. And the increase of lay participation was achieved despite the attempt of Methodist ministers to take over and give direction to the movement, having the ministerial aristocracy's inherent suspicion of any initiatives that could challenge their control of Conference and, thereby, the movement. What began as local and spontaneous efforts by well-meaning and benevolent laymembers was soon given structure and purpose by Adam Clarke and others in an inexorable Methodist "routinization of charisma" that occurred in both the SFS and the wider connection during the struggle for social control in the 1790s.[71]

The Nature of the Poor and Society's Reaction

Did Methodists have any concept of organized social change in response to the needs of the poor? The conservative views outlined above are not the full story. One has only to remember the example of more radical action of some Methodists in the struggle for penal reform and involvement in the anti-slavery movement. But these

---

71. Thomas R. O'Dea, *The Sociology of Religion* (Englewood Cliffs, N.J.: Prentice-Hall, 1966), 37.

actions were mostly the responses of individuals rather than the corporate action of the Methodist Conference.

Perhaps the importance of the work of Methodists in the SFS and among the poor was not primarily in what they hoped to achieve locally with individuals. Rather, the main significance of their work might have been in helping society at large recognize the conditions of the poor who were in danger of becoming invisible in an increasingly urbanized society. The vivid case studies in the annual reports served not only to highlight the laudable ways in which the poor were being relieved but also to introduce the question of what caused poverty to the new generation of those schooled in the harsher assumptions of political economy, the dominant social theory of the early nineteenth century.

In the end, neither the Methodists nor the SFS realized the progress they desired in tackling the problem of poverty through the imposition of "evangelical retribution and utilitarian optimism." The lesson learned from the SFS is that such limited and private voluntary approaches to the problem of poverty are unlikely to eliminate poverty. The same is true, in the long term, of the reform of the Poor Laws and massive state intervention. Nevertheless, the return to the more hands-on approach of the SFS and its more prominent place in the Wesleyan response to poverty was to be rediscovered by Hugh Price Hughes and the Forward Movement as well as the erstwhile Methodist William Booth and the Salvation Army in the last third of the century.

This creative interaction between compassion and evangelism was one of the fruits of Methodism through the SFS in the late eighteenth and early nineteenth centuries. Nevertheless, it is easy to exaggerate the importance or romanticize the impact of such works of compassion as exemplified by the SFS. In fact, money spent on voluntary relief was even less than that dispensed in public relief. The increasingly hard attitude toward the poor was based as much on economic grounds as on ideological ones. Given limited resources, which of the poor should benefit? Even within a narrow definition of *strangers* and *friendless*, choices must be made. And a convenient distinction, transmitted from the Puritans, made the task easier: Some endured a poverty that was undeserved and God-given, and some suffered indigence because of their own foolish and wicked actions, through laziness or drunkenness. The selectivity in determining recipients of relief was clearly shaped and formed by the prevailing orthodoxy: Poor relief was to be discriminatory so as not to encourage dependency. This approach stressed the value of work, and the aid programs rewarded those who would take advantage of such temporary relief to get back on their feet and help themselves out of their poverty. This understanding of poverty generally incorporated a view of children as degenerate, resistant to authority, and in need of correction.

From the softer humanitarian approaches of the late eighteenth century, the Methodists in the "age of unrest" became increasingly conformed to the role of church as guardian of morality. They consequently took an aggressive stance in the "reformation of manners" and the rooting out of social unrest in the cities, which were perceived to be places of moral and social danger. As David Bebbington notes, there was "a tight circumscription of the bounds of charity that sometimes has a harsh ring."[72] The presence of crisis management was more obvious than any systematic approach to poverty by way of either practical help or religious and economic thinking that underpinned such work.

Religion and the Working Classes

Kenneth Inglis has argued that, for the most part, the churches failed in their attempt to penetrate and convert the working classes because they paid too little attention to the environmental conditions (and one might add cultural distinctiveness) of the working classes or the causes of poverty.[73] Hugh McLeod, however, has demonstrated that the situation was much more complex. The poor did not necessarily need middle-class religion. They could and did help themselves in practical and strong expressions of mutual aid that did not depend on Christian benevolence. Extreme poverty tended not to produce conversions out of desperation but rather apathy and bitterness that sometimes turned to violence. The poor had their dignity, which was sometimes denied or undermined by visiting evangelists.[74] Therefore, we need not always be convinced, by the official religious records, of the necessity of interaction between the poor and the churches.

---

72. David Bebbington, *Evangelicalism in Modern Britain: A History from the 1730s to the 1980s* (London: Unwin Hyman, 1989), 121.

73. Kenneth Stanley Inglis, *Churches and the Working Classes in Victorian England* (London: Routledge & K. Paul, 1963), 260.

74. Hugh McLeod, *Religion and the Working Class in Nineteenth-Century Britain* (London: Macmillan, 1984), 11, 24.

Granted, most of the evident writing and preaching of the Methodists was very much an aping or echoing of the Anglican social thought. Nevertheless, there were perhaps more than a "few twinges of socially radical sentiment in churches."[75] Notable examples include Adam Clarke in the earlier period, who was sometimes out of line with the Wesleyan establishment, and Warren and Stephens in the latter part of the period at a time of growing social instability. The Methodist position is not primarily marked by its acceptance of the hierarchical nature of society and views of the relative merits of wealth and poverty (wealth as a millstone to be overcome and poverty as a means of grace) but rather by its stress on mutuality in society between classes and people, of brotherhood and the need to work for the rights of all with an equality of opportunity for all, irrespective of temptation and need. The issue of poverty heightened the conflict of interest between Christian morality and political economy in which the concerns for social justice came to prevail against the desire for personal salvation. In the period before 1840, the desire to save souls motivated Methodists more than the aspiration to create the kingdom of God on earth. The latter had to wait another half century before its case was heard with any force within Methodism. Still prevalent at this point was what Alan Wilkinson has highlighted as the more dualistic view of the world with a rather negative attitude toward the temporary inconveniences of this world compared with the eternal bliss in store for the faithful. Conversion and the personal acceptance of the Gospel were the only real antidotes for poverty in the minds of most Methodist ministers, for whom voluntary philanthropy was the only effective way of reaching the poor that was available to the churches.[76] The spontaneous philanthropy of the eighteenth century was dulled by the introspective nature of much of the Evangelical Revival that demanded conversions and changed lives. A price must be paid by the poor for their betterment.

But as Wilkinson also warns, evangelical social attitudes were far from uniform. The Methodists displayed some notable divergence from other churches in the more radical elements it harbored. The influence of Methodism on the cultural and social aspects of Chartism and the emergence of Trade Unionism and working-class organizations has rightly been recognized. Perhaps, as Gertrude Himmelfarb

---

75. Inglis, *Churches*, 251.

76. Alan Wilkinson, *Christian Socialism: Scott Holland to Tony Blair* (London: SCM Press, 1998), 8.

has recognized, there was a disparity between the theology of the church and its praxis: "Just as Methodism fostered a sense of fraternity that had only a peripheral relationship to its theology, so [the Church] provided a sense of fellowship that went well beyond its official program."[77]

What did the poor think of the work of the SFS and others? We can only surmise that the "labouring poor valued the social and psychological utility of religion more highly than confessional orthodoxy."[78] If there was no bread without the Bible, then the poor hosts swallowed without question the doctrinal niceties required to acquire bread, as the Visitors learned. For many, it was their only recourse. The State had failed them. The institutional church had failed them. Their working-class neighbors were often unable, through similar situations, to help them. They were unable to help themselves though others encouraged them to do so. Their only chance came from the voluntary workers who came in the name of no one but the Christ who impelled them to offer a saving word of grace, a tract, and a dole. Collusion and conversion were to be found in equal measure in a process that is difficult to assess.

We can, nevertheless, test the evidences of those who wished to be persuaded of the efficacy of engaging with the poor, whatever the cost. This study cannot unlock anything but the attitudes of the church toward the poor; it cannot discern the skepticism with which the laboring and non-laboring poor probably viewed the advances of the mostly middle-class visitors into their territories and lives, unannounced, sometimes welcome, often cursed. Any attempt to generalize in this area would be to disregard the very complex nature of the poor themselves, their circumstances and conditions, which varied greatly.[79] Methodism's flight to the suburbs in the period after 1840 was symptomatic of its disengagement at the sharp end of its mission work of which the SFS was one victim. The SFS was an example of a philanthropic effort born not of guilt but of confidence. Such confidence failed to produce a sustaining of the initiative in the 1840s when the efforts of Methodists turned to the heathen abroad rather than the sinners at home.

---

77. Gertrude Himmelfarb, *The Idea of Poverty: England in the Early Industrial Age* (New York: Alfred A. Knopf, 1983), 259.

78. David Hempton, *Religion and Political Culture in Britain and Ireland* (Cambridge: University Press, 1996), 59.

79. Rosemary O'Day, *The Family and Family Relationships: 1500–1900* (New York: St. Martin's Press, 1984), 232.

The Theological Framework

The Arminian "optimism of grace" that encouraged openness to all, irrespective of condition, broke through the societal manifestations of a more discriminatory and harsher attitude to the poor in a way that released the spirit of reckless generosity found in Wesley and the early Methodists. Why else would Methodists choose to be the visitors of the poor other than the pressing desire to save the souls of even the most deprived or depraved, with a selflessness that followed the example of Wesley himself, exhibiting "faith working by love"? To make members and to have the poor redeemed as part of their fellowship was of greater importance than to have them scrub themselves and their miserable dwellings clean of filth as well as sin. To make them useful members of society engaged in the worlds of work and education was a sure means of securing that objective.

In this effort, the SFS was perhaps the most useful agency that the Methodists were able to employ. Their work was a true mirror of Methodist societal and theological attitudes to the poor. They sometimes exhibited a bundle of contradictions: between an overbearing patriarchalism and a warm, enduring humane spirit of brotherhood and mutuality, and between a desire to see souls saved and a desire to see bodies preserved and enabled to live a more fulfilled life. They exhibited a widely recognized humanitarian attitude toward the relief of poverty and protested their lack of proselytism. Yet they were engaged in part of a process (along with Sunday schools and Tract societies) of aggressive evangelism among the most vulnerable of society, the poor. They lived in the optimistic confidence of post-millenarian evangelicals that individual conversions could not only change lives but also transform whole communities and even the nation. And yet they could still see cholera victims as examples of God's wrath on a godless world.

Conclusion

The work of the SFS and the writings of contemporary Methodists contain a mixed legacy—of Tory paternalism tinged with a radical social conscience that occasionally diverted from its conformity and of Wesleyan evangelical economics, which despised wealth but had to acknowledge its existence and benefits and had to come to terms with the responsibilities that wealth laid on the rich, for whom the poor existed in order to test their generosity and, thus, their faithfulness.

This mixture—of practical benevolence, generosity, and warm sympathy for the poor with a theological conservatism and evangelical priority that distanced itself from involvement in politics and the state—is a legacy with which Methodism has subsequently had to struggle in its relationship with the poor. Recognizing that it could no longer be a "church of the poor" and uneasy with its pretended role as a "church for the poor," the modern Methodist Church called its latest program of social action "Mission alongside the Poor." This title perhaps reflects a conscious decision to acknowledge both the ambiguities of the religious tradition and the significant Methodist emphasis on relationship with the poor.

At the heart of Wesley's approach was personal engagement with the sick and the needy wherever and whatever their condition. This focus was also at the heart of the work of the Strangers' Friend Societies in many towns and cities in Britain and Ireland for a critical half century. They carried the Wesleyan banner into the most deprived urban areas and brought relief to countless thousands. Their work is indicative of the concern for the poor, accompanied by whatever motives, social and religious, that those Methodists implemented at great cost to reputation and health.

CHAPTER EIGHT

From Revivalism to Socialism: The Impact of the Poor on Harry Ward

William J. Abraham

In its long and tangled contribution to the theory and practice of evangelism, the Wesleyan tradition has produced its fair share of unique individuals, not to speak of cranks. One thinks of Thomas Walsh, Richard Allen, Peter Cartwright, Billy Bray, William Booth, Phoebe Palmer, Gypsy Smith, and Harry Denman, for example. Few, however, can match the unique contribution of the person who shall detain us in this discussion. In his day, he was a street preacher, a flamboyant platform speaker, a prolific writer of books, editorials, and essays, an indefatigable organizer and campaigner, a beloved professor, and a social theorist. He was a friend of the poor, a champion of the rights of workers, and an enemy of war. He was acquainted personally with Mahatma Gandhi, his counsel was sought by Joseph Stalin, and he was lauded by Bertrand Russell. He loved tea parties with his friends and students; he was an expert rose gardener; and he loved to spend spare months in the wilds of Canada. He was deeply opposed by conservative Methodists, he was investigated by the FBI, and he was the butt of the criticism and wit of Reinhold Niebuhr. He had the honor of producing a creed that was adopted by The Methodist Church and that has had extra-ordinary influence on North American Christianity right down to our own day. In 1915, he wrote two books that symbolized what was to become a deep split in Western Christianity in the twentieth century—one was on the poor and the other on evangelism.[1] His name was Harry Ward.[2]

Review of Harry Ward's Life

Harry Ward was born in Turnham Green, England, into a conventional Methodist family on October 15, 1873. His father was a butcher and local preacher. His mother was something of a rebel, leaving the Church of England to become a dedicated Methodist. She was rewarded with a classically happy Methodist death, after a very painful illness, at the early age of forty-two. The young Ward worked initially for his father, who was a tough taskmaster over his employees, so much so that they labeled him a "sweater." For a short time, Ward attended a British public school, but his health declined, and he was forced to live in the New Forest area with two aunts. At the age of seventeen, he left England for good, emigrating to the United States so that he might gain the kind of university education that class prejudice in England at that time precluded.

Before he left home in 1891, Ward was already a local preacher in the Wesleyan connection, as an assistant in the work of the mission band and a class leader. He joined an uncle in Utah and continued his work as a preacher, admiring and emulating the Salvation Army in their commitment to street preaching. Thereafter, his education began in earnest. In turn, Ward attended the University of Southern California, Northwestern, and Harvard. He concentrated his studies in the fields of philosophy, political science, economics, and ethics. While at university, he was a skillful debater and orator. Surprisingly, Ward took virtually no formal training in theology, a fact that may account for his later refusal to answer specifically doctrinal questions in the heat of debate. This fact may also explain his general disdain for theology over against the social sciences in the training of ministers.

---

1. Harry F. Ward, *Poverty and Wealth from the Viewpoint of the Kingdom of God* (New York: The Methodist Book Concern, 1915) and *Social Evangelism* (New York: Missionary Education Movement of the United States and Canada, 1915).

2. I am grateful to my former colleague, Professor John Deschner, for first bringing Ward to my attention. I am indebted to the following for information on Ward: Robert T. Handy, *A History of Union Theological Seminary in New York* (New York: Columbia University Press, 1987); Eugene P. Link, *Labor-Religion Prophet: The Times and Life of Harry F. Ward* (Boulder: Westview Press, 1984); and Ralph Lord Roy, *Communism and the Churches* (New York: Harcourt, Brace and Company, 1960).

Ward turned down an offer to teach economics at Northwestern and began his long ministry among the poor in the Northwestern Settlement House in Chicago in 1898. During this tenure, he qualified to become a Methodist minister by taking the Conference Course of Study for certification. He was dismissed from work in the Settlement House in 1899, when anarchist impulses within ousted him from its leadership. He proceeded into two pastorates in the Chicago area from 1900 until 1904. There he engaged extensively again in street preaching. For the next six years, he was the minister at Union Avenue Methodist Church. During this time, Ward confirmed and strengthened his commitment to build the kingdom of God on earth through a comprehensive ministry of preaching and social action. All this was a natural expression of the evangelical theology he derived from his Wesleyan heritage.

It was during this time that Ward got to know Walter Rauschenbusch. Despite the distance that divided them, they became good friends, engaging in prolonged discussion, as and when they could, until Rauschenbusch died in 1918. During this time, Ward was also deeply involved in community projects, especially those connected with labor relations. With many of his friends he developed a lasting aversion to capitalism and a substantial commitment to socialism. Ward took the view that capitalism could be summarized accurately by the motto: "To the biggest beast the biggest bone."[3] In contrast to this position, he held that " 'the Labor Movement was the most advanced point at which the divine energy was operating in the higher evolution of man.' "[4] A world tour, which he took in 1908–1909 with a wealthy Chicago Methodist, did nothing to shake these convictions.

During this period, Ward produced the famous Social Creed of the Methodist Church. Link describes this document as a *magna carta* for church-labor relations.[5] The Creed fits snugly into Ward's interests and his work with the Methodist Federation for Social Service. Commentators generally agree that Ward was the crucial moving force in the attempt to express solidarity with the labor movement. The Social Creed itself began its life on the back of Western Union telegram forms. Others had a hand in the Creed, but there is no doubt that Ward was the chief architect and the creative mind behind it. He also piloted the Creed through both the Methodist Federation of Social

---

3. The phrase was that of a friend, Richard Ely.
4. Quoted in Link, *Labor-Religion Prophet*, 24.
5. Ibid., chap. 3.

Service and the Federal Council of Churches. The Creed itself enunciates a network of principles that Ward had already hammered out and embraced. The original Social Creed read as follows:

The Methodist Episcopal Church stands:
For equal rights and complete Justice for all men in all stations of life.
For the principles of conciliation and arbitration in industrial dissensions.
For the protection of the workers from dangerous machinery, occupational diseases, injuries and diseases.
For the abolition of child labor.
For such regulation of the conditions of labor for women as shall safeguard the physical and moral health of the community.
For the suppression of the "sweating system."
For the gradual and reasonable reduction of the hours of labor to the lowest practical point, with work for all; and for that degree of leisure for all which is the condition of the highest of human life.
For the release from employment one day in seven.
For a living wage in every industry.
For the highest wage that each industry can afford, and for the most equitable division of the products of industry that can ultimately be devised.
For the recognition of the Golden rule, and the mind of Christ as the supreme law of society and the sure remedy for all social life.[6]

With minor changes, this Creed was adopted by the Congregationalists, the northern Baptists, the southern Methodists, the Reformed and Episcopal denominations, and the Friends. In time, it was endorsed by the Central Conference of American Rabbis and by a number of Roman Catholic bishops. During the great steel strike of 1919, it was read from many pulpits and at labor conclaves. Ward was untiring in his labors to see the Creed embraced and applied. It became a central plank in the new evangelism that became fashionable in colleges and the YMCA. In all, Ward provided outstanding leadership in promoting the causes represented by the Social Creed he had originated.

By 1913, Ward had moved from the pastorate into teaching. He became the Professor of Social Service at Boston University School of Theology. By then, he was well-known as a labor evangelist, and he continued his campaigns for social evangelization. He was involved

6. Ibid., 47-48.

in the Men and Religion Forward Movement.[7] He had lobbied earlier for every Methodist annual conference to have an industrial evangelist to get the message of social evangelism to the middle and upper classes. In the first year and a half in his new position, Ward addressed 347 meetings, conducted thirty-six conferences in seventeen states, and traveled all over the continent. He produced the *Social Service Bulletin* to propagate his views, and he fought, albeit unsuccessfully, the Methodist Book Concern in Cincinnati over its labor practices. By the end of his stay in Boston and his move to Union Seminary in New York in 1918, he had become a Marxist in his social theory. He had also made friends with and been influenced by the great exponents of Boston Personalism, Borden Parker Bowne and Edgar Sheffield Brightman.

Ward spent the remaining years of his work as the Professor of Christian Ethics at Union. Although he was almost totally overshadowed by Reinhold Niebuhr, Ward more than held his own in teaching, in polemic, and in action. In the 1920s, he was well-known as an ardent proponent of the Social Gospel.[8] Outside his preaching and teaching, Ward was heavily involved in the American Civil Liberties Union, serving as the first chairman of its national board of directors from 1920 to 1940. In 1924–25, he took another trip around the world, meeting with Mahatma Gandhi, sharing the message of socialism with Chinese friends, and arguing for a revolutionary coalition of intellectuals, peasants, and farmers. Two Chinese papers printed his lectures in full. Link tells us that "Ward's lectures seemed to have played a small part in the vast Chinese Revolution."[9]

Perhaps most formative for Ward in this period was a trip to the Soviet Union for a sabbatical in 1931–32.[10] Although Ward never became a member of the Communist party, undoubtedly he was deeply drawn to communism as an alternative to capitalism. From the publication of his *In Place of Profit: Social Incentives in the Soviet*

---

7. In this movement, evangelists were sent out in teams who focused on six specific interests: evangelism, Bible study, missions, work for boys, social service, and community extension. For more on this movement, see *Bible Study and Evangelism*, vol. 3 of *Messages of the Men and Religion Movement* (New York and London: Funk and Wagnalls, 1912).

8. Link claims that Pauline Rauschenbusch, widow of Walter, looked to Ward as the successor to her husband. *Labor-Religion Prophet*, 73.

9. Ibid., 125.

10. Roy describes the significance of this visit in this fashion: "Ward's life reached a turning point in 1931. He went to Russia, spent almost a year there, and returned fired with ecstasy over what he had seen. The Soviet Union, he maintained, was bringing to the world a new concept that was in reality a fulfillment of the ethics of Jesus. Communism, he said, was systematically

Union[11] in 1933, he was an admirer and defender of the Soviet Union. This book followed on the heels of a duet of books that outlined Ward's account of the relationship between religion and the economic order.[12] Ward was already in trouble from various constituencies: He was now labeled a "commie" and "pinko." At one point, the *New York Daily News* called him the "Red Dean." By 1943, J. Edgar Hoover placed Ward's name on the list for custodial detention as a security risk in case of a national emergency. It remained there until his death.

Ward was not rattled in the least by this kind of opposition; if anything, he thrived on it. After retiring from teaching in 1941, he continued his labors in word and deed on behalf of the kingdom as interpreted in socialist categories. In 1947, Joseph Stalin sought his advice on how the Allies might restore war-torn Europe. Ward never wavered in his fundamental allegiance to socialism as the way for a new social order, even though the influence of Reinhold Niebuhr and Karl Barth created an entirely different theological climate from that of an earlier generation. In the 1950s, Ward fell out of favor at Union, and his name quietly dropped from the limelight. His last manuscript, "Jesus and Marx," was never published. Yet at his ninetieth birthday celebration in 1963, Ward stood and spoke for an hour before a galaxy of guests. Bertrand Russell was one of the many who sent a note acknowledging his courage and compassion.

After two years of constant care, Ward died in 1966. After his death, it came to light that Ward wanted "no lying eulogy—especially to the Lord in an all worship Memorial Service at Union."[13] However, Union did hold a memorial service in January 1967. By then some of those who attended had never heard much about him.

Ward's Conception of Social Evangelism

One reason we should know and hear of Ward stems from his work in evangelism. In his own way, Ward was deeply committed to evangelism. He began his ministry as a street evangelist. He was much

---

crushing the evil profit motive that spurred on the American economy and replacing it with incentives of service and sacrifice. The United States should set for itself the same goal." *Communism and the Churches*, 90.

11. Harry F. Ward, *In Place of Profit: Social Incentives in the Soviet Union* (New York and London: Scribner's, 1933).

12. Harry F. Ward, *Our Economic Morality and the Ethic of Jesus* (New York: Macmillan, 1929) and *Which Way Religion?* (New York: Macmillan, 1931).

13. Link, *Labor-Religion Prophet*, 304.

involved in this new form of evangelism that became popular for a time in mainline Protestant circles in the first two decades of the twentieth century. As we have already noted, he published a book on the subject in 1915. Without charting Ward's whole career in the field of evangelism, we will examine with some care his proposals for the social evangelism that became associated with his name.

As we proceed, it is important to note that Ward represents the culmination of a complex process that stretches far back into the nineteenth century. It has been common to see Ward and his generation as a bright and creative new wave of liberal Protestant tradition that can be contrasted with the more moribund, conservative forces that later crystallized into fundamentalism in the 1920s and that, thereafter, hogged the limelight in evangelism. We now know that this view is profoundly mistaken. Ward was not a particularly original thinker. Moreover, it is clear that some conservatives and many liberals of the turn of the century shared not just a common ancestry but a common set of themes.

In other words, the new theology that Ward represented had much in common with those conservative groups who were looking for a new outpouring of the Holy Spirit that would be a source of power for service and holy living.[14] Thus, both groups emerged out of the evangelical Protestantism of the nineteenth century. In fact, both groups were, in part, protests against the inability of the churches to reach the working class and the poor. Both were bored with the settled evangelical orthodoxy of the period; they tended to see it as an orthodox rationalism without life or heart.[15] Both shared a common cultural standing in the mainstream of social and ecclesial life. Both were interested in the working of the Holy Spirit. Both were fascinated by eschatological themes, especially that of the kingdom of God. Both expected to find in history a dialectic of divine judgment and promise. Both insisted on the importance of experience in the articulation of their theology. Both were impatient with calls for confessional regularity and were uneasy with theological speculation that was not anchored in the realities of daily experience. Both felt that there was the possibility of fresh discovery of new religious truth

---

14. For an excellent treatment of this theme see Grant Wacker, "The Holy Spirit and the Spirit of the Age in American Protestantism, 1880–1910," *Journal of American History* 72 (1985): 45-62.

15. This was also true of the English scene. The Cambridge University cricket star Charles T. Studd said of the Anglicanism of his youth that it was not "a religion that amounted to much. It was just like having a toothache." Ibid., 61.

in the modern age. The adversarial relationship that later developed and that has done so much harm in the field of evangelism was indeed implicit in the continuities they shared, but this tension arose precisely because each side was attempting to establish the superiority of one element or set of elements within a complex theological tradition. As Wacker puts it, "the relation between liberals and evangelicals in the 1880s and 1890s is best understood, not as a confrontation between aliens, but as a contest—albeit a deadly serious contest—between siblings who perceived and defined the issues in remarkably similar ways."[16]

How did Ward define the issues with respect to evangelism? His proposal was encapsulated in an attempt to forge a new conception of evangelism known as social evangelism. At heart, this approach represented a following-through on the evangelistic work of earlier generations. It involved the updating and enriching of earlier tradition by incorporating into evangelism the values of the social movement of the late nineteenth and early twentieth centuries.

> The mighty evangelism of the middle of the last century created as one of its by-products the moral standards of the formative community life of the Middle West. It turned licentious, drunken, brawling people into folks who began to organize their communities on the basis of purity, temperance, and a decent respect for the rights and opinions of others. The evangelism of to-day, even in the hands of its most individualistic exponents, attempts to exert a direct influence upon the community life. It brings its batteries to bear upon corrupt government, the liquor traffic, the social evil. Here is an attempt to bring within the scope of the evangel the fundamental social relationships of sex and property.[17]

As Ward saw it, the new evangelism must follow through on this basis and make the explicit redemption of the social order essential to its goal. It must be committed not only to the regeneration of the individual but also to the regeneration of society.

Ward marshals several reasons for this extension. It is a conscious development of what has always been unconscious and implicit in the work of evangelism. All the great evangelists from Girolamo Savonarola to D. L. Moody were actually social evangelists. Further, it is the only way that the church will be able to reach crucial segments

---

16. Ibid., 59.
17. Ward, *Social Evangelism*, 6-7.

of the modern world: "There are sections of our cosmopolitan population who have never heard the gospel of Jesus in its original simplicity, to whom its social interpretation and application is the easiest and sometimes the only approach."[18] Such an extension is in keeping with the new conception of society that has come to light with the development of sociology. Individuals are really cells of an organism that draw their life from their place in the organism and, hence, must be evangelized at the social level: "an effective evangelism must make its definite appeal to men in their social relations."[19] This extension of the work is in keeping with the gospel of the kingdom, for this message insists that one cannot have a relationship with God without a relationship with the neighbor. Finally, it fits with a proper account of the relation between the church and the community. The church does not exist to build up itself. It exists to build up the community. Hence there is a need to evangelize the community life. The object of church endeavor is to make the community religious. Such a community, then, will have become

aware of its organic nature, which has found its soul, repented of its sins, come to conscious realization of its powers and needs, and is coordinating its forces, including its churches, in harmony with a power greater than itself, for the working out of its salvation. This process is actually being accomplished in many a community, sometimes by a single church, sometimes by the federated churches. It must everywhere continue until the Church has poured the life of God into every function of the community, until that city appears in which God dwells with men and they are his people, and in it there will be no temple, "for the Lord God the Almighty, and the Lamb, are the temple thereof."[20]

Another way to see this approach is to envision the work of evangelism as the full christianization of the social order.

It now remains . . . to direct the forces of evangelism toward every part of the social order that remains unregenerate, to accomplish absolutely the Christian family, the Christian state, the Christian industry, and through these the Christian social order. *To put the dynamic of God's life into all the activities of man, to bring the social passion to a consciousness of its spiritual nature, to tie the social program to the eternities and fill it with the power of an endless life—this is the compelling task of the Church.*[21]

---

18. Ibid., 8.
19. Ibid., 18.
20. Ibid., 20-21.
21. Ibid., 24; emphasis as in the original.

169

The imperative for such an evangelism is manifold. It is directly derived from the mind and heart of Jesus. This grounding was lost in the imperial Christianity of the Roman Empire but was partially regained in the missionary movement of the nineteenth century. The latter has now completed its task geographically. What remains is to bring the organic world to Christ. Therein the program of Jesus to bring the kingdom of God on earth will be realized through the power of love. This goal is in the self-interest of the church. The church cannot stand still. It must either forge ahead to implement the vision of Jesus or degenerate into a vast institutional machine. If the church does not evangelize the social order, it will lose what little gains it has made in the lives of individuals. Worse still, it will find itself abandoned by God and shut off from God's activity in the community. Moreover, work among outcast groups clearly shows that many cannot be reached if we do not identify and eliminate the social causes that pull people down into misery and evil. Finally, only this kind of evangelism will truly match the deep needs that we can now identify. We now know from science that progress is not inevitable. Modern Western civilization is in deep trouble. It is weakened at its foundations by social waste, poverty, and disease. It is poisoned by sex, disease, alcohol, and by class, racial, and international strife. This situation can only be put right by divine action. "Without God there is no hope for the world."[22] The future lies in the hands of that remnant who will put God into the heart of our civilization.

In these circumstances, a purely individual gospel is not enough. To preach the simple gospel and then leave the rest to take care of itself is a totally inadequate approach. Even those who propose this tack are naively inconsistent. They know that people must choose consciously to enter the kingdom, but when it comes to the social world, they abandon this insight and settle for mere unconscious and indirect conversion of the social order. Such a policy is evasive when it comes to the fight against social injustice: it ignores the way evil gathers its corporate power and drags converted individuals back into the old life of sin; it is blind to the subtle forms of social wrong that degrade mature Christians; and it is selectively political, for it happily attacks the saloon but stays quiet about the need to move politically against other evils. Moreover, such a policy is empirically false. Changed individuals do not necessarily move to change the world. They develop a dual conscience to shield them from the harsh

---

22. Ibid., 43.

reality of social evil. In reality, they serve not Christ but Mammon. They recognize the authority of Christianity in only a segment of their lives.

What lies underneath this policy is a false view of the social world. Society is not just the sum of its individuals. It is constituted by a collective action and a social will. These realities, too, must be evangelized consciously and deliberately. This approach does not mean that one should ignore the evangelization of the individual. The individual person needs to be evangelized. But the evangelization of the individual cannot be fully accomplished without social evangelism.

> The one way of saving the social organism is through its constituent parts, which are individuals; the only way the individual can come to full salvation is by redemption of the social organism in which he subsists. To accomplish this joint end, men must be evangelized as *social beings*. They must be saved in all their group relationships, not as individuals abstracted from the world of reality, withdrawn from contact with their fellows and set apart in some arbitrary system of relationships with God. The fundamental error of those who insist that an evangel which talks about social conditions is neglecting the fundamental task of "getting the individual right with God" is that they are thinking of an individual who does not exist, except in the realm of theology.[23]

In this kind of evangelism, the life of the individual is not ignored but enlarged. There is a mutual interaction between the individual and the social organism. In social evangelism, there is a coordinate process in which both gain redemption and press on to perfection. The individual and the social order are reached together by the evangel. In this process, the appeal of the evangel to the individual must be a social appeal. Otherwise, all we produce are selfish Christians.

> *A sound personal salvation is accomplished only when the appeal is to lose life in order to find it, to join consciously with God in the saving of the world; not to attempt to appropriate the benefits of Calvary for personal ends, but to share in Calvary in order that the world may be redeemed.*[24]

What does this outlook mean for evangelistic methods? Essentially, this approach entails the extension of the old methods. The

---

23. Ibid., 56-57; emphasis as in the original.
24. Ibid., 64; emphasis as in the original.

aim of course has changed, and the aim of evangelism should determine the method. Moreover, the new aim of changing all of life will bring to our attention unreached groups in the population and unreached spheres in society that have been ignored. These new contexts will to some extent determine how to proceed. Evangelists will thus become aware of the poor, the working class, certain racial groups, recent immigrants, intellectuals, the luxurious rich, and the like. They will also become aware of government and industry. However, most of the old methods can be adjusted to fit the revised conception of evangelism. Thus, use can be made of mass meetings, open forums that discuss social and community questions, skillful advertising, and personal conversation. Crucial to this evangelism will be an evangel of deed. "The gospel of life is most effectively proclaimed in actual, living relationships."[25] This "new" method emulates the evangelism of early Methodism.

> It organized a ministry of service to all the needs of the people to whom it preached. Its methods are embodied in the instructions given by John Wesley to one of the preachers whom he sent to this country. "I turn you loose, George, on the American continent. Publish your message everywhere in the open face of the sun and *do all the good you can*."[26]

This method is also effective in practice.

> The preaching of the gospel to the poor involves both constructive and preventive philanthropy. These are phases of the evangel, and unless this be recognized both evangelism and philanthropy fail. The only effective effort for the misery group is that which brings spiritual forces to bear in practical fashion for the mending of broken lives. The best way to rehabilitate submerged individuals or families is to put them into the fraternal fellowship of a church that is flaming with the passion to realize the love of God in service to men.[27]

Only in this way, that is, by ministering to all the needs of the community, can the church secure the purpose of the social evangelism. This way, it will put God into the life of the community so that he will energize its every function. This result will not be achieved in an instant. Countering the overwhelming effects of environment takes

25. Ibid., 80.
26. Ibid., 82; emphasis as in the original.
27. Ibid., 83.

time, but the city of God can and will grow in our midst. A lay movement, without hierarchy or priesthood, that will manifest its own new apostles and martyrs in the workaday world will construct such a city.

This harnessing of old methods to new aims was no pipe dream. Ward was involved in a whole new impetus in evangelism that harnessed the methods of revivalism to fit the development of trade unions. In fact, Ward was drawing on a tradition of evangelism that has roots stretching back into the nineteenth century but has been lost from sight until recently. Thus, in the trade-union or labor evangelism that grew out of the Men and Religion Forward Movement, trade unionists deployed all the paraphernalia of revivalism to build up the unions.[28] They used camp meetings, preaching, state teams of workers, door-to-door canvassing, parades, music, labor sermonettes, decision cards, and inquiry rooms. The last two items were deliberately borrowed from Billy Sunday and D. L. Moody. Moreover, appeal was made to biblical truths, carefully crafted theological rhetoric, the life and teaching of Jesus, and even the psychology of conversion experience. So Ward was not whistling in the dark when he called for the extension of the old methods to the expression of the new evangelism.

Ward's desire to extend the old to embrace the new is also manifest in his account of the nature and content of the message of social evangelism. The heart of the matter is the application of the whole gospel to the whole of life. The evangelist will apply the one gospel to both the individual and the social. This task will involve convincing both the individual and the collective of sin, righteousness, and judgment. Thus, the evangelist will arouse and develop the social conscience, calling for a repentance that will not permit the individual to escape responsibility for the vast corporate wrongs of our time. This step, in turn, will bring forth the fruits of repentance. These fruits will be manifest in appropriate social action, in educating the community in the fundamental principles of social justice, in proclaiming

28. For useful descriptions and discussion of this fascinating phenomena, see Herbert G. Gutman, "Protestantism and the American Labor Movement: The Christian Spirit in the Gilded Age," *American Historical Review* 72 (1966): 74–101; Elizabeth and Kenneth Fones-Wolf, "Trade-Union Evangelism: Religion and the AFL in the Labor Forward Movement, 1912–16," in Michael H. Frisch and Daniel J. Walkowitz, eds., *Working-Class America: Essays on Labor, Community, and American Society* (Urbana: University of Illinois Press, 1983), 153-84; and Ken Fones-Wolf, *Trade Union Gospel: Christianity and Labor in Industrial Philadelphia, 1865–1915* (Philadelphia: Temple University Press, 1989).

God as the God of the poor, and in the removal of inequality in society. Failure to act in repentance entails sure and certain judgment.

> The Kingdom is organized around the law of love, and the scientist confirms it, declaring that the social organism develops only as fast as the altruistic instincts dominate the egoistic,—that self-preservation demands self-sacrifice. The consequences of the violation of this law must be proclaimed. This business of social evangelism is not a mealy-mouthed cant about love. There are stern facts here, terrible as fate, resistless as doom. The continuance of modern social sins means absolutely and inevitably the destruction of modern civilization. When the heart of society has been eaten out with greed and selfishness, and its body destroyed with sensualism and lust, legal and illegal, then it will know that "the soul that sinneth it shall die," social as well as individual.[29]

Ward is adamant about the bleak prospects for the West if it does not repent.

> Unless the principle of sex purity be established in the individual life and in the social code, the work of our hands comes to naught. Unless the principle of economic righteousness can be established so that none will take more than they create and each will get all that he produces, men's hands will be continually raised against each other, and there will be unending warfare. Unless we can put God into these formative relationships in life, religion is not established. When this is done, it becomes the partnership of men with God, not for the gain and benefit of a select few, but for the good of all. Nothing less than this is the realization of life, and unless religion dominates the fundamental social relationships, it fails and life fails with it,—there is nothing left but outer darkness.[30]

All of these steps pave the way for the proclamation of the social ideal in all its charm and power. The gospel of the kingdom gives us a new social possibility to be realized in human society. This prospect is a challenge to faith to believe in the program of God. Such faith laughs at impossibilities and cries "It shall be done."

> There are three steps in the development of the faith that will transform the kingdoms of this world by the spirit of Jesus. The evangelism of the Evangelical Revival developed a faith that, in the face of the

---

29. Ward, *Social Evangelism*, 108-9.
30. Ibid., 109-10.

FROM REVIVALISM TO SOCIALISM

great immorality of English society and the deadly formalism of English religion, dared believe in the complete transformation of the individual life. The evangelism of the Missionary Movement, in the face of the narrow provincial pride, the entrenched prejudices, and the armed jealousies and ambitions of modern nationalism, dared believe in the redemption of all mankind, asserted the spiritual equality and the resultant temporal rights of the so-called inferior races. The evangelism of the Social Awakening, in the face of all the brutalities and sordidness of our Christian civilization, develops a faith that here in this world of time and place, in the very muck and mire of life, with no other material than these weak human lives, the city of God can be built.[31]

The church must both proclaim this ideal in word and secure it in deed. The family, the state, and industry are to be reconstructed to fit this New World order.

What about results? These can be left to God. "To bear the Word is the supreme commission. To sow the seed is the primary task; to see the harvest is not essential."[32] Here the church should be like her master and trust that God's Word cannot return to him void.

The love of statistics possesses the modern churches as an evil spirit and unless it be exorcised it will presently carry them far from the path of Jesus and run them headlong into the oblivion in which the world of tomorrow will bury those religious organizations that can find no bigger goal than the development of their own ecclesiastical life.[33]

To be sure, there will be results. There will, for example, be the tangible amelioration of the community life. But this consequence is hard to measure. The full effects and the full value of social evangelism can only appear "when the work of men's hands is seen without the veil of time and sense."[34]

An Evaluation of Ward's Contribution to Evangelism

In coming to terms with Ward's proposals in evangelism, we have to explain the most conspicuous fact: They failed. They did not

31. Ibid., 117.
32. Ibid., 131.
33. Ibid., 135.
34. Ibid., 145.

survive, and they are now something of a historical curiosity. Even Ward himself seemed to have given up on them. Certainly by the time of his retirement from Union Theological Seminary, he had given up on the church. Link tells us that church attendance was not among the rituals of Ward's life.

> Granddaughter Robin Ward Savage asked him, "Do you go to church?" "No," was the quick response, "I only go when I am giving the sermon." "Why?" she pressed, and that brought the reply, "Because it is often too dull and boring."[35]

Link explains that this behavior was due to Ward's dislike of trivia, pomp, and escapism. It is hard to believe that this explanation clarifies the whole story, but that is beyond our ken. In my judgment, if Ward did not abandon his proposals on evangelism, he should have done so. Or at least he should have drastically overhauled them.

By making this suggestion, I mean absolutely no disrespect for Ward or his efforts. Ward's work highlights a host of issues in evangelism that deserve extensive discussion. He brings to our attention such matters as the place of the kingdom of God in our evangelism, the place of evangelism in the transformation of society, the role of the church in the preservation of Western civilization, the nature of true repentance, the place of judgment in the proclamation of the gospel, the relation between evangelism and church growth, and the special requirements of evangelism among the poor and wretched of the earth. His work has other effects too. It gives the lie to those who think that liberal Protestants have nothing of substance to say about evangelism, as if evangelism is the property of conservatives and evangelicals. It shows that those committed to the Social Gospel really did mean business about evangelism.[36] His work demonstrates, moreover, that such proponents did not believe in some doctrine of inevitable progress; they were as much realists about the harsh nature of the world as their later critics. Furthermore, Ward clearly anticipates developments in the theology of liberation that are beginning to surface at his death. We might even call him a proto-liberation theologian, although we can be sure that he would be amused at this kind of suggestion. Finally, Ward shows both courage and persistence

---

35. Link, *Labor-Religion Prophet*, 294.

36. This point is equally true of Ward's friend, Walter Rauschenbusch. For an excellent essay on the latter, see Winthrop S. Hudson, "Walter Rauschenbusch and the New Evangelism," *Religion in Life* 30 (1961): 412-30.

in his attempts to grapple with the new issues that emerged at the turn of the century. So Ward is an eloquent witness to the need for careful reflection about evangelism; he deserves our respect and attention.

The crucial problems in Ward are these: he is mistaken to think that we can make an easy conceptual shift from the regeneration of the individual to the regeneration of society; he is profoundly uncritical of the theory of social change that captures his allegiance; he has virtually no ecclesiology; he is working with a hopelessly reduced account of Christianity; and he is far too conservative in his analysis of evangelistic method. In turn, all of these problems can be traced to the legacy of the theological tradition he inhabited and inherited.

We can enter this domain by imagining the journey that Ward took over time. Ward began life as a street evangelist and conventional Methodist. The evangelist in this tradition was primarily a preacher; this role represented the fundamental method of evangelism he inherited.[37] Moreover, he was committed to personal conversion and the remnants of a doctrine of perfection. These foci provided both hope for the future and a yardstick for challenging the evils of life. His evangelistic work took him among the poor. His personalistic evangelism, however, did not work, or at least it was inadequate to meet the harsh realities of the social order. His first move in response was to enlarge the message. He simply extended the quest for regeneration so that it embraced the regeneration and perfection of the social order. His sense of the latter was confirmed and deepened by his work in economics and sociology. Ward now felt that he had a whole gospel for the whole of life. In terms of later jargon, he was committed to holistic evangelism. Yet he did not change drastically his evangelistic methods. He stuck to proclamation as represented by the revivalistic tradition, stretching this notion to mean proclamation in deed as well as word. The results were surely predictable. This approach did not work.[38] The world will not be changed by preaching or by a combination of preaching and the moralistic activity of either Methodist preachers or laity. Ward's own theory of society would even suggest this conclusion, for it is clear that he believed social environment to be almost determinative of the life of

---

37. I am presuming that this perception of evangelism was prevalent; the historical reality, in my view, was very different.

38. By 1916 already, trade-union evangelism had peaked. It did not work in the case of immigrant workers or in cases where factory owners were determined to break the power of the workers. Fones-Wolf, "Trade-Union Evangelism," 171-78.

the individual. Anyone as passionately committed to the redemption of the social order and as intelligent as Ward is likely in such circumstances to look for a more concrete and adequate analysis of the causes of the corporate evils of society. And like many others of his generation, he found the answer in Marxism. His visit to the Soviet Union confirmed that the Marxist theory was eminently practical and realistic in bringing salvation to the world. Once Ward had adopted this stance, it was unlikely that the new evangelism would be sustained. From the point of view of Marxism, there was a better and more concrete way to change the world. Socialism was the divinely driven force that could realize, here and now, the kingdom of God taught to us by Jesus. Ward had now found the real evangelism that would change the social order.[39]

We do not need to draw attention to the collapse of Ward's beloved Soviet Empire to know that there is something drastically wrong in all this. The seeds of destruction already lie buried in Ward's own hidden assumptions. We have already identified the chief problems. They merit further elaboration.

(1) Although Ward freely shifts from the regeneration or redemption of the individual to the regeneration and redemption of society, he is stretching the language of his Wesleyan tradition beyond its natural and appropriate boundaries. There is no way we can apply the language of the *ordo salutis* to the social order coherently. To be sure, we can make various metaphors stretch from the individual to society; this is precisely why Ward can write as he does. Where, however, are we to place such a crucial component of personal salvation as the internal witness of the Holy Spirit? How are we to talk of justification by faith in the realm of the social order? To raise these questions is to exhibit the absurdity of Ward's fundamental move in his definition of social evangelism.

(2) Ward is naive in his deliberations about the nature of the social sciences, hence he is uncritical in his commitment to Marxism. At the theoretical level, we might describe Ward as a naive realist in his epistemology of the social sciences. Things are as the social scientist tells us. This perspective simply ignores the role of anthropological assumptions at the foundations of the social sciences. More specifically, his conception of the role of law in the social order is

---

39. Note that I am not offering this narrative as a historical hypothesis about Ward's life. I am interested merely in unearthing the crucial conceptual issues that are at stake in the discussion.

178

heavily deterministic. This view is controversial theoretically, for it fails to take account of the role of the human agent in society. Theologically, it creates insoluble problems in the realm of theodicy. Morally, it is a disaster, for it cloaks sociopolitical proposals with an air of scientific certainty that they do not and cannot possess.

(3) One of the ironies of Ward's vision of evangelism is that despite his avowed commitment to the social sciences, he has nothing of substance to say about the crucial role of the church in evangelism. One would have thought that a sociologist would have been alert to this omission. Like many who come after him, Ward moves straight from proclamation to the reformation of society. He has no sense of the need for mediating institutions that will nurture the individual and the Christian congregation in changing the social order. Amazingly, despite his merciless excoriating of the ancient church for seeking to develop a Christian state, Ward's own proposal entails nothing less that a full-blown theocracy. Family, state, and industry are all to be ruled more or less directly by God. This prospect represents a return to the age of Christendom with a vengeance.

(4) This perspective should not surprise us, for Ward is working with a hopelessly reduced account of the gospel and of Christianity. The vast riches of the canonical traditions of the church, which together are needed to cope with the complexity, angularity, twistedness, and unpredictability of personal and social life, are whittled down to the bare bones. The kingdom of God, for example, is conveniently shorn of its apocalyptic dimensions and repackaged uncritically to fit with the cultural and intellectual trends of the day. It is small wonder that a later generation revolts in its efforts to retrieve lost and forgotten elements of the Christian heritage. We have yet to recover from the vast ecological damage that Ward's generation has wrought in its wasting of the forests of the tradition.

(5) Ward is blind to the methodological conservatism that he inherits from the nineteenth century's obsession with proclamation as the heart of evangelism. He completely misses the role of the church, more specifically the role of the small group, in the owning of the gospel for oneself. Getting the message straight is only half the issue; the other is devising a healthy catechumenate where people can come to genuine faith and be initiated into the costly demands of discipleship in society at large.[40]

---

40. I have argued this case in *The Logic of Evangelism* (Grand Rapids, Mich.: Wm. B. Eerdmans Publishing Co., 1989).

These problems are not accidental. They stem from a recurring feature of the Wesleyan tradition as it has played itself out in the arena of evangelism over the last two centuries. That feature is its failure to sustain the kind of deep doctrinal heritage that will secure the identity of the gospel and enable her evangelists to examine critically the competitors it must face in the modern world. To express the matter bluntly, despite his obvious intelligence, Ward is intellectually lazy when it comes to the hard theological and doctrinal issues that are central to evangelism. I have sometimes wondered whether this condition is a disease that can be cured. It will certainly not be cured merely by academic diligence or by more papers like this. Like it or not, however, we must find a cure if we are to correct the mistakes of the past. We must also find a cure if we are to grapple and resolve the theoretical and practical problems in evangelism that Ward has so vividly brought to our attention.

CHAPTER NINE

"The Poor Will Always Be with You": Can Wesley Help Us Discover How Best to Serve "Our Poor" Today?

José Míguez Bonino

When the fullness of time comes, anticipates Wesley, there is "no oppression to 'make (even) the wise man mad'; no extortion to 'grind the face of the poor.' "[1] Meanwhile, " 'the poor have you always with you,' " not as a mere fact to be passively accepted but as a permanent invitation to serve them, so that "you would no more ask, 'What shall I do?' "[2]

---

1. Sermon 4, "Scriptural Christianity," III.3, *Works*, 1:170.

2. Sermon 126, "On Worldly Folly," I.4, *Works*, 4:134. At several points, Wesley refers in similar terms to these words of Jesus, for instance, in Sermon 88, "On Dress," §14, referring to luxury: "Every shilling which you save . . . you may expend in clothing the naked, and relieving the various necessities of the poor, whom ye 'have always with you' " (*Works*, 3:254); and in Sermon 99, "The Reward of Righteousness," III.2, referring to works of mercy: "Occasions of doing this can never be wanting; for 'the poor ye have always with you' " (ibid., 413). Frequently, the idea of eschatological "reward" for works of mercy appears, as in the comment in *Explanatory Notes upon the New Testament* on Matt. 26:11, "Such is the wise and gracious Providence of God, that we may have always opportunities of relieving their Wants [of the poor], and so laying up for ourselves treasures in heaven." See also Charles Wesley's hymn on Matt. 26:11, "Ye have the poor always with you" (*Unpublished Poetry*, 2:46):

> Yes; the poor supply thy place,
>   Still deputed, Lord, by Thee,
> Daily exercise our grace,
>   Prove our growing charity;
> What to them with right intent
>   Truly, faithfully is given,
> We have to our Saviour lent,
>   Laid up for ourselves in heaven.

181

Poverty: the Poor

"Poverty" means, literally, a lack of something, having lost or been deprived of something. The range of possibilities is so wide that the temptation is always present to void the word of any concrete meaning by playing with contrasting or mutually neutralizing alternatives. But so also is the tendency to concentrate in such a way that one particular need appears as the only possible concern. Moreover, poverty is not only a complex and multifaceted phenomenon but also an interplay of historical—and therefore changing—conditions and situations. Thus, in the Puebla Conference of 1979, the Latin American Council of (Roman Catholic) Bishops spoke of Latin American poverty as "the faces of the poor," describing in detail the conditions of children, young people, native populations, peasants, and workers.[3] They could well have added women, people with disabilities, or religious minorities.

Wesley seems aware of this plurality of faces. In fact, he describes them many times. But he seems to use the term "poverty" (aside from the concept of "spiritual poverty") almost exclusively for conditions characterized by economic and social deprivation, which can be related to a variety of circumstances, such as unemployment, sickness, and imprisonment. In the ensuing discussion, we shall focus on this area, not because other forms of deprivation would not deserve attention, but because in the present Latin American conditions, as in the eighteenth-century British picture, these faces of poverty have a special claim on Christians.

Historians have an ongoing discussion of the social and economic conditions of eighteenth-century Britain. Many issues are far from settled, such as the social and economic impact of enclosures, the reasons for the growth of the population, the relation of the development of agriculture and the rise of an industrial society, and the birth of a new bourgeoisie. Moreover, the eighteenth century is not a homogenous period. Clearly identifiable ups and downs occurred in the forces and forms of production during the half century of Wesley's active life, from the 1730s to the 1780s. However, a new face of poverty was clearly emerging. In England, writes Gertrude Himmelfarb,

---

3. See Helen Bolkomener, ed., *Proceedings of the [Third] Latin American Bishops Conference* (CELAM): Puebla, Mexico, January 27–February 13, 1979.

in the period of only a century [the eighteenth century], circumstances conspired to create a highly differentiated poor. . . . This was not a matter . . . of raising or lowering the "poverty level". . . . The changes affecting the poor were changes in kind as well as . . . quantity, in ideas, attitudes, beliefs, perceptions, values. They were changes in what may be called the "moral imagination."[4]

The emergence of this "new poverty" has found dramatic expression in literature, probably beginning with some of Defoe's writings. These conditions gave rise to ethical concerns in some philosophers who, like the eighteenth-century Tory Samuel Johnson, would claim that "A decent provision for the poor is the true test of civilization."[5] We need not cite Wesley's descriptions of what he found from the early days of the Oxford Methodists to the evangelistic trips through the country, in visits to jails, homes, hospitals, in the gatherings of the missionary tours, or in the organizations and social programs of the societies. His diaries, sermons, treatises, and hymns contain the same pictures as the novelists or as the historians such as Hobsbawm, Hufton, and even Toynbee. Wesley's depictions, however, are fired with the mercy, anger, and commitment of his evangelical faith.

To what extent Methodism and earlier religious groups were significant in the birth and extension of the workers' movements (the organized resistance of the poor) is, as we know, a vexed question. In his well-known book, *Primitive Rebels*, Eric Hobsbawm allots religious groups a minor role in the eighteenth century: "In all these [industrialized] areas life was, for the working class, miserable, poor, nasty, brutish, short and above all insecure, and the religions they chose for themselves mirrored their situation."[6] For him, their role was minimal and, in any case, only transitional. He seems to admit, however, that the case of Methodism is a somewhat different phenomenon. He would certainly question Elie Halévy's well-known claim of a decisive social role for Methodism in the gradual and nonviolent transition to modernity.[7] Bernard Semmel, in turn, has argued that the initial participation of Methodist leadership in the workers' movement

4. Gertrude Himmelfarb, *The Idea of Poverty: England in the Early Industrial Age* (New York: Alfred A. Knopf, 1984), 18-19.
5. James Boswell, *The Life of Samuel Johnson*, 3 vols. (New York: Heritage Press, 1963), 1:452 (1770).
6. E. J. Hobsbawm, *Primitive Rebels: Studies in Archaic Forms of Social Movement in the 19th and 20th Centuries*, 2d ed. (New York: Frederick A. Praeger, 1963), 131.
7. Ibid., 128-29; see Bernard Semmel, ed., *The Birth of Methodism in England* (Chicago: University of Chicago Press, 1971). I also think that Halévy's thesis, to put it mildly, is greatly exaggerated.

at the end of the eighteenth and the beginning of the nineteenth centuries remained marginal or broke away from the central Methodist movement.[8] They were resisted by the leadership of Methodism that was already caught in the bourgeois mind-set, critically anticipated by Wesley himself, and that had embarked in the missionary enterprise related to the expansion of the British empire.

Wesley's Poor and Ours

Here, we are not concerned with the social impact of the Wesleyan movement but rather with Wesley's own stance toward the question of poverty and the poor—his understanding of it, his theological assessment of it, and his response to it. I am especially interested in those insights that seem to be relevant for our own Latin American Christian response to "our poverty" and "our poor." In this endeavor, we must avoid a direct transcription from eighteenth-century Britain to twenty-first century Latin America. The temptation to read Wesley in this manner (as we frequently do in our hermeneutics of Biblical writings) is especially strong when, in Wesley's writings, we find descriptions that "literally" fit into our own experiences. Who of us, who have moved about the outskirts of Latin American cities, will not want to repeat words like these?

> What shall [the poor] do who have none of these [that is, food, raiment, lodging]? Who as it were "embrace the rock for a shelter"? Who have only the earth to lie upon, and only the sky to cover them? Who have not a dry, or warm, much less a clean abode for themselves and their little ones? No, nor clothing to keep themselves, or those they love next themselves, from pinching cold, either by day or night? . . . God pronounced it as a curse upon man that he should earn [his food] by "the sweat of his brow". But how many are there in this Christian country that toil and labour, and sweat, and have it not at last? . . . Were it not that he is restrained by an unseen hand, would he not soon "curse God and die"? . . . Who can tell what this means unless he hath felt it himself?[9]

Such pictures might exactly fit many of our conditions. But they are set against a different background, a different social and economic

---

8. See Bernard Semmel, *The Methodist Revolution* (New York: Basic Books, 1973).
9. Sermon 47, "Heaviness through Manifold Temptations," III.3, *Works*, 2:227-28.

dynamic. Simply put, Wesley's picture belongs to a society that was moving into industrial capitalism. As Wesley himself recognizes in several writings, they are experiencing a growth in production, an expansion of business, and an appropriation of resources and markets through territorial expansion. A new social class is emerging, and many of the poor who have been rescued by the Methodist movement are coming into a new condition, through work and a clean and sober life. Britain was at the head of a "new world" that would sweep through northern Europe and the North American colonies. The workers' organizations, not without struggle and paying a high price, will claim and win their participation in the rich new world within the dynamics and structures of industrial capitalism. The service that Methodists and other evangelicals rendered to their society's poor—and Wesley's initiatives are good symbols for them—were adequate, fitting, and efficacious in the difficult interim period through which industrial capitalism was moving at that time. They helped people to integrate themselves actively into the new society that was emerging, to acquire the virtues and attitudes that were constructive for that society, and in many cases, to assume critical attitudes and initiatives to correct or moderate its negative tendencies.

But that picture is not the situation of our poor today. To be sure, the type of society that developed in the northern world has been the dream of the progressive elites of our countries since the beginning of this century. But, as we know, although many changes have taken place and some features of that society found their way into sectors of ours, we find ourselves, at the turn of the new century, further than ever from the model of a growing, dynamic, and open political economy. We have no time here to assess the political and economic history of Latin America throughout this past century. But at least two phenomena, which are shared by most so-called third world societies, deserve to be mentioned.

The first is clearly summarized by Professor Duncan Forrester:

> Because poverty is understood as primarily systemic, produced by inadequate political, economic and social organization, today's global interdependence of these systems makes poverty dependent upon a constellation of forces which transcend national boundaries and policies. Those peoples who are culturally, technologically, economically and politically powerful globally re-inforce their own (and one another's) power, at the expense of the half to three-quarters of the world's

185

people living in poverty. An adequate analysis of poverty and an effective strategy to diminish it have to be conceived globally.[10]

The second phenomenon—clearly related to the former, although also resulting from characteristics and deficiencies of the poor countries—is illustrated in the analysis and prospects of the last two decades made by the Economic Commission for Latin America (ECLA-CEPAL), an instrument of the United Nations hardly suspect of revolutionary leanings. It speaks of the 1980s as "the lost decade," characterized by a "marked process of globalization . . . of national economies," accompanied by a "fall in production, international indebtedness, regressive redistribution, fall in salaries and in the social expense (education, health, security) per inhabitant." In the later part of the 1980s and the first years of the 1990s, all countries went through processes of "adjustment": anti-inflationary programs, efforts to stabilize the balance of payments and obtain deferments in meeting the service of the debts, the shrinking of the state, and privatization. The results have been the growth of the debt, the loss in the purchasing power of the frozen salaries (no less than 30 percent in five years), increasing unemployment (which has now become structural), more regressive taxes, concentration of wealth in the highest two tenths of the population, and increasing marginality and criminality.

Lest we think all of this is due to the proverbial inefficiency of the Latin American "siesta people," we can see some of these signs, perhaps in a less dramatic way, in European societies and in the celebrated "tigers" of South East Asia.[11] In Latin America, CEPAL suggested a way of measuring success: the relation between growth and equity. In the report, it places seven countries in the category of "growth without equity," ten in that of "neither growth nor equity," and two in that of "equity without growth." In summary, Latin America has no country that combines growth and equity. Nobody dares today—and this view is joined by some of the more conspicuous economists of the developed world—to insist on the classic answer, "Let us grow, the market knows how to distribute and we'll see that the 'trickle down' effect will soon begin to function."

10. "Poverty," *Dictionary of the Ecumenical Movement* (Geneva: World Council of Churches Publications, 1991), 807.

11. Curiously enough, the concentration of wealth at the top 15 percent of the population, the loss in the salaries in the lower levels, and the percentage of people below the poverty line seems to be noted also in the United States in the midst of a flowering economy. See, for instance, Herman E. Daly and John B. Cobb, Jr., *For the Common Good: Redirecting the Economy toward Community, the Environment, and a Sustainable Future*, 2d ed. (Boston: Beacon Press, 1994),

In fact, recession is appearing in almost all Latin American countries (from annual growth of 4 percent to 7 percent in the nineties, we are now moving down to negative figures of minus 2 percent to minus 5 percent). The well-known ghosts of illiteracy, infantile disease, drug traffic, and delinquency, are not simply a passing "moment"—they are projecting themselves into at least the next decades. Although included in all political programs and speeches, the priorities indicated by CEPAL in 1994 fade further away: education, a greater investment in social expense, and conditions of competitiveness at the international level. I do not intend to paint an apocalyptic picture. Some of the international "gurus" are doing it much more effectively,[12] amazingly, as if they had no part or responsibility for what is happening and without suggesting any ways of turning the tide that they themselves promoted! There is no need to exaggerate. Reality is exaggerated enough, as anybody with open eyes can see. It is within this society that Methodists, and other churches and religious expressions, will have to operate in the next decades.

Wesley and "Our Poverty"

The contemporary poor clearly represent a different poverty in a different world from Wesley's. While our poor suffer just as those of eighteenth-century Britain, ours are in a qualitatively different condition in their social prospects, expectations, and attitudes. Even in our own terms, the "poor of the end of the century" are not the hopeful, militant, socially conscious poor of the 1960s. Can Wesley help us discern how can Christians minister to these "new poor"? A dialogue with Wesley would seem to be fruitful in at least four areas.

(1) Wesley is not content with describing and denouncing the condition of the poor or with simply practicing and commending works of mercy in their favor. Rather, he tries to understand the social, economic, and political conditions that produce poverty. Besides the much-quoted attempt to identify the "causes and cure of poverty," or the reasons for "the present scarcity of provisions" (1773), Wesley published a number of treatises ("Thoughts") that referred to

---

and Wallace C. Peterson, *Silent Depression: The Fate of the American Dream* (New York: W. W. Norton, 1994).

12. See, for instance, the recent analysis by Bill Gates, *The Road Ahead* (New York: Viking, 1995).

the specific conditions in the nation: public affairs, freedom, power, slavery, the state of the nation. He makes constant reference to the economic dimensions of moral and political issues. Even seemingly minor questions, like his views on dressing or on dissipation, he relates to a Christian's responsibility toward the poor. Naturally, some of his analyses and interpretations may sound simplistic or partial, and his political views are clearly conservative. There was not yet a systemic, much less an ideological, analysis. Adam Smith's classic, *Wealth of Nations*, the first "enlightened" attempt to understand the nature of the emerging economics, appeared in 1776, almost contemporary to Wesley's *Thoughts on the Scarcity of Provisions* (1773). Even Smith describes the capitalist economy without using the word "capitalism," and Marx and Engels had not yet been born. But it is particularly significant that, railing against what Warner calls "the typical judgement of the day [that] blamed the unfortunate for their own condition" (just as is frequently done today), Wesley retorted with anger after describing his own experience with the poor: "So wickedly, devilishly false is that common objection, 'They are poor because they are idle.' "[13]

Wesley is original and challenging in his courage to step beyond the boundaries of religion and take the risk to give to Christian mercy and justice a specific and operative project. Ironically, when Methodist (and other) Christians and churches in the so-called third world began in the 1960s and 1970s to relate their faith to concrete issues of social, political, and racial oppression and to commit themselves to specific initiatives for change, many of the leaders sitting in "Wesley's chair" were horrified at this mixing of faith and politics, or faith and economics. Clearly, Wesley's analyses of the eighteenth century cannot be applied directly to our present situation. Nor can we mechanically repeat those analyses of the 1960s. As we noticed a moment ago, our poor are caught in a new condition, shaped by the process of economic globalization, the weakening of the nation-state in relation to the transnational corporations, and the neoliberal

---

13. The first quotation is from Wellman Joel Warner, *The Wesleyan Movement in the Industrial Revolution* (New York: Russell & Russell, 1967), 455. The paragraph from which Wesley's words are taken deserves to be read in its entirety: "On Friday and Saturday I visited as many more [sick] as I could. I found some in their cells underground, others in their garrets, half starved both with cold and hunger, added to weakness and pain. But I found not one of them unemployed who was able to crawl about the room. So wickedly, devilishly false is that common objection, 'They are poor only because they are idle.' If you saw these things with your own eyes, could you lay out money in ornaments or superfluities?" *Journal* (9-10 February 1753), *Works*, 20:445.

ideology of a self-determined omniscient and omnipotent market. The question of poverty becomes for us the question of exclusion and, therefore, of structural unemployment and permanent deterioration of the social, educational, and health conditions of the excluded majorities in economies that are caught in a downward slope of recession.

In this situation, our "thoughts" today have to move in at least three directions: (a) the analysis and critique of the ideology that justifies the present form of globalization, a task that Wesley could only do, and did, in a symbolic way in his critique of luxury, dissipation, or unconcern (with the exception of slavery, where he was able to construct a powerful ethical and theological critique); (b) the discussion of possible alternatives in issues like foreign debts, equitable legislation on trade, construction of regional coalitions that have a greater possibility of negotiation of the laws of the market, and international legislation for the control of the financial market; and (c) the strengthening of "civil society" and especially of the forms of organization that give to the poor the possibility of participation in power. For these tasks Wesley is not an intellectual or political resource but an inspiration, an invitation to put in action, in relation to our poor, the best analytical tools, the most creative forms of association and action, and the persistent commitment that he tried to exercise in his ministry.

(2) The most devastating effect of the growing poverty by exclusion, which already affects not only the large majorities at the bottom of the social pyramid but also, increasingly, people in the two lower levels of the middle class, is its demoralizing effect on the people. Perhaps the most powerful symbol of this situation is the growth of structural unemployment. What happens to a teenager or a young college student who realizes that, upon completion of their study, his or her possibilities of getting a job, starting a family, or building a home are at least dubious and perhaps nonexistent? Such a situation immediately creates uncertainty about oneself: *who am I? who cares what I do? what am I good for?* The questions might not be verbalized; instead they are just a strange gut feeling of insecurity, anger, and despondency. A person who begins to lose self-respect will scarcely respect others. The roads to self-destruction—occasional changes (temporary jobs), begging, trying to sell useless and unwanted trash from house to house, tramping around, prostituting, drinking, distributing and using drugs, delinquency—these increasingly seem to

189

be the only roads open. One's own failure and devaluation leads to indifference toward and devaluation of another. Who will care for the other if he/she cannot love and respect him/herself?

Wesley had seen this condition (not always for exactly the same reasons) as he moved around the country and knew its destructive effects. How can one restore these people to a "human" condition, to a sense of their dignity? Basically, he settles on two responses. One is social, and the other is theological. The latter rests on two pillars: prevenient grace and the invitation of the gospel. Both responses are powerfully expressed in two letters: one to a drunkard and the other to "an unhappy woman" (a prostitute). "Are you a man!" he asks the former.

> God made you a man; but you make yourself a beast. . . .
> O do not aim at any excuse! Say not, as many do, "I am no one's enemy but my own." If it were so, what a poor saying is this, "I give none but my own soul to the devil." Alas! is not that too much? Why shouldest thou give him thy own soul? Do it not. Rather give it to God.[14]

And to the second he says:

> "Know ye not, that ye are the temples of God?" Was not you designed for the Spirit of God to dwell in? . . .
> Know you not, that your body is, or ought to be, the temple of the Holy Ghost which is in you? . . .
> . . . You yourself are ashamed of what you do. Are you not? Conscience, speak in the sight of God! . . . Dare, for once, to lay your hand upon your breast, and ask, "What am I doing? And what must the end of these things be?" . . .
> "But you have no friend; none at least that is able to help you." Indeed you have: One that is a present help in time of trouble. You have a friend that has all power in heaven and earth, even Jesus Christ the righteous. He loved sinners of old; and he does so still. . . . Say, Amen! Lift up your heart, and it shall be done."[15]

Gustavo Gutiérrez has defined the condition of the excluded as "the non-person." Wesley addresses the non-person in the perspective of grace: God's Holy Spirit is already present in you—you may not be a person for those around you or for yourself. But you are a person for God. Be therefore who you are! Claim the fullness that is

---

14. *A Word to a Drunkard,* §§1, 8, *Works* (Jackson), 11:169-70.
15. *A Word to an Unhappy Woman,* §§3–5, 8, *Works* (Jackson), 11:172-73.

yours; that is the good news of the Gospel! In our countries, millions of poor people are hearing this message and responding to it. They hear it from the evangelists preaching in the square; or in the home of a neighbor, a relative, or a coworker who invites them to "the meeting in my house"; or in the pastor who visits them in prison. What Wesley offers to this effort is an understanding of human life and of God that corresponds to this message of hope. In other words, he provides an anthropology that vindicates the dignity of any human being and a soteriology that invites people to develop fully the potential of that dignity.

(3) The subjective question of how people experience the condition of poverty also has a social correlate: how society experiences the ethical question of poverty and the poor. Eighteenth-century England was aware of the issue. Several "ethical societies" for the reformation of behavior, such as The Society for the Reformation of Manners, were created early in the century, and some "Propositions" were published. Several people, such as William Law, had forcefully expressed their concern over the corruption of society and the need for an ethical reform. Wesley, in fact, understood his call to "spread scriptural holiness" not merely as an individual question or even as the rescue of groups but as an instrument to "reform the nation." Regardless of how one views the immediate or long-term social and moral consequences (positive and negative) of the evangelical movement that swept through Great Britain and the American colonies, Wesley's mission seems undoubtedly to have had a significant impact on the self-understanding of the British mind, values, and behaviors.

Today, the dimensions of the social question are a very serious concern. A struggle for and with the poor does not rest only on the transformation of economic and social structures, which is indispensable, but also on the transformation (both among the poor and in the larger society) of the ideological and ethical self-understanding of that society—what Thomas Luckmann calls "the horizons of meaning" that inspire and justify the goals, ways of acting, and "moral arrangements" of a society.[16] As our Latin American hybrid cultures face the encounter of premodern, modern, and postmodern trends with the claims of neoliberal market ideology as "the only alternative" or "the new world order," religion has to play its role as both a comforting and prophetic presence, as both assurance and challenge. At precisely this point, the Wesleyan way of understanding human

16. See Luckman, *The Invisible Religion* (New York: Macmillan, 1967).

life and the invitation to a socially aware and personal committed faith that provided the dynamic of the early Wesleyan movement is both an inspiration and a source of insight for our Christian testimony.

(4) Finally, we should note the significance of Wesley's (perhaps somewhat abused) emphasis on "social holiness." This point concerns the ways in which Wesley tried to make the social dimension of holiness operative in practical ways in the organization of groups, the networks of relations, and the creation of institutions to meet specific needs—economic, educational, and social. In a larger sense, one can speak of a participation in the weaving of the civil society. The struggle against poverty is tied in Latin America (though certainly not only in Latin America) with a number of issues in which the role of civil society is of primary significance: the struggle for a participatory democracy; the strengthening of Latin American social, economic, and cultural ties over against the self-destructing nationalisms; and the organization of associations and groups to combat corruption both in government and in private economic life.

Christian churches have, in Latin America, an unprecedented opportunity to participate in this process, specifically in the growing number of Protestant evangelical communities and in the base Catholic movements and communities among the poor and middle sectors of society. Wesley's example should be an inspiration for us insofar as his theology rests on an organic unity between the personal encounter with Christ in the power of the Spirit and the commitment to a life of active love and service. Theologically, we could speak of a simultaneous process of justification and sanctification. In practical terms, at a moment of evangelistic growth, this combination protects us against what could be called a religious consumerism without ethical consequences, which is present in some mass evangelism. In this sense, Wesley's bringing together works of piety and works of mercy, against the dominant tendency to keep them separate, has great theological significance. In fact, as Professor Rieger has shown, Wesley goes even further by understanding works of mercy, in terms of responsibility for the poor, as a test of the authenticity of our piety.[17] Such a relationship ought to protect our piety from an introverted and escapist spirituality, and our mercy from an evangelically

---

17. Joerg Rieger, "The Means of Grace: John Wesley, and the Theological Dilemma of the Church Today," *Quarterly Review* (Winter 1997–98): 377-93. See also "Spiritualitat der Befreiung? John Wesleys Sorge für die Armen und Gnadenmittel," *Theologie für die Praxis* 21.1 (1995): 17-35.

aseptic neutrality that, far from respecting the freedom of the poor (as it is sometimes claimed), robs mercy of its deeper dimension: the invitation to live, joyfully, a new life in Christ.

We should also, however, be aware of the danger in that participation, both in Methodism and even more in other massive evangelical movements. This unity of religion and social activism, inspired by the numerical strength and dynamism of evangelical churches, has already become a temptation for some in their attempts to occupy places of political power or initiate evangelical political parties. In a society that has suffered from ecclesiocratic control, the social participation of Christians could easily be confused with the attempt simply to seek political power. Although, in the British conditions at Wesley's time, there was not much risk that Methodists could do that, his theology does not seem to be guarded enough against this confusion. Perhaps some carefully protected doses of Lutheran "two Kingdom theology" would not be bad for our overconfident evangelical movements. Participation in the development of civil society keeps its Christian and evangelical character in so far as it is clear that civilian society is civilian.

Contemporary Issues and Models of Ministry with the Poor, the Underrepresented, and the Ignored: A Panel Discussion

Introductory Comments, Joerg Rieger

Before we look at contemporary issues and models of ministry, we need to give an account of where we are at this point in our exploration of the relation of the Wesleys and the poor. A common theme has emerged in many of the presentations and discussions: Love of the poor is inextricably connected to love of God. We are all well aware of the relation of this insight to Jesus' own concern for the love of God and the love of neighbor, which he saw as the sum of the commandments. A well-known passage, 1 John 4:20, puts a similar insight into the following words: "Those who say, 'I love God,' and hate their brothers or sisters, are liars; for those who do not love a brother or sister whom they have seen, cannot love God whom they have not seen." Here is certainly one of the biggest challenges for the ministry of the church today. We need to remind ourselves that even well-meaning and orthodox claims to love God easily turn into lies unless they are tied to love for brothers and sisters.

Once this point is clear, however, we need to face yet another challenge. There is always a danger of idealizing and romanticizing the poor, and the call to love them does not necessarily overcome this problem. At a time when love is often seen as not much more than a nondescript feeling of sympathy, it is easy to convince ourselves that we love those who are less fortunate, at least as long as they do not impose on us. The same is true in our relationship with God. But what if love is different—what if love implies respect as well? To learn how to respect poor people cuts through idealization and romanticization, and opens the way to learning about their real struggles and hopes and how these challenge us. A similar dynamic applies to our relation with God as well: Learning how to respect God (something that might well be trained in the context of learning how to respect others) helps us to become aware in new ways of where God is at work and how this challenges our lives.

At this point, new relationships can be built that end the works-righteousness that is at times a temptation of those who care about the poor. The question is not what we can do for those who are less well off—efforts which often end up turning other people and even God into our own image—but how we can experience God's grace together. Grace, we are beginning to realize, comes to us in unexpected ways in relationships where we begin to open up to those who are different from us—to brothers and sisters whom we see and, closely related, to God whom we do not see, to paraphrase 1 John. Only if we give up our attempts to assimilate both the poor and God to ourselves will we be able to move to the next step.

Already, John Wesley knew of the dangers of a church that forgot about the poor. At one point, he reminds us that "religion must not go from the greatest to the least, or the power would appear to be of men" (Journal, May 21, 1764). But is that not the way we generally proceed in the mainline churches when we develop our models of ministry? Is that not the way we understand terms such as *charity* and *ministry*, as moving from the haves to the have-nots? If Christianity works the other way around, however, we need to develop new models. One example is the West Dallas Project at Perkins School of Theology, which I helped initiate a few years ago. Here, faculty and students interact with people in a neighborhood suffering from oppression, mainly along the lines of race and class. Our experiences show how theological reflection, Christian praxis, and even spiritual formation are transformed in this context. We have found that meeting God in West Dallas can indeed change one's life. In the following contributions the panelists will introduce other models that transform lives.

An important question that has been raised throughout this conference is, Who are the poor? One of the epigraphs in my recent book, *Remember the Poor: The Challenge to Theology in the Twenty-First Century* (Harrisburg, Pa.: Trinity Press International, 1998), states that "*the* poor do not exist." There is a danger in universalizing the term and thus forgetting that poor people have actual faces, names, and stories. We can only form true bonds of solidarity if we develop actual relationships to people at the margins of our world. Like Wesley, we must not begin with generalizations but with close encounters with real people who are suffering. It is in these relationships that we become aware of what the contemporary issues are and of the pressing need to analyze the cruel realities of poverty today. The church needs to realize that at a time when the global economy is booming and some people are doing very well, the poor still become poorer, even in the United States. There are between 5,000 and 10,000 homeless people on the streets of Dallas alone, and child poverty—one of the most atrocious forms of poverty—is still on the rise even in our own country. On a global level, more than 30,000 children die every day from preventable causes such as hunger and disease.

To remember the poor, therefore, is not a matter of special interest for those who feel especially called to this sort of thing. Let me close the circle with another reference to Jesus' summary of the commandments, particularly to his reminder that we need to love our neighbors as ourselves. We need to understand that our neighbors are not just recipients of charity but that they are part of who we are and that loving them "as ourselves" implies loving them "as being part of ourselves." We can neither be fully human nor fully Christian (and certainly not fully Methodist) without the "least of these" who are a part of who we are—a notion that will radically reshape how we think about ministry now and in the future.

The following panel draws together people from various walks of life. Paul Escamilla is currently a pastor at Walnut Hill United Methodist Church in Dallas, Texas, after having served Munger Place United Methodist Church, an inner-city congregation in Dallas, for several years. Minerva Carcaño is director of the Hispanic American Program at Perkins School of Theology, Southern Methodist University, and an ordained United Methodist pastor. Dr. Stuart Jordan, an ordained pastor of the Methodist Church in Great Britain, is Secretary of the London Committee of the Methodist Church. His office supports the ministry and mission of Methodist churches in London with a focus on the situation in inner London.

Paul Escamilla

Whenever people of means come together to discuss people who are of less means, words easily become so much watered-down soup. Therefore, as a person of means and a pastor of a congregation of means, I am diffident in beginning this conversation on issues and models of ministry with the poor.

Any discussion by the North American church of models of ministry to the poor and of the most pressing issues in a specific congregational context must begin with confession. We are, after all, responsible for the wealth we have attained, and as successful as we have been in securing that wealth, we have been less successful in managing it faithfully.

In this, a Wesleyan forum, we can remember John Wesley's supreme concern regarding the American Methodists, namely, that new, economically subsisting Christians risked becoming responsible and industrious in their affairs to the point that they would eventually gain a certain wealth and that such wealth would threaten the practice of true religion.

History confirms Wesley's prophetic eye. It is not only the neglect of the poor for which we must confess when we gather to talk about "helping the poor" but also the neglect of our own poverty of spirit. When we pray, "Give us each day our daily bread," we have neither practiced the implied meaning of "us" in any meaningful way, nor needed the ear of the one to whom we make that petition. Therefore, any confession we make regarding our financial prosperity must have two aspects—acknowledging that on the one hand, we have neglected the poor, and on the other, we have shaken free of our dependence on God as well. Any congregation of means that is not aware of the deep and painful complicity of its privileged situation will not in any faithful or redemptive way begin to engage the world's need—or its own.

When confession becomes constitutive of a congregation's life and practice, conversion can follow. By conversion I mean precisely the repentance to which the Bible calls us and the transformation it promises. Beginning to take steps to move our trust toward God rather than mammon is at the same time to step out not only in awareness but also in compelling interest toward those among us who are poor.

It has been my observation that the best context within which "conversion to the poor" takes place is the context of being among the poor. Mission trips, whether across town, across the country, or across borders; whether for a Saturday morning, a week, or a month, have awakened many hearts and minds to a new way of seeing reality and of participating in Christian faith. Such ventures have the simple function of exposing people to people, who in the process discover they are different and yet not so much so. The disequilibrium of such encounters has proven in my experience to have converting and transforming consequences. Therefore, as a pastor, I am more and more interested in opportunities that place our congregation among people of little or no means. The words which open E. M. Forster's *Howard's End* put the matter simply yet profoundly: "Only connect."

We often approach the poor ostensibly with the intention, in the words that are frequently used, of doing ministry "*to* the poor." However, it is precisely when that objective is confounded or forgotten that conversion and transformation become possible. We go with our gift baskets, hammers, canned goods, tutoring skills, and medical equipment to minister *to* the poor. Yet it is only when these are set aside, and human encounter happens without the benefit of our tools of advantage, that the "helping" role becomes secondary, and the relational opportunity emerges. It is then that we can begin to see the truth of the Vincentian motto: "Go to the poor not because they need you but because you need them."

The Dutch painter, Hugo Vanderges, is known for a portinari altarpiece on the subject of the traveling magi. In the painting, the three resplendent kings, seeking the Christ child, pause to ask directions of a poor beggar, and he is pointing the way! To regard our life together as being given direction by those we have disdained or forgotten—that is, in my judgment, the most pressing issue for the church. Whatever models, grand or modest, serve to awaken that awareness are worthwhile.

We've been asked what theological resources have been useful in developing our ministry with the poor. They are many, and some are even found in writing. Books such as Joerg Rieger's *Remember the Poor: The Challenge to Theology in the Twenty-First Century* (Harrisburg, Pa.: Trinity Press International, 1998) and William K. McElvaney's recent *Eating and Drinking at the Welcome Table: The Holy Supper for All People* (St. Louis: Chalice Press, 1998) are two examples. Other resources have arms and legs, as when certain people interpret ministry theologically even as they engage in it. Again, Rieger has invested himself in communities of need off as well as on the page and done a good job of interpreting that practice; John Perkins is in town this week from Jackson, Mississippi, where he leads an intentional Christian residential community that seeks to be modest in its lifestyle for the sake of the gospel. Further east, Bob Lupton in Atlanta is inviting people of wealth to "reneighbor"—that is, to reverse "white flight" urban exodus in order to rediscover the power of an economically mixed community. In our own front yard, Kathy Dudley witnesses to the power and possibilities of life between rich and poor intertwined.

Issues in ministry with the poor? successful models? theological resources? In the context of a subject that offers no comfortable answers, these are silencing questions. Nonetheless, I appreciate a moment for us to reflect on these questions together.

Minerva Carcaño

End of the Social Compact

There was a time in this country when to speak of the American Dream was to understand that there was an implicit social compact. This social compact meant that society was committed to the security and dignity of its workers. This compact promised that if families worked hard, paid their dues, and played by the rules, they would earn the rewards of an income sufficient to support a family, buy a house, send their children to college, and retire with dignity. Employers, government, and labor unions in the post–World War II era shared responsibilities and made mutual commitments to the welfare of families. Employers, in negotiation with labor unions, provided employment opportunities for families through which they received wages, pensions, and health care benefits. Government regulated work-related relationships through institutions such as the National Labor Relations Board. The government also established broad, national commitments to the well-being of families through policies. The Employment Act of 1946 gave the federal government the responsibility for promoting employment. The Housing Act of 1949 committed the nation to "a decent home and suitable living environment for every American Family." The G. I. bill opened higher education to millions of people. The Civil Rights Act of 1965 broadened the promise of the American Dream to many who had been excluded.

Today, however, families now find that this social compact has been broken. Even though they are working harder, they are earning less. Some families have two and three family members working, some two and three jobs, and still barely meeting their basic needs. Even though they play by the rules, they can no longer count as much on the security of their work. When one factors in the cost of living and inflation, the 1990s have witnessed the first generation of workers in this century to live poorer than its parents.

Some of the manifestations of this broken social compact include: the downsizing of companies without adequate care for workers; the movement of U. S. industries to places in the world outside of the U. S. where labor is paid less, causing subsequent unemployment of U. S. workers and raising the issue of fair wages for employees in other countries; and the reorganization of the workforce in some companies from hired full-time employees to temporary workers, consultants, and part-time workers in order to reduce wages and avoid paying benefits.

Or to view it from another perspective, according to the Center on Budget and Polity Priorities, by the mid-1990s the richest 20 percent of families with children had average incomes over thirteen times as large as the poorest 20 percent of families, and 2.9 times as large as the middle 20 percent of families. From the early 1970s to the mid-1990s, the gap between the top fifth and the bottom fifth of families grew by 65 percent.

Poverty in the U. S., as it is in the new global economy, is a systemic problem that will only worsen unless strong moral, ethical, and practical forces are brought to bear on companies and government.

Racial and Cultural Diversity of the Poor

Poverty in this country is further complicated by the diversity of race and cultures. It is one thing to reach out to another who is like us in the color of our skin, in the use of our language, in the appreciation of our culture, but quite another matter if the person is of another color, speaks another language, and expresses life's joys and pains through different means. Learning how to welcome and accept the gifts of another who may be very different from us is an increasing challenge in this country with its growing diversity. Needless to say, racism continues to be an obstacle to true community in this country—the kind of community that does not ignore the poor, but rather views the poor as neighbor and co-citizen deserving of freedom from want and suffering.

Ministry as Program Rather than as a Way of Life

Before coming to Perkins, I served an ecumenical parish. The parish included United Methodists from the New Mexico and the Rio Grande Annual Conferences, Presbyterians (USA), Congregationalist, and Mennonites. The congregations were concerned about self-revitalization but also had a genuine concern for reaching out to Hispanic immigrants. As lead pastor of the cooperative, I had the dubious privilege of having clergy status in three denominations.

From that ministry setting, I gained the important insight that the United Methodist Church has become a denomination of programs that all too often have replaced discipleship. Programs and programming have become our way of doing ministry to the point that people no longer know how to be disciples of Jesus Christ without a neatly organized program. Furthermore, the energies of new and old members are directed not toward learning and practicing the disciplines of piety and mercy but on learning complex institutional programmatic structures. It is no wonder that we lead people to burnout and then lose them.

Models of Ministry to the Poor, the Underrepresented, and the Ignored

I would like to share some models of ministry to the poor, the underrepresented, and the ignored that I believe have something to teach the church and the academy. I also want to share a word about what I believe to be at the core of effective ministry to the segment of society that has been of central concern to the conference in which we have been participating. The three models that I want to share with you are the covenant groups of Wesley United Methodist Church of El Paso, Texas, the South Albuquerque Cooperative Ministry of Albuquerque, New Mexico, and Perkins School of Theology's own Urban Ministry Steering Committee.

1. Covenant Groups of Wesley UMC of El Paso, Texas

This covenant group ministry organizes neighborhood persons who gather for Bible study, worship, prayer, and fellowship in a home. The focus of these home covenant groups is not to gain new members for existing churches or to start new churches. Rather, these covenant groups work very intentionally on the central commitment of equipping disciples of Jesus Christ. Of secondary concern for these groups is the task of maintaining the institutional church. These home covenant groups are very similar to the original Wesley classes and not unlike the Latin American base communities. They are supportive communities that care for each other spiritually and practically. The home covenant group members hold each other accountable in Christian discipleship and care for each other. Home covenant group meeting offerings are used for the purchasing of food products in bulk and made available to poor neighbors at a minimal cost, which is then reinvested in the purchase of other foods. The love of Christ and the discipleship zeal of these home covenant group members is amazing and inspiring. These home covenant groups have the potential of leading institutional reform for our churches and helping United Methodists reconnect with their Wesleyan roots.

2. South Albuquerque Cooperative Ministry

The South Albuquerque Cooperative Ministry is the ecumenical parish that I referred to above. This cooperative brings together four congregations that are learning how to pool their resources for more effective ministry and are serving and walking with the Hispanic immigrant community in their city. In its eighth year, this ministry has begun to practice living as the greater body of Jesus Christ. While each congregation is strongly committed to its own denomination, each now also holds its relationship with other Christians as a highly important value. Striving to reconcile the body of Jesus Christ is of importance to them in their faith development and also of value to them in their Christian witness to others. In the process of this cooperative ministry, all four congregations have been revitalized and have established some exciting relationships with the poor of Albuquerque, including joint work in the areas of education, immigration services, broad-based community organizing, and youth ministry with and among the poor.

3. Urban Ministry Steering Committee

Perkins School of Theology has established a steering committee for urban ministry. It is an important step for Perkins as it affirms that the urban setting and the urbanizing of society must be considered in the school's curriculum and scholarship. Perkins' commitment to urban ministry also affirms that the academy is called upon to serve the church and community in relevant ways that are grounded in societal reality. In its work, the Perkins Urban Ministry Steering Committee has partnered with annual conference Shalom Zones, the Industrial Areas Foundation, and African American pastors' associations to bring the experiences of these organizations to the academy and the church through conversations and days of learning. The steering committee is also working in helping the seminary address the urban ministry agenda in its curriculum. A primary goal of all this work is to equip seminarians to serve as present and future church and community leaders in an urbanizing society.

The Core Has to Do with Relationships

Finally, it is important to say that, whether one is considering a contemporary issue or a potential model for ministry, the core always has to do with relationships. I learned this lesson as a young child.

When I was in fourth grade my father lost his job. We lived in the Rio Grande Valley of Texas, an area known even today for its Third World poverty. It is also important for you to know that I am a third-generation Methodist.

In an effort to resolve a very desperate situation my parents decided that we needed to move to a small town in the northern part of Texas where an uncle and his family lived. My uncle had apparently found a job for my father in the town's grocery store.

We moved to this new town, and on the first Sunday morning, as was our custom, we arose early and prepared for church and then went in search of the Methodist church. In a town of two thousand it was not difficult to find the church. My father parked right in front of the church, but then we simply sat in the car. As a child who loved to go to church, I was anxious to join this new church, but my parents weren't making any effort to get out of the car and join the congregation. I caught both of my parents staring at the people who were arriving for church and then I also caught the stares of those who were arriving. They were not warm stares. No one came over to welcome us. In fact, quite the contrary. Even for a child it was obvious that we were not welcomed at this church. Without a word, my father began to drive away. "But they don't even realize that we are Methodists, too," I thought to myself. "If they knew that we were Methodists like them, they would welcome us." I was sure of this. My parents seemed to think otherwise; so we left.

The next morning a Sunday school teacher from the local Baptist church came to visit us. She brought us cookies and told us how glad her church was that we had moved to their town and that she would love to have us in her Sunday school class. For the entire time that we lived in that town we attended the Baptist church. The pastor of the church invited us to become members, but my mother held firm to her Methodist relationship, and thus we remained Methodists in a Baptist church.

What I learned from this experience is that the sharing of faith, and particularly the sharing of faith with those who are poor, underrepresented, and ignored, is always about relationship. In contemporary society and church life, relationship with such as these is the greatest challenge and opportunity.

Stuart Jordan

Speaking from a very different context, let me briefly set the scene for my remarks. The twenty London Mission Circuits, which cover the area of central and inner London, currently comprise some seventy congregations and six thousand Methodist members. As a group of churches they are shaped by two distinctive factors in particular.

In the first instance, the earliest London Missions were set up as an expression of the Forward Movement from the middle of the 1880s with a conscious intention of meeting the needs of "the poor, the underrepresented, and the ignored" in inner London. In the meantime, they have developed a whole range of social and community projects as an essential element of their Christian presence in an urban context. At present, over seventy such projects are run directly by those churches while many more are offered space and hospitality on church premises. Those specialist ministries have always been subject to change in response to changing social needs and public policies with new models such as credit unions or supplementary schools complementing most established work with the young, lone parents, the elderly, or the homeless.

That traditional emphasis in ministry is currently under some pressure. Externally, a relentless trend towards professionalization means that many church-based projects are having to adapt their work to meet the needs of service agreements, quality controls, inter-agency partnerships, and the like, which have become the prerequisites of public funding. Internally, the increasing mobility and changing nature of the congregations have often decimated the pool of volunteers on which such projects have always depended and undermined congregational ownership of such work. As a result, the practical viability, as well as the theological underpinnings, of these ministries are often under review.

Secondly, these congregations have experienced a radical demographic change over the last forty years. Significant arrivals of Caribbean Methodists in the 1950s and 1960s and then of West African Methodists from since the 1970s have totally revitalized the inner London churches, many, indeed most, of which might have otherwise closed. That process has had many positive and enriching consequences. It has also brought such issues as poverty, underrepresentation, police relations, immigration, or racially motivated violence directly to the attention of many congregations and their members.

Against this background let me suggest three models of engagement we need to address within our London context that seem to resonate with the concerns of this conference.

Spirituality and Care: An Integral Program

Throughout the conference, we have been reminded of the integral nature of the Wesleys' project and of the bifocal vision that saw "works of mercy" as an essential counterpart to "works of piety."

That integral vision needs to be rediscovered and embodied if we are to avoid the real risk of many traditional social projects becoming ever more isolated from the worshiping life of the congregation.

Unless the integral links are made and kept in good repair, such projects could be denied the prayerful, as well as practical, support of the church; opportunities for understanding such activities as holistic expressions of mission could be lost; and the spiritual and theological development of the congregations could be impoverished—since active engagement with the demanding issues raised may be real catalysts for growth.

Parables of a New Community

Increasingly, the language of social exclusion is complementing, if not replacing, the more narrowly focused language of poverty in British political life. In turn, that expression provokes a concern for strategies and policies aimed at increasing genuine social inclusion. As part of that process, the churches need to recognize their potential as parables of inclusive community: as places of meeting beyond barriers of age, gender, race, culture, or class.

In many congregations, that encounter takes place week by week at a basic level—services of worship where representatives of ten, fifteen, twenty nationalities come together. We need greater intentionality, however, if those opportunities are to serve a wider concern. We are good at laying on splendid international meals and at exploring the visual expressions of cultural life. We need to move further though, to recognize and examine the profound differences and difficulties that can exist: the clashes of style, of stereotypes, of expectations. We need to become "laboratories of the Spirit" since such congregations have unique opportunities to learn lessons about multicultural coexistence which others need to hear.

To pursue such a vocation is also to be true to the inclusive gospel of the Wesleys. In societies that speak of, and practice, social exclusion, the creation of such inclusive, parabolic communities is a contemporary embodiment of the underlying Arminian convictions. There is little point in the theoretical belief that "all" may come, unless all are, in practice, made welcome.

Harvesting the Experience

In 1985, the Church of England published *Faith in City*, a major report on the state of British cities. It had an impact largely because it was able to draw on the presence, insights, and stories of local churches and clergy in many different urban locations. It bore the credibility of eyewitness testimony. It was an exercise in harvesting people's experience.

Wesley's recurrent injunction to "visit the poor" also recognized the transforming power of firsthand experience. Such literal visitation may no longer be appropriate in most cases, but by "harvesting the experience" of those who are socially excluded, by reflecting on and marshalling the stories of those many individuals whose lives interact with our urban congregations, the churches may be able to arrange for the poor to visit others—namely the policy-makers and others whose decisions affect their lives.

There are increasing possibilities within the British context for the churches to contribute to such a process. The faith communities are being actively courted by national as well as local politicians as significant players in local community partnerships. Congregations and representative individuals are vested with a credibility and significance that we are sometimes ourselves the last to recognize.

Fulfilling that role, however, will undoubtedly require new priorities and new methods. Denominational leaders, for example, will need to work together on community issues in a more urgent and focused way if the church's voice—and more importantly the voice of those on whose behalf we sometimes claim to speak—is to be heard at all.

It is doubtful whether any conference can be of direct benefit to the poor and the excluded, about whom so much is said. If it provokes any of us and our churches to reclaim more of the tradition of the Wesleys' concern for the poor that we have rehearsed together, however, it will have proven to be worthwhile.

APPENDIX TWO

For the Charles Wesley Society meeting
Perkins School of Theology
Southern Methodist University, Dallas, Texas
October 14-17, 1999

Happy the multitude

Charles Wesley

Carlton R. Young

all were of one heart and mind. To him and to each
soul of har - mo - ny and love; one soul did all the
lost in char - i - ty Di - vine; the dif - ference base of
noth - ing had, yet all po - sessed; with ev - ery com - mon

oth - er joined, they all were of one heart and mind. ____
mem - bers move, the soul of har - mo - ny and love. ____
thine and mine was lost in char - i - ty Di - vine. ____
bless - ing blessed they noth - ing had, yet

all pos - sessed.

Acts 4:32: The multitude of them that believed, were of one heart, and one soul; neither said any of them, that aught of the things which he possessed, was his own, but they had all things in common. Neither was there any among them that lacked.

APPENDIX THREE

The Poor and the People Called Methodists: An Exhibit

The following exhibit items re-create the exhibit from the conference held at Southern Methodist University. A similar exhibit can be found online at *http://rylibweb.man.ac.uk/data1/dg/methodist/poor/*.

Introduction—The Poor and the People Called Methodists

From the beginning, the Wesleyan movement, like Christianity itself, was largely a movement of and for the poor. An Oxford don, John Wesley attempted to imitate the life and ministry of Christ to the marginalized and disenfranchised. He brought together evangelical zeal and social outreach in a manner that focused on the needs of the working class.

The Methodists in Wesley's day translated their basic message of "love of God and neighbor" into a mission of help and hope in the community of faith in which the poor were included as children of God. The Wesleyan program of outreach to society is a defining element of the Methodist heritage.

Part One—The Poor in Eighteenth-century England

Virtually half the population in eighteenth-century England were poor according to government standards of that day. An even larger percentage of Methodists could be classified as the working poor, not earning enough to support themselves and their families adequately.

211

Poverty in England at that time was caused by three major problems: underemployment, economic displacement, and infirmity. Economic depravity was not as severe as in some other areas of Europe—there were almost no transient beggars or starving, homeless people in England.

Some English politicians and economists of the day, however, felt that many people were not making a positive contribution to the national wealth. These "poor" were identified and defined in terms of economic worth, and national programs were developed to relieve the infirm, employ the hardy, and assist the needy, thereby strengthening the national economy.

Workhouses, charity schools, the poor tax, and parish programs of assistance that were established to help solve the "problem" were often ineffective and insufficient. Many who had never considered themselves "poor" now developed a reliance upon government entitlements. In the eighteenth century, the various attempts at legal and political solutions failed to relieve the situation.

1. CRITIC OF PROGRAMS TO ASSIST THE POOR

John M'Farlan, *Inquiries Concerning the Poor*, Edinburgh: Dickins, 1782.

M'Farlan, a minister of Canongate, Edinburgh, begins his work by pointing out that poverty has a number of unavoidable and adventitious causes but that the most frequent causes are sloth, intemperance, and other vices. He proceeds with the assumption that charities are designed "to relieve absolute want." He then criticizes those programs that seem to promote a social and political agenda beyond that basic goal.

M'Farlan also criticizes the orphan hospitals for attempting to educate the poor children. His argument is that there are productive working people in society who are not able to read, while these institutions are trying to educate indigent children who have the "least title to such advantage." Any consequent attempts to advance themselves, nevertheless, will likely be unsuccessful since there are already many candidates for most positions. The result will be a servile class that is even more unhappy and, therefore, more unfit for their "proper stations."

2. CRITIQUE OF M'FARLAN'S OBJECTIONS

Thomas Tod, *Observations on Dr. M'Farlan's Inquiries Concerning the State of the Poor*, Edinburgh: 1783.

Tod, an Edinburgh merchant and treasurer for the orphan hospital, responded to M'Farlan's *Inquiries* with this small book, which the title page indicates was "published for the benefit of the orphans."

The author does not agree with M'Farlan's traditional English view that the bulk of mankind is assigned by Providence to "labour, toil, and fatigue, with coarse food and homely lodgings." He views M'Farlan as a Mandevillian in the sense that he wants to keep poor children "in darkness, ignorance, and slavery."

3. AN ECONOMIC THEORY OF WEALTH

Adam Smith, *An Inquiry into the Nature and Causes of the Wealth of Nations*, 2 vols., London: Printed for W. Strahan, and T. Cadell, 1776.

Smith's study propounded a theoretical framework for the mercantile economic system that was tied to the developing British colonial empire. Wesley did not agree with one of the essential features of Smith's work, namely the assumption that the surplus accumulation of wealth was an essential element of fiscal security for individuals and the nation. (See Wesley's sermon on the Use of Money, exhibit 11.)

4A. POVERTY AND THE POOR LAWS

Joseph Townsend, *Dissertation on the Poor Laws, by a Well-wisher to Mankind*, London: C. Dilly, 1786.

Townsend practiced medicine early in his career, became a clergyman, and was eventually well-known as a geologist. He was for a time enamoured by the Calvinist Methodists in Lady Huntingdon's connection and even preached in her chapel in Bath. His sister, Judith, married one of Lady Huntingdon's preachers, Thomas Haweis.

His *Dissertation* is a political tract, attacking the Poor Laws—those in place and those contemplated. The Poor Laws were designed to take care of the infirm and to furnish work for the underemployed, not to provide maintenance for the unemployed. The original theory and design may have been admirable to some, but in practice it failed miserably.

Townsend viewed the Poor Laws as, in effect, providing a guaranteed wage for the indigent and lazy, promoting "drunkenness and idleness cloathed in rags," paid for by the industrious farmers who were thus oppressed themselves by poverty. Very few people were raised out of poverty by the parish welfare system, partly because those who dominated the economic system in England, like Townsend, did not really want the lower classes to have any upward mobility.

The *Dissertation* expresses one of Townsend's basic views: that the natural relationship between servant and master must be acknowledged and preserved by legislators. One of his "purple passages" has been highlighted by an early reader: Ashley Montagu has said of this book, "Never were there a more important ninety-nine pages written."

4B. CONTINUING CRITICISM OF THE POOR LAWS

John Baker Holroyd, Earl of Sheffield, *Observations on the Impolicy, Abuses, and False Interpretation of the Poor Laws; and on the Reports of the Two Houses of Parliament*, 2d ed., London: Printed for J. Hatchard, 1818.

The Earl of Sheffield was a British statesman who was thirty-two years younger than John Wesley. He was a leading authority on commerce and agriculture and led the Board of Agriculture and the Board of Trade in the early nineteenth century. He was active in suppressing the Gordon Riots in 1780, and as a member of Parliament from Bristol, he opposed William Wilberforce's motion to abolish slavery in 1791—positions that put him in opposition to Wesley's stated views.

Sheffield's pamphlet on the Poor Laws is typical of criticism in many places and periods: that the system had strayed from its original purpose. Of course, commentaries on the English Poor Laws hardly ever said that the patchwork of legal provisions was ideal or the implementation effective.

Sheffield's argument is, however, more pervasively negative and more strongly worded than most. He saw the system as "defective in its very principle and still more in practice," having within itself the potential of destroying the country. He decries the "system of compulsory charity" with a stream of pejorative adjectives: oppressive, ruinous, insufferable, uncontrolled. He vents some of his most virulent criticism on the "wretched establishments falsely called workhouses." His vindictiveness merely added heat to the discussion of the problem, however, and did little to effect a cure.

5. THE STATE OF THE PRISONS

John Howard, *The State of the Prisons in England and Wales with Preliminary Observations and an Account of some Foreign Prisons and Hospitals*, Warrington: Eyres, 1777.

Wesley was very impressed and influenced by the philanthropist John Howard, calling him "one of the greatest men in Europe." Howard tried very hard to improve the state of institutions in Great Britain, a difficult effort that Wesley felt was enabled by "the mighty power of God." Howard, as a young man, heard Wesley preach and was moved by the sermon.

Later in life, Howard indicated that he was encouraged by Wesley "to go on vigorously with my own designs. I saw in him how much a single man might achieve by zeal and perseverance; and I thought, why may not I do as much in my way, as Mr. Wesley has done in his, if I am only as assiduous and persevering? I determined I would pursue my work with [more] alacrity than ever."

6. CENSUS OF POOR CHILDREN IN LONDON

An Abstract of the Annual Registers of the Parish Poor, London: 1799.

This very scarce publication provides summaries of the yearly lists of poor children in each parish in and around London for the year 1798. The age range is "from birth until apprenticed out," which appears to be under six years of age.

The numbers are large, especially in some parishes such as St. James, Westminster (now just off of Picadilly Circus). The total number of children born and/or received in workhouses for the year is 8,185, of whom 906 were deemed "illegitimate" and 514 named as "casualties."

There are some pathetic facts revealed here, such as the number of young children who died under the care of nurses in the workhouses or parish houses: 287 of the 389 who were being housed in the environs of London. Of the 1,787 children under six years of age "sent to the country to be nursed," 110 died during that year, while 366 were "apprenticed out or put out to service."

The population of the workhouses seems to be quite transient. While 2,157 were sent home with their mothers that year, 568 were "discharged to the Foundling Hospital," and 1,214 were sent back to the parish (for some sort of alternate care), the workhouses still contained 2,861 children who "remain alive" at the end of the year.

7. PROPOSAL FOR IMPROVING THE WORKHOUSES

William Bailey, *A Treatise on the Better Employment, and more Comfortable Support, of the Poor in Workhouses; together with some observations on the growth and culture of flax: with divers new inventions, neatly engraved on copper, for the improvement of linen manufacture, of which the importance and advantages are considered and evinced*, London: Dodsley, 1758.

William Bailey presented this modest work to the Society for the Encouragement of Arts, Manufactures, and Commerce, suggesting guidelines for improving the efficiency of workhouses and promoting methods for encouraging linen manufacture therein. His charts indicate that he anticipated a workhouse of 150 people to include 11 people who would attend and instruct children, 5 to cook and clean, 6 tailors, 8 to wash and mend, 20 elderly, sick, and children who could do no work, 20 who could earn one penny per day, 20 who could earn two pence a day, and 60 healthy people who could start earning six to ten pence per day and within four or five years earn eighteen pence per day.

His proposed Rule 9 for the Governors of workhouses states: "He shall summon the foremen and forewomen of each employment every night, or as soon as they leave work, to know how much work they and their respective companies have performed that day, and enter the same in his list." He shows a variety of tasks for 100 people in the house, ranging from spinning flax to making gloves, brushes, and brooms.

8. ACCOUNT OF THE RELIGIOUS SOCIETIES

Josiah Woodward, *An Account of the Societies for Reformation of Manners, in London and Westminster, and other Parts of the Kingdom; with a persuasive to persons of all ranks, to be zealous and diligent in promoting the execution of the laws against prophaneness and debauchery, for the effecting a national reformation*, London: Aylmer, 1699.

Woodward was an early proponent and historian of the religious society movement, which incorporated piety, charity, and learning in their national program. Samuel Wesley, Sr., and John Wesley both were corresponding members of the Society for Promoting Christian Knowledge, which encouraged the establishment of charity schools ("free schools") throughout the nation to assist the education of poor children.

The Society for the Reformation of Manners (i.e., "morals"), here described by Woodward, focused on the enforcement of laws pertaining to public and private morality. Their reputation for snitching on their neighbors to the local authorities gave the religious society movement a bad name and contributed to its eventual decline after the first third of the eighteenth century.

9. CHARITY SERMON FOR THE SPCK AND ANNUAL REPORT

John Heylyn, *A Sermon Preached at St. Sepulchre's; . . . to which is annexed An Account of the Origin and Designs of the Society for Promoting Christian Knowledge*, London: J. Downing, 1734.

Charity Sermons were often preached in order to raise a special collection for a particular charity. In this case, Heylyn was preaching at the annual celebration of the charity schools, many of which were founded and supported by the Society for Promoting Christian Knowledge and are listed in an appendix.

Also appended to the published sermon was the annual report of the SPCK, which included a brief account of its origin and designs and a listing of its publishing inventory of "books for the poor."

The "design" of the schools was explained in such a fashion (as indicated in the displayed page) that the benefactors would be assured that the schools would not become seedbeds of discontent. They were not trying to upset the economic apple cart by raising chimney sweeps (and others) out of their low estate, but rather they simply hoped to make good honest Christian chimney sweeps out of the little wretches, well instructed in the duties of servants and submission to superiors.

10. JOHN WESLEY'S THEOLOGY OF CHARITY

John Wesley, Sermon 91, "On Charity" (III.8), in *Arminian Magazine* 8 (1785): 70-76.

The published sermon on charity, based on Paul's "love" chapter in 1 Corinthians, was used on at least one occasion as the basic text for preaching a charity sermon. There is a unique transcript of the sermon on that occasion, which varies slightly from the printed version published two years earlier. The oral sermon appears to have included some different stories and a special appeal at the end for his listeners to contribute "upon the present occasion" to the Finsbury Dispensary, a clinic that served the poor in the area of Wesley's City Road Chapel.

In the concluding portion of the published sermon, Wesley stresses the last verse in his text, 1 Corinthians 13:3, pointing out that even the greatest of benefactors (several types of which he lists) cannot expect that good works (beneficence) would *replace* holy tempers but should *spring from* them.

11. JOHN WESLEY ON THE ECONOMICS OF CHARITY

John Wesley, Sermon 50, "On the Use of Money," in *Sermons on Several Occasions*, Bristol: Grabham, 1760.

The first of a series of sermons by Wesley on the topic of money and riches, this sermon contains his well-known principle "Gain all you can, save all you can, give all you can." The third point is the most crucial for Wesley: to help Methodists avoid the pitfalls associated with the accumulation of surplus wealth.

Many Methodists, following Wesley's injunctions to work hard and be frugal, had raised their economic status and were no longer poor. He therefore found it necessary to remind them that good Christians are concerned about their neighbors and share any goods that are beyond the range of "necessities." He speaks harshly of those who accumulate the "superfluities" of life when many do not have the necessities, much less the "conveniencies" of life, and some are at the "extremities."

The message was apparently a difficult one to get across as he felt compelled to repeat some of the same basic principles in subsequent sermons on "The Good Steward" (1768), "The Danger of Riches" (1781), "On Dress" (1786), "On Riches" (1788), and "The Danger of Increasing Riches" (1790).

The 1760 volume of *Sermons on Several Occasions* contains the first printing of this sermon. Although Wesley had earlier produced three numbered volumes with the same title, this one is not numbered "four."

12. JOHN WESLEY ON THE CAUSES OF POVERTY AND SCARCITY

John Wesley, *The Present Scarcity of Provisions*, London: Hawes, 1773.

This rare item contains a political tirade by Wesley that, in part, counteracts the views of Townsend and M'Farlan (exhibits 1 and 4). From his extensive traveling throughout the country, he concludes that the problems of hunger and unemployment are not caused, as many claimed, by poor people who are lazy and indolent. The three main culprits are distilling, taxes, and luxury.

His argument is that there is no food because there is no work available; and there is no work because employers can't hire workers—they can't afford to because there is no market for their goods because so much money has to be spent on food.

He then goes on to explain his views on why food is so dear (because of grain prices), why land is so expensive, why taxes are so high (because of the exorbitant national debt), and why everything else is so expensive (because taxes are so high). The solution to these problems, for Wesley, entails finding work for the poor.

Part Two—Methodist Mission of Relief and Assistance

Wesley realized that poverty was a relative concept. While he recognized that many people revel in the superfluities of life at the same time that others do not even have the necessities, he felt that everyone should be concerned about helping anyone who was less fortunate. Poverty could not be defined simply by an economic formula nor was it necessarily the product of widespread laziness, as many officials thought.

Wesley's rule with regard to money, applicable to all levels of society, was to gain all you can, save all you can, and give all you can—with an emphasis on the third point. This point was also applied across the Methodist connection by establishing collections and funds for relief and assistance that were shared among the whole movement.

Wesley's concerns for those in need became institutionalized in the Methodist movement in areas where the less fortunate had the greatest needs: nutrition, housing, clothing, medical care, education, and finance. The constellation of programs and institutions that he established in these areas became the model for the Methodist mission of social outreach for succeeding generations.

13. EARLY ACCOUNT OF METHODIST WORK WITH THE POOR

The Oxford Methodists; being some account of a society of some young gentlemen in this city, so denominated, London: 1733.

This anonymous booklet is the first printed pamphlet that gives notice to the Methodists. It purports to be an investigative report commissioned by the worried father of a prospective student who does not want his offspring corrupted by religious fanatics. Much of the substance of the author's description of the Oxford Methodists is drawn from John Wesley's own letter to another student's father, Richard Morgan, Sr., defending the nature and design of the Methodists' work at the University. Wesley's diary indicates that he tried unsuccessfully to trace the author's source.

The charges of enthusiasm and zeal were thrown at the Methodists throughout the century for both their evangelical preaching as well as their philanthropic program to assist the poor. Even John Wesley's father was somewhat skeptical of their widespread program to assist the poor in and around Oxford.

The pamphlet contains quoted material from a letter of advice from Samuel Wesley, Sr., to his son John, cautioning him to be careful to avoid "blind zeal" in their endeavors, such as in their work with the poor in the villages near Holt just beyond Worcester. Samuel also passes on further advice from another friend who suggests that "you may walk uprightly and safely, without endeavouring to out-do all the good bishops, clergy, and other pious good men of the present and past ages."

14. METHODIST MISSIONS IN BRISTOL

Historical Tablets in John Wesley's Chapel, Broadmead, Bristol, Bristol: Dorian, 1930.

Wesley's work with the poor is the focus of two tablets that were placed in the New Room, Bristol, when it was remodeled in 1930. The New Room was the first preaching-house built by Wesley (1739) for the Methodist work. The historical tablets, thirty in all, were subsequently published in this book, which at the time was said to have been printed on the largest sheets ever placed in a book.

Tablet Eight, on "Wesley's Philanthropy," recounts incidents in his life where he provided medicine, clothing, housing, and other necessities of life for the poor. Bristol, rife with poverty and one of the centers of Methodist work, was a port city, notorious as the center of the English slave trade to America and the rest of the world.

Tablet Nine, on "Care for the Poor," recounts instances of Wesley's efforts in Bristol to feed and care for poor Methodists as well as those beyond the Society. The Stranger's Friend Society, though not founded by Wesley, was strongly supported by the Methodists.

15. SONGS FOR THE POOR

a. *Hymns for the Use of Families*, No. 132, "For a Family in Want," Bristol: Pine, 1767.
b. *Short Hymns on Select Passages of the Holy Scriptures*, 2 vols., Bristol: Farley, 1762, 2:139-40.

The hymnody of Methodism does not focus on their work with the poor as much as one might expect, probably because most of the people who were singing these hymns were the poor themselves. Lines such as, "Gladly of that little give / Poor thyself, the poor relieve," are therefore not out of place in that context.

The greater tendency exhibited in the hymns is to idealize the poor and spiritualize the value of poverty. Those who are unable to depend on this world's goods are more easily able to trust in God, "the portion of the poor." As Charles Wesley wrote in another hymn:

> The poor in every age and place
>   thou dost, O God, approve
> to mark with thy distinguished grace,
>   to enrich with faith and love.

Although Christian Perfection was the hallmark doctrine of the Methodists, Charles points out that before Jesus said, "Be ye perfect," he said (using poetic paraphrase), "Be poor." For Charles, then, the goal of the Christian life is "perfect poverty."

16. JOHN WESLEY'S CHARITABLE ACTIVITIES AT OXFORD

John Wesley, MS Oxford Diary I, Colman Collection, Methodist Archives, John Rylands University Library of Manchester.

Wesley began keeping his diary in 1725 in this small volume. Interspersed among the notes on daily activities, he frequently included miscellaneous information and financial records.

Some pages show part of his financial accounts relating to charitable activities, including the money collected in December 1730 and January 1731 for the work with the poor and the prisoners and expenditures from December 1730 to March 1731.

The money was collected quarterly, in this instance from his brother Charles, William Morgan, Bob Kirkham, and himself—the four who would be called "Methodists" by mid–1732—along with John's brother Samuel and four other gentlemen.

Many of the people listed as recipients of their beneficence are also mentioned in John's daily diary accounts. Two entries indicate money given "to the turnkey and felons by times," as well as threepence "distributed at the C[astle prison]" and the same "at Bocardo [jail]."

17A. JOHN WESLEY'S CHARITABLE GIVING AT OXFORD

John Wesley, MS Financial Accounts, Methodist Archives, John Rylands University Library of Manchester.

One of Wesley's MS notebooks contains primarily his personal financial accounts for 1731–33, including summaries of his traveling expenses for 1732, his debts paid, and his charitable giving.

The recipients of his gifts include prisoners at the Castle prison and children in the Grey Coat school (contributions totaling one pound), two quarterly payments of eight shillings to Mrs. Plat for teaching school, eighteen shillings for "physic" (medicine), four lines of gifts to his family, six lines of gifts to "my children" (distinguished from the Grey Coat school), including three shillings for flax.

The total giving for the year (including some listed on the following page) was 15 pounds, 19 shillings, and 6 pence, more than 15 percent of his total expenditures of 91 pounds, 14 shillings, and 3 pence.

17B. COLLECTION FOR THE POOR OF THE LONDON SOCIETY

John Wesley, *An Extract of the Rev. Mr. John Wesley's Journal* (entry for 7 May 1741), Bristol: Pine, 1774.

Very early in Wesleyan revival, John Wesley realized that many of the people in the Methodist societies were elderly, orphaned, sick, or unemployed and in need of food, clothing, housing, medicine, and other basic necessities. Collections within the societies provided for the most needy. Clothing, food, and money were the most common requests.

The collection in May 1741 also was used to purchase wool and set up a small cottage industry in knitting among the unemployed women of the society. This practice followed a precedent he had set while at Oxford, where he purchased wool for the orphans in the workhouse.

This particular copy of the *Journal* is from an unusual set of Wesley's *Works* (1771–74) that was bound by its contemporary owner in tree calf leather with gold tooling, a very expensive binding. Most eighteenth-century Wesleyan material, printed for and purchased by Methodists, is more plainly bound, if bound at all.

18. WESLEY'S BEGGING FOR THE POOR

John Wesley, *An Extract of the Rev. Mr. John Wesley's Journal* (entry for 4 January 1785), London: New Chapel, 1789.

In his *Journal*, Wesley frequently mentions occasions when he does what he calls "the unpleasing but necessary work of going through the town, and begging" for the poor. He was not, however, standing on a corner with a tin cup. The results of his begging during the first week of 1785 testify to his success in soliciting 200 pounds from well-heeled friends, the equivalent of $30,000 today. His diary indicates that he spent about thirty hours in these personal solicitations that week.

On another occasion he bemoans that his begging during one day resulted in only six or seven people giving ten pounds each. Ten pounds was a sizable sum, approximately equivalent to $900 in today's currency. The principle of begging is clearly enunciated in the "Large Minutes" where Wesley suggests that the preachers should "beg from the rich to buy books for the poor."

These benevolences—for food, clothing, shoes, housing—were intended for the poor who were in "pressing want" in the Methodist societies, in London about ten percent of their membership. He makes it clear on some occasions that these gifts were intended "for them whom I knew to be diligent and yet in want."

19A. METHODIST STEWARDS TO ASSIST THE POOR

John Bennett, MS Minutes of 1744 Conference, Methodist Archives, John Rylands University Library of Manchester.

These Minutes of the first Methodist Conference were recorded by John Bennett, one of Wesley's preachers, who later married Grace Murray (who was betrothed to John Wesley at the time).

Included in these minutes are the description of the office of Steward and the rules of a Steward. Two of their main tasks were to "receive the weekly contributions" and to "send relief to the poor."

Among the rules for this position is the injunction to "Give none that ask relief an ill word or ill look. Do not hurt them, if you cannot help them."

19B. INSTRUCTIONS TO THE STEWARDS

John Wesley, *Extract of the Rev. Mr. John Wesley's Journal* (entry for June 4, 1747), London: Cock, 1754.

In 1747, Wesley streamlined the work of the stewards in the London Society, reducing the number from sixteen to seven and giving them eleven specific instructions in everything from organization to demeanor.

Rules are generally developed to solve particular problems. One can therefore perceive several of the problems behind these rules, including persistent contention, loud debates at their meetings, and discourtesy ("sour looks or harsh words") toward the poor.

One instruction is a variation of a rule in the *Minutes* (see previous document). Apparently, not all of the poor who requested help could be assisted: "If you cannot relieve, do not grieve, the poor."

20. METHODIST POOR FUND LEDGER

West Street Chapel (Seven Dials, London) Poor Fund ledger, 1764–96, Methodist Archives, John Rylands University Library of Manchester.

West Street Chapel, a disused Huguenot Chapel leased by Wesley starting in the mid–1740s, was the first consecrated building acquired by the Methodists in eighteenth-century England. The stewards of each society were expected to account for the money collected during the year. This book contains the records of the West Street Society.

On the left page is an itemized account of money collected at the Chapel in 1768 by class leaders, in poor boxes, and through special collections "at the door," entered by date.

On the right page is an account of when and how the money was distributed by the stewards. The most frequent entry is "paid sundry poor." Also noted are payments to Mr. Collins at the Foundery School and to Mr. Wheeler for "stock binding."

21. JOHN WESLEY ON CLEANLINESS

John Wesley, Sermon 91, "On Dress," in *Sermons on Several Occasions*, 8 vols., London: Paramore, 1788.

The main point of this sermon is in keeping with his other tirades against the accumulation of riches—that Christians should not wear gold, jewels, or costly apparel when others are in rags. Wesley apparently often heard Methodists say, "But I can afford it," to which he retorts, "No Christian can afford to waste any part of the substance which God has entrusted him with."

On the other hand, in this same sermon he also points out that "slovenliness is no part of religion" and quotes a favorite proverb (sometimes attributed to him): "Cleanliness is next to godliness." In a letter to a friend in Ireland in 1769, he had made this point even more strongly: "Let none ever see a ragged Methodist." The spiritual relevance of his point was drawn out further in his comment, "Mend your clothes, or I shall never expect you to mend your lives."

Recognizing both the slimness of his preachers' resources and the divisive tendencies that were present in his movement, Wesley specified in his will that any preacher who remained in the Methodist connection at least six months after their leader's death would be given a copy of this eight-volume collection of his *Sermons*.

22. WESLEY'S ADVICE TO VISIT THE POOR

John Wesley, MS Letter to Brian Bury Collins, June 14, 1780, Bridwell Library, Southern Methodist University.

Brian Bury Collins, an ordained deacon in the Church of England, was assisting in the Methodist work in Everton at the time of this letter. His involvement with the Wesleyans as a traveling preacher caused his bishop to delay his final ordination as a priest for several years.

One of Wesley's primary rules in working with the poor is clearly stated to Collins at the end of this letter: Visit the poor in their humble lodgings in order to know them. He enlarges on this theme in his correspondence with Miss March, where he says, "Go and see the poor and sick in their own poor little hovels. Take up your cross, woman! Remember the faith! Jesus went before you, and will go with you." Wesley viewed such visiting, though perhaps not pleasant, as a means of grace.

One of the perils of this practice was the possibility of contracting "the itch," which seems to have afflicted Wesley on occasion (mentioned by Hawes in exhibit 29; see also exhibit 28).

23. WESLEY'S ADVICE TO JOHN NEWTON

John Wesley, MS Letter to John Newton, April 1, 1766, Bridwell Library, Southern Methodist University.

John Newton, of Olney, was a friend whom Wesley tried to involve more closely in the Methodist movement. He was a former slave trader who, after converting to Christianity, became an evangelical Anglican clergyman and is probably best known for writing the hymn, "Amazing Grace." This letter continues a dialogue on the doctrine of sanctification, on which Wesley thinks there is not "an hair's breadth difference" between them.

At the end of the letter, Wesley clearly reiterates two of the three main points of his guidelines on the use of money (enunciated six years earlier in a sermon): Save all you can, and give all you can.

His closing attestation would be confirmed in his own experience. Toward the end of his life, on July 16, 1790, he decided to stop keeping his financial accounts (which he had kept since 1725), "being satisfied," as he noted after the last entry, "with the continual conviction that I save all I can, and give all I can, this is, all I have."

24. WESLEY'S ACCOUNTING TO A BENEFACTOR

John Wesley, MS Letter to Ebenezer Blackwell, Feb. 4, 1751, Bridwell Library, Southern Methodist University.

Ebenezer Blackwell was a London banker and friend of the Wesleys, who entrusted large sums of money to Wesley for his work with the poor. He no doubt would have approved the exactness of Wesley's accounting for the five guineas (five pounds, five shillings) that Blackwell had given to Wesley in 1751 for this work. Wesley was careful to avoid the charge of becoming rich on the gifts of benefactors, claiming that if when he died he had more than ten pounds to his name, people could say "that I lived and died a thief and a robber."

The purposes of the distributions, as listed, range from enhancing the lending stock at the Foundery to helping sick families. Food, fuel, clothing, and rent were constant needs for many people who were short of resources. Two business people were assisted as well as several sick families and "an ancient woman in great distress."

25. WHITEFIELD'S ORPHAN-HOUSE IN GEORGIA

George Whitefield, *An Account of the . . . Orphan-House in Georgia; . . . to which is prefixed a plan of the building,* London: Strahan, 1741.

As Whitefield left England in 1738 to succeed John Wesley as priest in Savannah, Georgia, he wrote, "What I have most at heart is the building [of] an orphan-house." His orphan-house, called Bethesda ("House of Mercy"), which he hoped would become "an oasis of religion in a desert of paganism," became the focus of his charitable solicitations up and down the Atlantic seaboard for many years (see next exhibit).

The Trustees of the colony gave him five hundred acres for the project, much to the chagrin of many other colonists, who also were annoyed by his monopolizing the available tradesmen in the area, by his desire for more free land, and by his attempts to introduce African slavery in a slave-free colony. "The Plan Elevation of the Present and Intended Building of the Georgia Orphan House & Academy" shows the proposed facility.

Whitefield eventually had a falling-out with the Trustees of the Colony of Georgia over their reticence to give him more free land and to allow him to use slaves. As unsuccessful leverage, he threatened to move his operation to Pennsylvania. Later in the decade, he did found a school in Philadelphia, which eventually became part of what is now the University of Pennsylvania.

26. WHITEFIELD'S ATTEMPTS TO RAISE MONEY FOR ORPHANS

John Wesley, *Hymns and Sacred Poems*, Philadelphia: Bradford, 1740. Old St. George's United Methodist Church, Philadelphia, Pa.

This early American publication of a Wesley hymnbook (first published earlier that year in London) was no doubt taken to the printers by George Whitefield, who was the only Methodist leader in America at that time. The title page indicates that the proceeds from the sale of the books would assist the work of the poor in Georgia, where Whitefield had established an orphanage.

In 1764, Whitefield tried to change the orphan-house into an academy, which brought down the wrath of Wesley on his friend: "Can anything on earth be a greater charity, than to bring up orphans? What is a college or an academy compared to this? . . . You had land given and collected money for an orphan-house; are you at liberty to apply this to any other purpose—at least while there are any orphans in Georgia left?"

Bethesda School for Boys still operates in Georgia as a continuation of Whitefield's vision.

27. WESLEY'S MEDICAL CLINICS

a. John Wesley, *A Plain Account of the People Called Methodists*, Bristol: Farley, 1749.

With evident pride, Wesley tells the story of the origins of the medical clinic for the poor that he established at the Foundery in the late 1740s. The intent was to provide for members of that Methodist society, but of the hundred or so who came each month during the first few months, several were people that Wesley had never seen.

He was criticized by some for stepping over the bounds of the medical profession, which is why, here, he explains that, although he had long-studied anatomy and physick, he hired an apothecary and a surgeon to take the difficult cases so as "not to go out of my depth." The story of Mr. Kirkman's cure, recounted in this exhibit, was a typical illustration of the success experienced by this ministry.

Wesley's Foundery clinic is sometimes called the first free public medical dispensary in London. He later provided similar services at Newcastle and Bristol. They were all closed within a decade for lack of donations to keep up with the demand.

b. John Wesley, *An Extract of the Rev. Mr. John Wesley's Journal* (entry for June 6, 1747), in vol. 29 of *The Works of the Rev. John Wesley*, Bristol: William Pine, 1771–74.

This entry for June 6, 1747, in Wesley's *Journal*, recounts the success of the medical clinic that he had established at the Foundery. Following Wesley's calculations, more than three hundred came two or three times; about twenty who came regularly experienced no change in their condition; more than two hundred were "sensibly better"; and fifty-one "thoroughly cured." One wonders what happened to the other twenty-nine.

The importance of this entry, for Wesley, is indicated by an asterisk at the beginning of the paragraph. This method of notation, used throughout the thirty-two volumes of this first edition of the Works, is explained by Wesley in the Preface to the first volume: "I placed a mark before those passages which I judged were most worthy of the reader's notice." He used this method very sparingly however—even his account of Aldersgate contains no asterisks.

28. WESLEY'S FOLK MEDICAL REMEDIES

Primitive Physick; or, An Easy and Natural Method for Curing most Diseases, London: 1747.

This first edition of Wesley's collection of home remedies for common illnesses was a successor to a brief publication in 1745 of *A Collection of Receits for the Poor*, the title of which clearly demonstrates his primary interest in producing such a handbook. The work went through nearly two dozen editions in Wesley's lifetime, expanding the number of remedies as the century wore on.

Wesley was especially critical of the apparent collusion of doctors and apothecaries to milk the public for all they were worth in times of personal medical distress. The remedies he included in this publication, he claimed, were not the result of untried medical theories of doctors but were the product of generations of successful use. Those recipes followed by an "I" were "said to be infallible." In later editions, many recipes marked with a "T" were thus designated as "tried."

Wesley also describes several cures for "the itch," a common ailment among the poor. Many of his cures entailed the use of concoctions that some of his critics felt were totally useless, if not harmful (see the next exhibit). One wonders how a shirt steeped in powdered brimstone would smell after being worn for five or six days.

29. HAWES' CRITIQUE OF WESLEY'S MEDICAL WORK

William Hawes (apothecary), *An Examination of the Rev. Mr. John Wesley's Primitive Physic; shewing that a great number of the prescriptions therein contained, are founded on ignorance of the medical art, and of the power and operation of medicines; and that it is a publication calculated to do essential injury to the health of those persons who may place confidence in it; interspersed with medical remarks and practical observations*, London: 1776.

Hawes was, for a time, president of the Royal Society, which, among other things, promoted the search for an effective means of resuscitating drowning victims.

His object was to discredit Wesley's "injudicious collection of pretended remedies." In the introduction, he defends the medical profession from Wesley's attacks, and then proceeds to dismantle many of Wesley's 1,012 remedies one by one.

He cannot resist some sarcastic compliments for Wesley, such as his comments on Wesley's remedies for "the itch." He makes no comment on one of Wesley's innovative suggestions for rescuing drowning victims—mouth to mouth resuscitation.

30. KINGSWOOD SCHOOL

Minutes of the Methodist Conferences, London: 1862. Conference of 1783, q. 15.

Throughout his life, Wesley was interested in the education of children, including children of the poor. He supported the work of the established charity schools and set up schools himself for poor children, starting at Oxford.

Kingswood School, established originally in 1739 by George Whitefield for the children of the colliers near Bristol, was taken over by Wesley and reopened as a school for preachers' children in 1748. Although not strictly speaking "for the poor," this school demonstrated a curriculum and program that Wesley felt was essential for all children—a mixture of academic rigor, personal discipline, and vital religion.

The report of his disappointment with the work at Kingswood, in the Minutes of 1783, demonstrates the difficulties entailed in promoting his ideal. The rules for the children included rising at 4:00 A.M. and retiring at 8:00 P.M., starting the day with two hours of private and public devotion and ending the day with an hour of private devotion and an hour of public evening prayers, having no time during the day for play (the options for recreation were walking or working) and spending from 7:00 to 11:00 A.M. and 1:00 to 5:00 P.M. "in school."

This document also contains an interesting expression of concern at this point in Wesley's life that the children in his school not be left free to roam and mix (much less fight) with the colliers' children in Kingswood.

31. COKESBURY COLLEGE

Thomas Coke and Francis Asbury, *An Address to the Friends and Annual Subscribers for the Support of Cokesbury-College, and to the Members of the Methodist Society: to which are added, the rules and regulations of the College*, New York: W. Ross, 1787.

Thomas Coke and Francis Asbury tried to transplant the Wesleyan method of education, found in Kingswood School, to America in 1787 with the founding of Cokesbury College, named for the two leaders. The student body was composed of three groups: sons of preachers, sons of subscribers to the school and of members of the Methodist societies, and orphans. The first and last categories were to be "boarded, educated, and cloathed *gratis*."

The rules, outlined in this rare publication from 1787, bear a noticeable similarity to the rules of Kingswood. Recreation possibilities are a bit broader, including "gardening, walking, riding and bathing without Doors; and the carpenter's, joiner's, cabinet-maker's, or turner's business within doors." There was, however, to be no "play" as such allowed, "for those who play when they are young, will play when they are old."

The College burned twice before the enterprise was abandoned in 1795. The support of education by Methodists in America continued, however, as the denomination proceeded in the following two centuries to found more schools, colleges, and universities than any other Protestant denomination.

32. KNOWLEDGE AND VITAL PIETY

Children's Hymn ("Kingswood Hymn"), *Hymns for Children*, no. 40, Bristol: Pine, 1768.

This hymn is remembered most for its couplet, "Unite the pair so long disjoined, / Knowledge and vital piety." It is less often noted that the hymn was written "For Children" and was originally entitled, "At the Opening of a School in Kingswood."

The inherent fusion of "learning and holiness" furnishes the framework for this hymn as an expression of the interconnected nature of wisdom and love, perhaps most poignantly expressed in one of Wesley's sermons: "without love, all learning is but splendid ignorance." This double focus is at the heart of Wesley's educational program, which was designed to discriminate and teach "the knowledge fit for man to know."

33. INEXPENSIVE METHODIST PUBLICATIONS

John Wesley, MS Letter to Christopher Hopper, Nov. 20, 1769, Bridwell Library, Southern Methodist University.

One important means of education and evangelism for the Wesleys was the production of inexpensive tracts. Wesley realized that, as he tells Hopper in this letter, most Methodists are poor. But he still felt that they could (or should) spend a penny every other week for a tract

Most of the Wesleyan publications were penny pamphlets (or sometimes less), but a penny in those days was a substantial amount for a poor person. To the rich, a penny was only the price of a watch key; to the poor it was the value of a bag of sugar or a loaf of bread. The cost of this material was therefore thought by most of the poor to be beyond their means.

34. METHODIST TRACT SOCIETY

John Wesley, *The Important Question*, London: Paramore, 1785 ("not to be sold, but given away").

By 1782, Wesley had apparently changed his views expressed in the 1769 letter to Hopper. He then instituted a plan to distribute pamphlets to the poor through a Methodist Tract Society. The Wesleyan tracts were to be purchased in bulk by more wealthy supporters and then given free to the poor.

These inexpensive publications often bear the marks of cheap production—poor inking, bad alignment, and inelegant paper.

35. METHODIST LENDING PROGRAM

Foundery Lending Stock receipt, 1764, Methodist Archives, John Rylands University Library of Manchester.

This printed note is the record of a two-pound loan to R (Robert or Rebecca?) Lander, a member of John Bugbee's class, in October 1764. The load steward was Mr. Ward and security for this particular loan was given by John Bakewell.

The loan program was established in 1748 when Wesley raised thirty pounds to provide seed money to help small businesses, primarily the tradesmen, merchants, and manufacturers. The money, up to twenty shillings per person, was loaned at no interest for a period of three months, to be paid back weekly. Two hundred fifty-five people were assisted in this manner during the first eighteen months. Over the years, the limit for loans was gradually raised until it reached five pounds.

This note is a rare relic of an important part of the Methodist program to assist the poor, who were more often than not business people who were underemployed or going through hard times.

36. BENEFICIARY OF THE LENDING PROGRAM

James Lackington, *Memoirs of the Forty-five Years of the Life of James Lackington, the Present Bookseller*, 9th ed. cor. and much enl., London: Printed for the author, 1794.

Some editions of this work bear the subtitle, *who, from the humble station of a journeyman shoemaker, by great industry, amassed a large fortune and now lives in a splendid stile, in London.*

Lackington was, for a time, a member of the Methodist society that met at the Foundery in London, having "caught the infection" as an apprentice cobbler. At age twenty-six, he decided to start in business as a bookseller. He benefitted from the lending program that Wesley established by borrowing five pounds, interest free, with which he purchased some antiquarian books. These, combined with a small stock of books that he already owned, got him started and within six months his stock was increased five-fold.

Within two years, Lackington became disillusioned with the Methodists and left the society. He felt that many of the preachers proclaimed one thing about their dealings with the poor yet practiced another. His book trade flourished, however, and he soon became one of the richest book dealers in London.

Lackington's memoirs contain many references to the Methodists, several of them quite critical of their ideas and practices, as is evident in the account of the prayer meeting displayed in this exhibit.

Abbreviations

Letters (Telford)	*The Letters of the Rev. John Wesley, A.M.* Edited by John Telford. 8 vols. London: Epworth Press, 1931.
Minutes (Mason)	*Minutes of the Methodist Conferences, from the First, held in London, by the Late Rev. John Wesley, A.M., in the Year 1744.* London: John Mason, 1862.
Unpublished Poetry	*The Unpublished Poetry of Charles Wesley.* Edited by S T Kimbrough, Jr. and Oliver A. Beckerlegge. 3 vols. Nashville: Kingswood Books, 1988–92.
Works	The Works of John Wesley. Begun as *The Oxford Edition of The Works of John Wesley.* Oxford: Clarendon Press, 1975–1983. Continued as *The Bicentennial Edition of The Works of John Wesley.* Nashville: Abingdon Press, 1984–; 15 of 35 vols. published to date.
Works (Jackson)	*The Works of John Wesley.* 14 vols. Edited by Thomas Jackson. London: Wesleyan Reading Room, 1872 (reprint, Grand Rapids, Mich.: Zondervan Publishing House, 1958).

Contributors

William J. Abraham is Albert C. Outler Professor of Wesley Studies at Perkins School of Theology, Southern Methodist University. His books include *Canon and Criterion in Christian Theology* (1998), *Waking from Doctrinal Amnesia* (1995), *The Logic of Evangelism* (1989), *The Coming Great Revival* (1984), and *The Divine Inspiration of Holy Scripture* (1981).

José Míguez Bonino, retired presbyter of the Iglesia Evangélica Metodista Argentina (IEMA), is Emeritus Professor of Systematic Theology and Ethics of the ISEDET (Protestant School of Theology in Buenos Aires, Argentina). His books include *Faces of Latin American Protestantism* (1997), *Towards a Christian Political Ethics* (1983), *Faces of Jesus: Latin American Christologies* (1984), and *Revolutionary Theology Comes of Age* (1975).

Ted A. Campbell is President of Garrett-Evangelical Theological Seminary in Evanston, Ill. His books include *Methodist Doctrine: The Essentials* (1999), *Christian Confessions: A Historical Introduction* (1996), *John Wesley and Christian Antiquity* (1991), and *The Religion of the Heart* (1991).

237

Richard P. Heitzenrater is William Kellon Quick Professor of Church History and Wesley Studies at The Divinity School, Duke University, and General Editor of the *Bicentennial Edition of the Works of John Wesley*. His books include *Wesley and the People Called Methodists* (1995), *Mirror and Memory: Reflections on Early Methodism* (1989), *The Elusive Mr. Wesley* (1985), and (with W. R. Ward) Wesley's *Journal and Diaries* (vols. 18–24 of the *Works*).

S T Kimbrough, Jr. is Associate General Secretary for Mission Evangelism of The General Board of Global Ministries of The United Methodist Church. He is a member of the Center of Theological Inquiry in Princeton, N. J., and was the founding president of the Charles Wesley Society. His books include *A Heart to Praise My God: Wesley Hymns for Today* (1996), *Songs for the Poor* (1996), *Charles Wesley: Poet and Theologian* (1992), and *The Unpublished Poetry of Charles Wesley* (1988–92).

Gareth Lloyd is the Archivist for The Methodist Church of Great Britain. The archives, deposited at the John Rylands University Library of Manchester, constitute the world's finest collection of early Methodist material. His books include *Methodist Biographical Index* (1998), various published *Catalogues* of collected papers in the John Rylands Library (such as Thomas Coke, Joseph Benson, Charles Wesley, the Wesley family), and *Early Methodist Personal Papers, 1750–1850* (2000).

Tim Macquiban is Director of the Wesley & Methodist Studies Centre at the Westminster Institute of Education, Oxford Brookes University, England. He is British Secretary of the Oxford Institute of Methodist Theological Studies and a vice-president of the World Methodist Historical Society. His books include *Issues in Education: Some Methodist Perspectives* (1996), *Pure, Universal Love: Reflections on the Wesleys and Inter-faith Dialogue* (1995), and *Methodism in its Cultural Milieu* (1994).

Randy L. Maddox is Paul T. Walls Professor of Wesleyan Theology, Seattle Pacific University, Seattle, Washington. His books include *Rethinking Wesley's Theology for Contemporary Methodism* (1998), *Responsible Grace: John Wesley's Practical Theology* (1994),

Aldersgate Reconsidered (1990), and *Toward an Ecumenical Fundamental Theology* (1984).

Joerg Rieger is Associate Professor of Systematic Theology at Perkins School of Theology, Southern Methodist University, and founder of the West Dallas Project to build relationships between diverse people and to revitalize theological reflection. His books include *God and the Excluded* (2000), *Theology from the Belly of the Whale* (1999), *Remember the Poor* (1998), and *Liberating the Future* (1998).

Index

LaVergne, TN USA
16 December 2010
209094LV00004B/18/P